ADVENTURES AMONG BIRDS

Adventures Among Birds is a manifesto for the life of birds. From childhood memories of his first caged bird and his growing passion for them, slowly growing throughout his adolescence in Argentina, to the beauty of the diversity of bird life in England, Hudson's delight at this particular aspect of nature is palpable.

It is in his protests against the hunting of birds for sport that his love for birds is most clearly shown. Their behaviour towards one another convinces Hudson of their friendship, and his powers of observation paint a picture of interaction and emotion between birds that is almost human.

Told with an unrelenting passion for its subject, Hudson's book is sure to draw you in with its countless beautiful descriptions in miniature.

BY THE SAME AUTHOR

Afoot in England
Argentine Ornithology
Birds of La Plata
Birds in London
Birds and Man
Birds in Town and Village
Birds in a Village
The Book of a Naturalist
British Birds
Hampshire Days
Hind in Richmond Park

Idle Days in Patagonia
Land's End: A Naturalist's
  Impressions in West Cornwall
Men, Books and Birds
The Naturalist in La Plata
Nature in Downland
Osprey; or, Egrets and Aigrettes
Rare, Vanishing & Lost British
  Birds
A Shepherd's Life: Impressions
  of the South Wiltshire Downs

COLLINS NATURE LIBRARY

ADVENTURES AMONG BIRDS

BY

W. H. HUDSON

With an introduction by
Robert Macfarlane

Collins

First published in 1913 by Hutchinson & Co.

This edition published in 2012 by Collins
An imprint of HarperCollins*Publishers*
77–85 Fulham Palace Road
London W6 8JB

www.harpercollins.co.uk

10 9 8 7 6 5 4 3 2 1

Author's note: A considerable portion of the matter contained herein has appeared in the *English Review, Cornhill Magazine, Saturday Review, Nation,* and a part of one chapter in the *Morning Post.* These articles have been altered and extended, and I am obliged to the Editors and Publishers for permission to use them in this book.

A catalogue record for this book is available from the British Library.

ISBN: 978-0-00-746640-5

Printed and bound in Great Britain by Clays Ltd, St Ives plc
Typeset by Susie Bell – www.f-12.co.uk
Cover design © HarperCollins*Publishers.* Designed by Bird
Cover photograph © Laura Ruth/Getty Images

Once I was part of the music I heard
On the boughs or sweet between earth and sky,
For joy of the beating of wings on high
My heart shot into the breast of a bird.

I hear it now and I see it fly,
And a life in wrinkles again is stirred,
My heart shoots into the breast of a bird,
As it will for sheer love till the last long sigh.

Meredith

CONTENTS

INTRODUCTION
BY ROBERT MACFARLANE

Among the titles that W. H. Hudson considered for this book was *The Adventures of a Soul, Sensitive or Not, Among the Feathered Masterpieces of Creation.* You can see why he didn't use it in the end, but there's much of the man – and much of the finished work – still to be heard here: whimsy, passion, a hint of persiflage, a dash of feyness and an unembarrassedly spiritual regard for nature in general and birds in particular.

Birds were friends and family to Hudson. They brought him uncontrived joy, conviviality and kinship. In his weird way-book *Afoot In England* (1909) he referred to birds as 'feathered people'; here again he speaks of birds as his 'people', to whom he feels closer than to the world's 'human inhabitants'. He loved birds 'with . . . tenderness and sympathy' and he celebrated them both for themselves and for 'that glorious gladness' which the sight of them produced in him. Any birdwatcher – from ultra-twitcher to lunchtime pigeon-feeder – will recognise that gladness, a version of what Ceri Levy has nicely called 'The Bird Effect'. *Adventures* is about that effect: about how encounters with birds can shape and shift us, and about the flights that birds make through our imaginations and memories. The book's aims are modest but ardent: 'to reveal, to testify, [and] to endeavour to convey to others some faint sense or suggestion of the wonder and delight which may be found in nature'.

Adventures is what would now be called 'hybrid' in form. It mingles memoir, travelogue, meditation and nature writing, along with audacious passages of sympathetic fiction (as when Hudson imagines his way into the mind of a migrating redwing, or reconstructs a vision of the Lincolnshire fenlands as they might have looked five thousand years ago). Each chapter has a different totem bird – the pheasant, the raven, the goldfinch, the ring ouzel – and in this manner it is a travel book structured by species rather than geography. The result is a medley – episodic, anecdotal and digressive – that is united by its avian obsession and by its author's other passions. For Hudson is invigoratingly open about both his hatreds (Italians, gamekeepers, cats, motorcyclists and Chepstow, 'a small parasitic town much given to drink') and his loves (nightingales, grass, 'Northerners' – who are apparently much given to a 'poetical feeling' – the colour green, wild geese and natterjack toads).

Its faults as a book are worth acknowledging so that its qualities can be reliably identified. It starts slowly (one longs for Hudson to lean on the crank-handle and get the engine going sooner), and once started up it can sound here and there like the grumpy harrumphs of a walking-stick-waving, clay-pipe-smoking, bushy-bearded nature crank. In common with numerous English travelogues of the early twentieth century, a number of its chapters were published first as stand-alone essays in periodicals (*The English Review, The Cornhill Magazine*) before being stitched together to make a whole. It is unmistakably of its era: this is a book written at a time when a chap might correspond with other chaps called Mr Walter Herries-Pollock and Mr Mansel Roydell-Bouverie, and when a further chap called Mr Charles Witchell might spend years 'recording in musical notation no fewer than seventy-six blackbird strains'.

But at the core of the book is the testimony of an intense and eccentric man concerning his relationship with birds. Its finest sections are born, like the best nature writing, of long acquaintance and fierce looking. It asks difficult questions about the metaphysics of our relations with birds, but also about the pragmatics of their right to life. Hudson considers – as Henry David Thoreau had put it half a century earlier – how we might 'leave some life pasturing freely where we never wander', while also recognising and valuing

the 'tonic' with which the experience of wildness provides us. These
are not questions that have receded in importance in the century
since Hudson was writing.

William Henry Hudson (1841–1922) grew up on the Argentinian
pampas in the Province of Buenos Aires, one of six children of
immigrant American sheep-farmers. He and his siblings led
untrammelled lives as children. The vast grasslands surrounding
their cabin became their school. During those years Hudson developed an intricate and self-taught knowledge of flora and fauna, and
a taste for remoteness and solitude that never left him. Argentina
was also the land where he 'first knew and loved birds'; it made him
'one whose chief pleasure from childhood has been in wild birds and
who delights in bird voices above all sounds'. How tame England
must have seemed when, after the death of his parents, he left South
America and settled in London in the mid-1870s.

   Actually, 'settled' is the wrong word, because although Hudson
spent the rest of his life in England, he was allergic to what he
called 'attachment'. He was nomadic by instinct and practice, sceptical of ideas of home and belonging, and far more fond of passing
through and moving on than of digging in and staying put (though
he lived much of his English life in a London house in Westbourne
Grove with a woman who began as his landlady and became his
wife). *Adventures*, like many of his other books, is animated by his
commitment to movement. In a paragraph of Lawrentian baroque-
ness he speculates about how people form 'attachments' to places:
our 'vegetative nerves' have the 'queer trick' of 'throwing out countless invisible filaments to fasten themselves like tendrils to every
object . . . or to root themselves in the soil'. Such rapid affiliation
alarmed Hudson, however, and he remarks that he himself always
'severs these inconvenient threads before they get too strong'.
It's a revealing passage, and a reminder that Hudson needs to be

understood at least in part as a writer not of ruralist nostalgia, nor even of exile, but of something far more modern: displacement. It's of course no coincidence that birds – mobile, migrant – should be the object of his obsession. 'One of the greatest pleasures in life – my life, I mean,' he remarks with disarming candour, 'is to be present, in a sense invisible, in the midst of the domestic circle of beings of a different order, another world, than ours.'

Hudson's method as a walker was to keep to the margins and to keep in motion. When he was able to escape London he tended to head south and west to the chalklands of England, or up to the North Norfolk coast, where in autumn the wild geese from Spitsbergen and Siberia landed – and still land – to 'relax their intense wildness'. He enjoyed tramping and traipsing, and then sitting and watching; he would find his way on foot to 'quiet places', before taking up brief residence in a stand of reeds by a riverbank, in a 'small isolated copse by a tiny stream', or 'at the lower end of a long sloping field'. Like J. A. Baker – the author of *The Peregrine* (1967), the stone-cold classic of twentieth-century birding literature – Hudson was a hedge-haunter and a field-farer, but unlike Baker he was a loner rather than a misanthrope.

The only people Hudson hated were those he considered the enemies of birds. *Adventures* opens with a salvo against those 'wholesale killers' – the hunters and sportsmen of wildfowl and songbirds. Strong stuff, but then Hudson – who was a founder member of the RSPB – knew the dangers that birds faced and continue to face: hundreds of thousands of guns are still fired each hunting season in Europe alone, and tens of millions of birds are killed by shot, mist-net and lime-stick. It's clear that Hudson felt himself to be living through an era of decline tending to extinction in bird populations in Britain, brought about by the damage to habitat from agriculture, and the depredations of cats and gunmen. His own body of work, enormously influential in its day, now appears as a junction-point in the history of nature writing: converging the attentive devotions of Gilbert White and Richard Jefferies, but also anticipating the noisier activism of later-twentieth-century environmental writers. Certainly there are seeds of both Edward Abbey and Rachel Carson in Hudson's audacious combining of scientific detail, lyrical rhapsody, livid polemic and elegiac mysticism.

Adventures – like several of Hudson's other works – is rich with incidents of 'extra-natural' experience, to borrow Hudson's own term. The most intense of these moments concern his dreams of metempsychosis or transmigration. Like Baker, Hudson seems to have experienced often and powerfully the desire to swap species and become a bird. His most frequent fantasy, alluded to several times here, involves the dispersal of his physical body, its evaporation into 'air, essence, energy or soul', and then his re-condensation into avian form. Various elements are recognisable in Hudson's extra-naturalism: shades of Platonism (there in his interest in 'pure form'), relics from pagan Celtic culture (*Buile Suibhne*, for instance, the fourteenth-century Irish poem often translated as *Sweeney's Flight*, in which an Ulster king called Sweeney is cursed by a Christian priest and transformed into a creature of the air, compelled to wander the remote places of Ireland), the Romantic aerial fantasias of Shelley and Byron, and also a sturdy deep-English mysticism that is at ease with the time-slips and shape-shifts made possible by landscape (the mysticism of Masefield and his mummers, of Kipling's Pook's Hill, in which the children time-travel 'by right of Oak, Ash and Thorn', through the portal hard under the chalk hill).

Various triggers prompt Hudson's extra-natural episodes: bright colours, fog and mists, the play of light upon water, 'the magical effect of heat haze'. Like Nan Shepherd, Hudson was fascinated by optical illusions and by transitional weather. He was acutely colour-sensitive: the 'Ham stone' of Sherborne Abbey leaves him feeling 'yellow all through', as if his 'very bones are dyed yellow'; the green colour of grass, by contrast, 'is so . . . necessary to my well-being . . . that when removed from the sight of it I am apt to fall into a languishing state, a dim and despondent mind, like one in prison or sick . . .'. Some of the book's most memorable passages are almost Fauvist in their dabs and daubs of colour, as when he describes 'gulls resting in [a] field, white and pale grey, their beaks turned to the wind . . . like little bird-shaped drifts of snow lying on the green turf, shining in the sun'. The sight one day of a flotilla of white ducks bobbing in a blue lake induces in him a visionary fugue in which he imagines the human dead inhabiting a 'country of the sky', up to which they 'fly like birds'.

At the book's beautiful ending that flow of that migration is reversed, as Hudson watches wild geese descend from the 'far-up country' of the air to make their landings on the salt-marshes and shallows of North Norfolk. The sight of the geese's 'marvellous wild-wing display' leaves him 'pulled two ways', 'in, or between, two minds'. Observing them on a 'perfect November morning', under 'a clear sky' and in 'a clear sharp air', he feels himself drawn almost out of his body, caught between gravity and levity, flight and earth. In a passage that is itself poised somewhere between vaudeville and Audubon he notes that at such a moment 'it is only necessary for a man to mimic the actions of a crane or stork by lifting his arms and taking a couple of strides and a hop forward, to find himself launched into space, rising to a vast height, on a voyage of exploration.' Such a happy, hopeless pantomime, Hudson writes with both longing and resignation, 'is the nearest we can get to the state of being a bird.'

Robert Macfarlane

NOTES

I have not supplied specific page references when quoting from
Adventures Among Birds, so all un-referenced quotations should be
assumed to have their origins in the book. The few other sources for
quoted material are given below.

page xi
'feathered people': W. H. Hudson, *Afoot In England* (London:
Hutchinson, 1909), p. 138.

'The Bird Effect': see http://www.thebirdeffect.com/

pages xii–xiii
'some life pasturing freely' and 'tonic': Henry David Thoreau,
Walden, ed. J. Lyndon Shanley (Princeton: Princeton University
Press, 1971 [1854]), p. 318.

page xv
'by right of Oak, Ash and Thorn': Rudyard Kipling, *Puck of Pook's
Hill* (London: Macmillan, 1906), p. 13.

1 THE BOOK: AN APOLOGY

A preliminary warning – Many books about a few birds – People who discover well-known birds – An excuse for the multiplicity of bird-books – Universal delight in wild birds – Interview with a county councillor – A gold-crest's visit to a hospital – A rascal's blessing – Incident of the dying Garibaldi and a bird

The book-buyer in search of something to read before making his purchase as a rule opens a book and glances at a few lines on the first page, just to get the flavour of it and find out whether or not it suits his palate. The title, we must presume, has already attracted him as indicating a subject which interests him. This habit of his gives me the opportunity of warning him at the very outset that he will find here no adventures of a wild-fowler, if that's what he is seeking; no thrilling records of long nights passed in a punt, with a north wind blowing and freezing him to the marrow in spite of his thick woollen clothing and long boots and oilskins, and the glorious conclusion of the adventure when he happily succeeds in sending a thousand pellets of burning lead into an innumerable multitude of mallard, widgeon, teal, pochard, and pintail; how for several successive winters he repeated the operation until the persecuted fowl began to diminish so greatly in numbers that he forsook that estuary or haunt on the coast to follow them elsewhere, or transferred his attentions to some other far-distant point, where other wholesale killers had not been before him. No, this is not a sporting record, despite the title, and if long titles were the fashion nowadays, it would have been proper to call the book 'The Adventures of a Soul, sensitive or not, among the feathered masterpieces of creation'. This would at all events have shown at once whence the title was derived, and would have better served to indicate the nature of the contents.

It all comes to this, that we have here another book about birds, which demands some sort of apology.

In England, a small country, we have not too many species – two or three hundred, let us say, according to the number of visitants we include or exclude; all exceedingly well known. For birds are observed more than any other class of creatures, and we are not only an observant but a book-writing people, and books have been written on this subject since the time of Queen Elizabeth – as a fact the first book (1544) was before her time – and for the last century have been produced at an ever-increasing rate until now, when we have them turned out by the dozen every year. All about the same few well-known birds! To many among us it seems that the thing is being over-done. One friend expostulates thus: 'What, another book about birds? You have already written several – three or four or five – I can't remember the number, I don't know much about the subject, but I should have thought you had already told us all you know about it. I had hoped you had finished with that subject now. There are so many others – Man, for instance, who is of more account than many sparrows. Well, all I can say is, I'm sorry.'

If he had known birds, I doubt that he would have expressed regret at my choice of a subject; for many as are the observers of birds and writers on them in the land, there are yet a far greater number who do not properly know them, and the joy they are or may be to us.

The people who discover birds are now common with us, and though the story of their discoveries is somewhat boring, it amuses at the same time. A lady of your acquaintance tells you the result of putting some crumbs on a window-sill – the sudden appearance to feed on the crumbs of a quaint fairy-like little bird which was not a sparrow, nor robin, nor any of those common ones, but a sparkling lively little creature with a crest, all blue above and yellow beneath – very beautiful to look at, and fantastic in its actions. A bird she has never seen before though all her life has been passed in the country. Was it some rare visitor from a distant land, where birds have a brighter plumage and livelier habits than ours?

Two or three years ago a literary friend wrote to me from the north of England, where he had gone for a holiday and was staying at a farm, to say that he wished me there, if only to see a wonderful bird that visited the house every day. It was probably a species, he thought, confined to that part of the country, and perhaps never seen in the south, and he wanted very much to know what it was. As I couldn't go to him he would try to describe it. Every morning after breakfast, when he and his people fed the birds on the lawn, this strange species, to the number of a dozen or more, would appear on the scene – a bird about the size of a thrush with a long sharp yellow beak, the entire plumage of a very dark purple and green colour, so glossy that it sparkled like silver in the sunshine. They were also sprinkled all over with minute white and cream-coloured spots. A beautiful bird, and very curious in its behaviour. They would dart down on the scraps, scattering the sparrows right and left among themselves over the best pieces; and then, when satisfied, they would fly up to the roof and climb and flit about over the tiles and on the chimneys, puffing their feathers out and making all sorts of odd noises – whistling, chattering, tinkling, and so on.

I replied that the birds were starlings, and he was rather unhappy about it, since he had known the starling as a common bird all his life, and had imagined he knew it too well to take it for a strange and rare species. But then, he confessed, he had never looked closely at it; he had seen it in flocks in the pastures, always at a distance where it looks plain black.

If the lady who discovered the blue-tit, or nun, and my friend who found out the starling, would extend their researches in the feathered world they would find a hundred other species as beautiful in colouring and delightful in their ways as those two, and some even more so.

Much, too, might be said on the subject of many books being written about birds. They are not necessarily repetitions. When a writer of fact or fiction puts his friends and acquaintances in a book, as a rule it makes a difference, a decline, in the degree of cordiality in their relations. That is only, of course, when the reader recognises himself in the portrait. He may not do so, portraits not always being 'pure realism', as Mr Stanhope Forbes says they are. But whether the reader recognises his own picture or not, the writer himself experiences a change of feeling towards his subject. It is, to put it brutally, similar to that of the boy towards the sucked orange. There is nothing more to be got out of it. It need not be supposed for a moment that the fictionist is friendly towards or interested in his fellow-creatures for the sake of what he can get out of them – that, like the portrait-painter, he is on the look-out for a subject. He has no such unworthy motive, and the change in his feeling comes about in another way. Having built up his picture he looks on it and finds it an improvement, and infinitely more interesting than the original, and the old feeling inevitably changes – it is transferred from the man to the picture. These changes in feeling never occur in the case of the feathered friends we have made, and find pleasure in portraying. We may put them again and again in books without experiencing any diminution in our feelings towards them. On the contrary, after doing our best we no sooner look again on the origi-nals than we see how bad the portrait is, and would be glad to put it out of sight, and forget all about it. This lustre, this peculiar grace, this expression which I never marked before, is not in the picture I have made; come, let me try again, though it be but to fail again, to produce yet another painting fit only for the lumber-room.

After all it does not need a naturalist nor an artist nor a poet to appreciate and be the better for that best thing in a wild bird, that free, joyous, joy-giving nature felt by every one of us. The sight of a wild, free, happy existence, as far as the fairies' or angels' from ours, yet linked to us by its warm red blood, its throbbing human-shaped heart, fine senses, and intelligent mind, emotions that sway it as ours sway us. A relative, a 'little sister', but clothed for its glory and joy in feathers that are hard as flint, light as air and translucent, and wings to lift it above the earth on which we walk. Is there on earth a human being who has not felt this? Not one!

I remember going once to see a member of a county council to try to enlist his interest in the subject of bird protection for his county. I was told that he was the biggest man on the council and had immense weight with his fellow-members on account of his wealth and social position, that without getting him on our side it would be difficult to obtain an order. He was certainly a big man physically, a very giant in stature, with a tread like that of an elephant when he entered the vast dim room into which a servant had conducted me. So huge a mass, so heavy and stolid, as he stood there silently, staring at me out of his great expressionless boiled-gooseberry-coloured eyes, waiting to hear what I had to say to him. I said it, and handed him some papers, which I wanted him to look at. But he was not listening, and when I finished he held out the papers for me to take them back. 'No,' he said, 'I have too many calls on me – I can't entertain it.' 'Will you kindly listen,' I said, then repeated it again, and he muttered something and taking the papers once more inclined his head to indicate that the interview was over, and, thanking him for his ready sympathy, I went my way to someone else.

My next visit was to an enthusiastic sportsman. I told him where I had been, and he exclaimed that it was a mistake, a waste of time. 'That chunk of a man is no good,' he said. 'If he sees a roast goose on the table he knows what it is and he can distinguish it from a roast turkey, and that's all he knows about birds.' Perhaps it was all he knew, from the natural history point of view at all events; yet even this 'chunk of a man' had doubtless felt something of that common universal joy in a bird, which makes the bird so much to us, for by-and-by it was with his help that the order for the county was obtained.

Here is a little incident in which we can see just the feeling a bird is able to inspire in us. A friend writes to me:

> *I have just heard from Miss Paget, who says her most interesting news is the visit of a gold-crested wren at the Connaught Hospital. It flew in through one of the open windows and at once became friendly with the patients, perching on their fingers and being fed by them to their great delight. Then, having cheered them for a day and night, it flew away and has not been seen since. The men long for its return, for nothing has pleased and refreshed and brightened them so much in their wearisome hours as its companionship.*

Miss Rosalind Paget is so well known for her work in the military hospitals that I hope she will forgive me for giving her name without her permission when relating this incident.

But the effect of the bird is due as much to the voice as to the dainty winged shape, the harmonious colouring, and the graceful easy motions in the air. That peculiar aerial vibrant penetrative character of bird-notes moves us as other sounds do not, and there are certain notes in which these qualities are intensified and sometimes suggest an emotion common to all mankind, which pierce to the listener's heart, whatever his race or country may be or his character or pursuits in life.

I here recall an incident of my young days in a far land, less civilised than ours. I had a neighbour in my home for whom I had little love. He was a greedy rascal, a petty rural magistrate with an itching palm, and if justice was required at his hands it had to be bought with

money like any other commodity. One summer afternoon he rode over
to my home and asked me to go for a walk with him by the river. It
was a warm brilliant day in early autumn, and when we had walked
about a couple of miles along the bank to a spot where the stream was
about fifty yards wide, we sat down on the dry grass under a large red
willow. A flock of birds was in the tree – a species of a most loquacious kind – but our approach had made them silent. Not the faintest
chirp fell from the branches that had been full of their musical jangle
a few minutes before. It was a species of troupial, a starling-like bird
of social habits, only larger than our starling, with glossy olive-brown
plumage and brilliant yellow breast. *Pecho amarillo* (yellow breast) is
its vernacular name. Now as soon as we had settled comfortably on
the grass the entire flock, of thirty or forty birds, sprang up into the
air, going up out of the foliage like a fountain, then suddenly they all
together dropped down, and sweeping by us over the water burst into
a storm of loud ringing jubilant cries and liquid notes. My companion
uttered a sudden strange harsh discordant laugh, and turning away
his sharp dry fox-like face, too late to hide the sudden moisture I had
seen in his eyes, he exclaimed with savage emphasis on the first word
– '*Curse* the little birds – how glad they are!'

That was his way of blessing them. He was a hardened rascal,
utterly bad, feared and hated by the poor, despised by his equals; yet
the sight and sound of that merry company, its sudden outburst of
glorious joy, had wrought an instantaneous change in him that was like
a miracle, and for a moment he was no longer himself, but what he had
been in the past, in some unimaginably remote period of his existence, a
pure-hearted child, capable of a glad, beautiful emotion and of tears.

I will remark in passing that the actual words of his *blessing*
are hardly translatable; for he didn't call them 'little birds', but
addressed them affectionately as fellow-mortals of diminutive size –
'little children of a thousand unvirtuous mothers' was more nearly
his expression.

One is reminded of a famous historical incident – of the exclamation of the dying Garibaldi, when a small bird of unrecorded species
alighted for a moment on the ledge of his open window, and burst
out into a lively twittering song. 'Quanto è allegro!' murmured
the old passing fighter. The exclamation would have seemed quite
natural on the lips of a dying Englishman, but how strange on his!
Does it find an echo in the heart of the people he liberated, who
appreciate a bird not for its soul-gladdening voice but for its flavour?
It can only be supposed that Garibaldi during his furious fighting
years in the Argentine Confederation, in the forties of the last
century, had become in some ways de-Italianised – that he had been
infected with the friendly feeling towards birds of his fellow 'pirates
and ruffians', as they were called, and of the people generally, from
his enemy the Dictator Rosas himself, the 'Nero of South America',
down to the poorest gaucho in the land. They, the fighters, were
mostly ruffians in those days in a country where revolution (with
atrocities) was endemic, but they did not kill or persecute 'God's
little birds', as they called them. The foreigners who did such things
were regarded with contempt.

Garibaldi was beaten again and again, and finally driven from
the Plate by a better fighter – an Englishman of the name of Brown;
but the beaten 'pirate' lived to liberate his own country and to see
his people going out annually in tens of thousands to settle in the
land where he had fought and lost. How melancholy to think that
from the bird-lover's point of view they have been a curse to it, that,
but for the wealthy native and English landowners who are able
to give some protection to wild life on their estates, the detestable
swarm of aliens would have made the land they have populated as
birdless as their native Italy.

2 CARDINAL: THE STORY OF
MY FIRST CAGED BIRD

The past recalled by a sound – A caged cardinal – A memory of
childhood – The clergyman's cardinal – My first caged bird – History
of its escapades and ultimate fate

A once familiar but long unheard sound coming unexpect-
edly to us will sometimes affect the mind as it is occasionally affected through the sense of smell, restoring a past
scene and state so vividly that it is less like a memory than a vision.
It is indeed more than a vision, seeing that this is an illusion, something apparently beheld with the outer or physical eyes; the other is
a transformation, a return to that state – that forgotten self – which
was lost for ever, yet is ours again; and for a glorious moment we are
what we were in some distant place, some long-vanished time, in age
and freshness of feeling, in the brilliance of our senses, our wonder
and delight at this visible world.

Recently I had an experience of that kind on hearing a loud glad
bird-note or call from overhead when walking in a London West-End
thoroughfare. It made me start and stand still; when, casting up my
eyes, I caught sight of the bird in its cage, hanging outside a first-floor
window. It was the beautiful cardinal of many memories.

This is a bird of the finch family of southern South America
– about the size of a starling, but more gracefully shaped, with a
longer tail; the whole upper plumage clear blue-grey, the underparts
pure white; the face, throat, and a high pointed crest an intense brilliant scarlet.

It had actually seemed to me at the moment of hearing, then
of seeing it, that the bird had recognised me as one from the same
distant country – that its loud call was a glad greeting to a fellow-
exile seen by chance in a London thoroughfare. It was even more
than that: this was my own bird, dead so many, many years, living
again, knowing me again so far from home, in spite of all the
changes that time had wrought in me. And he, my own cardinal, the
first cardinal I ever knew, remembered it all even as I did – all the
little incidents of our life together; the whole history was in both our
minds at that same moment of recognition.

I was a boy, not yet eight years old, when my mother took me
on one of her yearly visits to Buenos Ayres. It was a very long day's
journey for us in those pre-railroad times; for, great and prosperous
as that city and republic now are, it was not so then, when the
people were divided, calling themselves Reds and Whites (or Blues),
and were occupied in cutting one another's throats.

In Buenos Ayres we stayed at the house of an English missionary
clergyman, in a street near the waterside. He was a friend of my
parents and used to come out with his family to us in the summer,
and in return my mother made his house her home for a month
or so in winter. This was my first visit, and I remember the house
was like a luxurious palace to my simple mind accustomed to rude
surroundings. It had a large paved courtyard, with ornamental
shrubs and orange and lemon trees growing in it, and many prettily
decorated rooms; also a long passage or balcony at the back, and, at
its far end, facing the balcony, the door of the study. This balcony at
the back had an irresistible attraction for me, for on the wall were
hung many cages containing beautiful birds, some unknown to
me. There were several canaries, a European goldfinch, and other
kinds; but the bird that specially attracted me was a cardinal in fine
plumage, with a loud, glad, musical call-note – just such a note as
that with which the bird in a London thoroughfare had pierced my

heart. But it did not sing, and I was told that it had no song except that one note, or not more than two or three notes, and that it was kept solely for its beauty. To me it was certainly most beautiful.

Every day during our six or seven weeks' visit I used to steal out to the balcony and stand by the hour watching the birds, above all the cardinal with his splendid scarlet crest, thinking of the joy it would be to possess such a bird. But though I could not keep away from the spot, I was always ill at ease when there, always glancing apprehensively at the closed door at the end – for it was a glass door, and in his study behind it the clergyman, a grave studious man, was sitting over his books. It made me tremble to think that, though invisible to me in that dim interior, he would be able to see me through the glass, and, worse still, that at any moment he might throw open the door and come out to catch me gazing at his birds. Nor was this feeling strange in the circumstances, for I was a timid, somewhat sensitive little boy, and he a very big stern man with a large clean-shaved colourless face that had no friendliness in it; nor could I forget an unhappy incident which occurred during his visit to us in the country more than half a year before. One day, rushing in, I stumbled in the verandah and struck my head against the door-handle, and, falling down, was lying on the floor crying loudly with the pain, when the big stern man came on the scene.

'What's the matter with you?' he demanded.

'Oh, I've hit my head on the door and it hurts me so!' I sobbed.

'Does it?' he said, with a grim smile. 'Well, it doesn't hurt me,' and, stepping over me, he went in.

What wonder that I was apprehensive, would shrink almost in terror, when by chance he came suddenly out to find me there, and, after staring or glaring at me through his gold-rimmed glasses for a few moments, would pass me by without a word or smile! How strange, how unnatural, it seemed that this man I feared and hated should be a lover of birds and the owner of that precious cardinal!

The long visit came to an end at last, and, glad to return to the
birds I had left – to the purple cow-birds, the yellow-breasted and
the crimson-breasted troupials, the tyrant birds, the innumerable
sweet-voiced little crested song-sparrows, and a hundred more –
yet sad to leave the cardinal which I admired and had grown to
love above all birds, I was taken back to my distant home on the
great green plains. So passed the winter, and the swallow returned
and the peach-trees blossomed once more; the long, long dry hot
summer season followed; then autumn – the three beautiful months
of March, April, and May, when the sunshine was soft and we were
among the trees, feasting on ripe peaches every day and all day long.

Then again winter and the annual visit to the distant town;
but none of us children were taken on this occasion. My mother's
return after one of these long absences was always a great joy
and festival to us children. To have her with us again, and the
toys and the books and delicious things she brought us, made us
wild with happiness; and on this occasion she brought me something compared with which all the other gifts – all the gifts I had
ever received in my life – were as nothing. She had a large object
covered from sight with a shawl, and, drawing me to her side,
asked me if I remembered my visit to the city over a year ago,
and how the birds at the parsonage had attracted me? Well, our
friend the clergyman, she went on to say, had gone back to his own
country and would never return. His wife, who was a very gentle,
sweet woman, had been my mother's dearest friend, so that she
could hardly speak of her loss without tears. Before going away
he distributed his birds among his closest friends. He was anxious
that every bird should have an owner who would love it as much as
he had loved it himself and tend it as carefully; and remembering
how he had observed me day after day watching the cardinal, he
thought that he could not leave it in better hands than mine. And
here was the bird in its big cage!

The cardinal was mine! How could I believe it, even when I pulled the shawl off and saw the beautiful creature once more and heard the loud note! The gift of that bird from the stern ice-cold man who had looked at me as if he hated me, even as I had certainly hated him, now seemed the most wonderful thing which had ever happened in the world.

It was a blissful time for me during that late winter season, when I lived for the bird; then, as the days grew longer and brighter with the return of the sun, I was happier every day to see my cardinal's increasing delight in his new surroundings. It was certainly a great and marvellous change for him. The cardinals are taken as fledglings from the nests in forests on the upper waters of the Plata river, and reared by hand by the natives, then sent down to the bird-dealers in Buenos Ayres; so that my bird had practically known only a town life, and was now in a world of greenest grass and foliage, wide blue skies, and brightest sunshine for the first time. By day his cage was hung under the grape-vines outside the verandah; there the warm fragrant wind blew on him and the sun shone down through the translucent red and green young vine-leaves. He was mad with excess of joy, hopping wildly about in his cage, calling loudly in response to the wild birds in the trees, and from time to time bursting out in song: not the three or four to half a dozen notes the cardinal usually emits, but a continuous torrent, like the soaring lark's, so that those who heard it marvelled and exclaimed that they had never known a cardinal with such a song. I can say for myself that I have, since then, listened to the singing of hundreds of cardinals, both wild and caged, and never heard one with a song so passionate and sustained.

So it went on from day to day, until the vine-leaves, grown large, spread a green roof to keep the hot sun from him – a light roof of leaves which, stirred by the wind, still let the sparkling sunbeams fall through to enliven him, while outside the sheltering vines the bright world was all before him. If any person, even the wisest, had

then told me that my cardinal was not the happiest bird in the world
– that not being free to fly he could not be as happy as others – I
should not have believed it; consequently it came as a shock to me
when one day I discovered the cage empty – that my cardinal had
made his escape! The cage, as I have said, was large, and the wires
were so far apart that a bird the size of a linnet or siskin could not
have been confined in it; but for the larger cardinal it was a safe
prison. Unfortunately one of the wires had become loose – perhaps
the bird had loosened it – and by working at it he had succeeded in
bending it and finally had managed to squeeze through and make
his escape. Running out into the plantation I was soon apprised of
his whereabouts by his loud call-note; but though he could not fly,
but only hop and flutter from branch to branch – his wings never
having been exercised – he refused to be caught. I was advised to
wait until he was hungry, then to try him with the cage. This I did,
and, taking the cage, placed it on the ground under the trees and
retired a few paces, holding it open by means of a string which when
released would cause the door to fly to. He became greatly excited
on seeing the cage, and being very hungry soon came down to
the ground and, to my joy, hopped up to it. But he did not go in: it
seemed to me that he was considering the matter, if the state he was
in of being pulled in opposite directions by two equally importunate
impulses may be so described. 'Must I go in and satisfy my hunger –
and live in prison; or stay out and keep my freedom and go hungry?'
He stood at the door of the cage, looking in at the seed, then turned
and looked at me and at the trees, then looked at the seed again,
and raised and lowered his shining crest and flirted his wings and
tail, and was excited and in two minds and a quandary; finally, after
taking one more look at the tempting seed, he deliberately flew or
fluttered up to the nearest branch, then to another, and so on, till
he had gone to the very top of the tree, as if to get as far from the
tempting cage as he could!

It was a great disappointment, and I now determined to hunt him down; for it was late in the day, and he was not a cunning wild bird to save himself from rats and owls and black and yellow opossums and other subtle enemies who would come presently on the scene. I hunted him from the first tree on to the next, then to another, until I had driven him out of the plantation to an open place, where he fluttered over the surface until he came to the bank of the huge ditch or foss, about twelve feet deep and half as wide as the Regent's Park canal. He would drop into it, I thought, and I would then be able to capture him; but after a moment's rest on the bank he rose and succeeded in flying across, pitching on the other side. 'Now I have him!' I exclaimed, and, getting over the foss, I was quickly in hot pursuit after him; for outside the foss the earth spread out level and treeless, with nothing but grass and giant thistles growing on it. But his wings were now getting stronger with exercise, and he led me on and on for about a mile, then disappeared in a clump of giant thistles, growing on a warren or village of the vizcachas – the vizcacha being a big rodent that lives in communities in a dozen or twenty huge burrows, their mouths placed close together. He had escaped down one of these holes, and I waited in vain for him to come out, and in the end was compelled to go home without him.

I don't know if I slept that night, but I was up and out an hour before sunrise, and, taking the cage, set out to look for him, with little hope of finding him, for there were foxes in that place – a family of cubs which I had seen – and, worse still, the large blood-thirsty black weasels of that country. But no sooner was I at the spot where I had lost him than I was greeted with his loud note. And there he was, hopping out from among the thistles, a most forlorn-looking object, his plumage wet and draggled, and his feet thickly covered with wet clay! And he was glad to see me! As soon as I put the cage down he came straight to it and, without a moment's hesi-tation, hopped in and began feasting on the seed.

It was a happy ending. My bird had had a lesson which he would not forget; there would be no more tugging at the wires, nor would he ever wish to be free again. So I imagined. But I was wrong. From that time the bird's disposition was changed: ever in a restless anxious state, he would flit from side to side of his cage, chirping loudly, but never singing – never one note; the gladness that had made him sing so wonderfully had quite gone out of him. And invariably, after hopping about for a few moments, he would go back to the wire which had been loosened and bent – the one weak spot which was now repaired – and tug at and shake it again. And at last, greatly to my surprise, he actually succeeded in bending the same wire once more and making his escape!

Once more I went to look for him with the cage in my hand, but when I found him he refused to be tempted. I left him for a day to starve, then tried him again; and then again many and many times on many following days, for he was now much too strong on the wing to be hunted down; but though he invariably greeted and appeared to welcome me with his loud chirp, he refused to come down, and after excitedly hailing me and flirting his feathers for a few moments he would fly away.

Gradually I grew reconciled to my loss, for, though no longer my captive – my own bird – he was near me, living in the planta-tion and frequently seen. Often and often, at intervals of a few or of many days, when my lost, yet not wholly lost, cardinal was not in my mind, I would come upon him, sometimes out on the plain, feeding with a flock of purple cowbirds, or yellow-breasted trou-pials, or some other species; and when they would all rise up and fly away at my approach, he alone, after going a little distance with them, would drop out of the crowd and pitch on a stalk or thistle-bush, just, as it would appear, to look at me and hail me with his loud note – to say that he remembered me still; then off he would fly after the others.

That little action of his went far to reconcile me to his loss – to endear him still more to me, changing my boyish bitterness to a new and strange kind of delight in his happiness.

But the end of the story is not yet: even at this distance, after so many changing and hardening years, I experience a certain reluctance or heaviness of heart in telling it.

The warm bright months went by and it was winter again – the cold season from May to August, when the trees are bare, the rainy south wind blows, and there are frosty nights, frosts that would sometimes last all day or even several days. Then it was that I missed my bird and wondered often what had become of him. Had he too flown north to a warmer country with the swallows and other migrants? It could not be believed. But he was no longer in the plantation – that little sheltering island of trees in the level grassy sea-like plain; and I should never see him more or know what his fate had been.

One day, in August, the men employed about the place were engaged in a grand annual campaign against the rats – a sort of spring-cleaning in and out of doors. The shelter of the huge old foss, and of the trees and thickets, wood-piles, many outbuildings and barns full of raw or untanned hides, attracted numbers of these unpleasant little beasts and made it a sort of rats' metropolis; and it was usual to clear them out in early spring before the new grass and herbage sprang up and covered the ground. They were suffocated with smoke, made deadly with brimstone and tobacco, pumped into their holes. I was standing by one of the men who was opening one of the runs after the smoking process, when I caught sight of a gleam of scarlet colour in a heap of straw and rubbish he was turning over with his spade, and, jumping down, I picked up the shining red object. It was my lost cardinal's crest! And there too were his grey wing and tail feathers, white feathers from his breast, and even some of his bones. Alas! he had found it too cold to roost in the naked trees in the cold wind and rain, and, seeking a more sheltered roosting-place on the ground, had been caught and carried into its den and devoured by a rat.

I experienced a second and greater grief at his miserable end – a feeling so poignant that the memory has endured till now. For he was my loved cardinal – my first caged bird: And he was also my last. I could have no other, the lesson he had taught me having sunk into my heart – the knowledge that to a bird too the world is very beautiful and liberty very sweet. I could even rejoice, when time had softened my first keen sorrow, that my cardinal had succeeded in making his escape, since at the last he had experienced those mirac-ulous months of joyous existence, living the true bird-life for which nature had fashioned and fitted him. In all the years of his captivity he could never have known such a happiness, nor can any caged bird know it, however loudly and sweetly it may sing to win a lump of sugar or a sprig of groundsel from his tender-hearted keeper and delude him with the idea that it is well with his prisoner – that no injustice has been done.

3 WELLS-NEXT-THE-SEA, WHERE WILD GEESE CONGREGATE

A restful spot – The marsh and the pine wood – Wild geese on the
marsh – Their tameness there – Alarums and excursions – Their
intelligence – Bird-sanctuary at Holkham

There are few places in England where you can get so much
wildness and desolation of sea and sand-hills, wood, green
marsh, and grey saltings as at Wells, in Norfolk, the small
old red-brick town, a mile and a quarter from the beach, with a
green embankment lying across the intervening marsh connecting
town and sea. Here you can have it all in the space of a half-day's
prowl or saunter – I cannot say 'walk', seeing that I am as often
standing or sitting still as in motion. The little village-like town
in its quietude and sense of remoteness from the world is itself a
restful place to be in; going out you have on the land side the quiet
green Norfolk country of winding roads and lanes, old farm-houses
and small red villages which appear almost deserted. As I passed
through one the other day, the thought was in my mind that in
this village not one inhabitant remained, when all at once I caught
sight of a very old man, shrunk and lean and grey, standing in a
cottage garden behind its grey palings. His clothes, too, like his hair
and face, were a dull grey, so like the hue of the old weathered and
lichen-stained wood of the palings as to make him almost invisible.
It was an instance of protective resemblance in the human species.
He was standing motionless, leaning on his stick, peering at me out

of his pale dim eyes as if astonished at the sight of a stranger in that lonely place.

But I love the solitariness on the side towards the sea best, the green marsh extending to Holkham on your left hand, once a salt flat inundated by the sea, but long reclaimed by the making of that same green bank I have mentioned – the causeway which connects Wells with the beach. On the right side of this bank is the estuary by which small ships may creep up to the town at high tide, and the immense grey saltings extending miles and miles away to Blakeney. Between the flats and the sea are the sand-hills, rough with grey marram grass; then the beach, and, if the tide is up, the sea; but when the water is out, you look across miles of smooth and ribbed sands, with no life visible on its desolate expanse except a troop of gulls resting in a long white line, and very far out a few men and boys digging for bait in the sand, looking no bigger than crows at that distance. Beyond the line of white gulls and the widely scattered and diminished human forms is the silvery-grey line of the sea, with perhaps a sail or two faintly visible on the horizon.

What more could anyone desire – what could add to the fascinations of such a retreat A wood! Well, we have that too, a dark pine wood growing on the slopes of the sand-hills on the land side and extending from the Wells embankment to Holkham a couple of miles away. Many an hour in the late afternoons and evenings have I spent in that perfect solitude listening to the sea-wind in the pines when the sound of wind and sea were one, and finding the deep shelter warm and grateful after a long ramble over the sands and dunes and marshes.

For I go not to Wells in 'the season', when days are long and the sun is hot, the scattering time for all those who live 'too thick', when even into this remote spot drift a few of the pale town-people with books in their pockets and cameras and green butterfly-nets in their hands. The wild geese are not there then, they are away breeding in

the Siberian tundra or Spitzbergen; and for that wild exhilarating
clangour which they make when passing overhead to and from the
sea, and for the cra-cra of the hooded crow – his harsh war-cry and
curse on everything – you hear lark and titlark, dunnock and wren,
with the other members of the 'feathered choir' even as in all other
green places.

Autumn and winter is my time, and at no other place in the
kingdom can the grey geese be seen to better advantage, despite the
fact that to this spot the wild-fowler comes annually in numbers,
and that many of the natives, even the poorest, possess a gun and
are always on the look-out for geese. The birds come in undiminished numbers, probably because they find here the one green spot
on which they can repose in comparative safety. This spot is the
reclaimed marsh or meadowland which I have mentioned as lying
between the Wells embankment and Holkham. It is not a perfect
sanctuary, since the geese are shot a few times during the winter by
the lord of the manor and his guests; but the dangerous days are so
few and far between at this place that the geese have come to regard
it as a safe refuge, and are accustomed to congregate daily in large
numbers, two or three thousand or more being often seen together.

How intelligent these noble birds are! The whole human population of the country round are against them, waiting for them
morning and evening in various hiding-places to shoot them down
as they pass overhead to and from the sea. This incessant persecution has made them the wariest of all wild birds and most difficult
to approach. Yet here, where their enemies are most numerous,
where they keep the sharpest watch when feeding and roosting, and
when on the wing fly high to keep out of range of those who lie in
wait for them – on this one green spot they drop down to rest and
feed by the hour and pay but the slightest attention to the human
form and the sights and sounds of human life! This camping-
ground is backed by the sand-hills and pine wood; on the opposite

side is the coast road and sight of people driving and walking, and nearer still the line of the railway from Lynn to Wells. The marsh, too, is fed by cattle and horses and sheep; there is the shepherd with his dog, and others from the farms going about; but the geese do not heed them, nor do they show alarm when a train rushes past a couple of hundred yards away puffing out steam and making a mighty noise on that flat moist earth. They have made the discovery that there is no harm in it notwithstanding its huge size, its noise and swift motion.

To find at this spot that I was able to look at a flock of a thousand or two of geese at a short distance has been one of my most delightful experiences in bird-watching in England. I had heard of their tameness from others, but could hardly credit it until witnessing it myself. The best time was in fine weather as we occasionally get it in October and November, when the wind is still and the sunshine bright and warm, for the birds are then in a drowsy state and less vigilant than at other times, especially after a moonlight night when they have been feeding on the stubble and pastures. You can then get quite near to them and see them at their best, and with a good binocular bring them as close to your eyes as you like. It is a very fine sight – this assemblage of large wild birds on the green turf sitting or standing in every attitude of repose. At a distance they look almost black; seen closely one admires the shading of their plumage, the dark upper barred greys and browns, and the buff colouring on neck and breast and pink beak and legs. The sight is peculiarly fine when, as frequently happens, great numbers of birds of other species gather at the same spot as if a parliament of the feathered nations were being held. Rooks and crows, both black and hooded, and daws are often there in hundreds; lapwings too in hundreds, and black-headed gulls and starlings and wintering larks, with other small birds. The geese repose, the others are mostly moving about in search of worms and grubs. The lapwings are quietest, inclined to repose too; but at intervals they all rise up and wheel about for a minute or so, then drop to earth again.

As I stand motionless leaning on a gate watching them, having them, as seen through the glasses, no more than twenty yards away, I note that for all their quietude in the warm sleepy sunshine they are wild geese still, that there are always two or three to half a dozen who keep their heads up and their eyes wide open for the general good, also that the entire company is subject at intervals to little contagious gusts and thrills of alarm. It may be some loud unusual noise – a horse on the road suddenly breaking into a thunderous gallop, or the 'hoothoot' of a motor-car; then the enraged scream of a gull or carrion-crow at strife with his neighbour; the sleepers wake and put up their heads, but in a few moments they are reposing again. Then a great heron that has been standing motionless like a grey column for an hour starts up and passes swaying and flapping over them, creating a fresh alarm, which subsides as quickly as the first. By-and-by a fresh flock of geese arrive, returning from some inland feeding-ground, where the gunners have been after them, flying high with a great clamour which you hear before they become visible. Arrived at the refuge, they wheel round and begin their descent, but do not alight; again they rise to circle about and again descend, and when close to the earth, every bird dropping his bright-coloured legs to touch the ground, suddenly they change their minds and rise to wheel about for a minute or two and then go right away out to sea.

It was no doubt my presence on several occasions which prevented them from settling down with the others; for it was no harmless shepherd or farm-labourer which they perceived looked on standing motionless by the gate watching their fellows, a suspicious-looking object in his hand. It might be a gamekeeper or sportsman whose intention was to send a charge of shot into the crowd. But this going away of the flock instead of alighting would prove too

much for the others: they would now be all awake; the suspicion
would grow and grow, every bird standing up with outstretched
neck; then they would draw closer together, emitting excited cackling sounds, all asking what it was – what had frightened their
fellows and sent them away – what danger invisible to them had
they spied from aloft And then they would spring simultaneously
into the air with a rushing noise of wings and tempest of screams,
and rising high go straight away over the sea, soon vanishing from
sight, only to return half an hour later and settle down once more in
the same green place.

To the naturalist, to any bird-lover in fact, a large gathering of
big birds is, of all sights, the most exhilarating, especially in this
country where the big birds have been diligently weeded out until
few are left. At Wells I had two matters in my mind to enhance the
pleasure experienced. One was in the thought of the birds' striking
intelligence, as shown by their changed demeanour during their
daily visits to that camping-spot on the marsh where they relax
their extreme wildness. It is often borne in on me in observing
birds that the position of a species or family in the scale of nature
from the point of view of the anatomist and evolutionist is not a
criterion of its intelligence. Thus the Anatidæ, or ducks, which in
any natural classification would be placed far below the crows and
parrots, are mentally equal to the highest of the bird order. It was
purely the intelligence of these geese which made it possible for me
to observe them so nearly at that spot, which was no sand-bar with
the protecting sea all round it, but a small space in the very midst of
the enemies' country.

It gave me even a higher pleasure to think that there are still
a few great landowners in England, like the present and the late
Lord Leicester, who do not look on our noble bird life as something
to be destroyed for sport, or in the interests of sport, until it has
been wiped out of existence. It is not only the geese which receive

protection here. Ducks in thousands are accustomed to winter in the park at Holkham. All breeding species, from the beautiful sheldrake to the small redshank and ringed dotterel, are protected as much as they can be in a place where everyone has a gun and wants to get something for the pot. In summer the common and lesser tern have their breeding-place on the sand-hills, and a watcher is placed there to prevent them from being disturbed and harried by trippers and egg-stealing collectors. One curious result of the protection given to the terns was that two or three years ago two pairs of black-headed gulls started breeding close to them. It was as if these gulls had observed what was being done and had said to one another: 'This is not a suitable breeding-place for gulls, though a proper one for terns who prefer sand and shingle; but what an advantage to have a man stationed there to protect the nests from being harried! Come, let us make our nests here, just on the border of the terns' gullery, on the chance of our eggs coming in for protection too.' The experiment turned out well, and last summer no fewer than sixteen pairs nested and brought off their young at that spot.

4 GREAT BIRD GATHERINGS

Mr Richard Lydekker's search for the crested screamer – Extirpation
of birds in La Plata – Persecution of sea birds in England – The fight to
save our birds – Our delight in the spectacle of great bird-gatherings

This chapter, is nothing but a digression, suggested by what
goes before; for the subject touched on in the account of
the wild geese on the east coast is one which stirs the
naturalist and bird-lover deeply – the delight of witnessing immense
congregations of birds, especially those of large size and noble
appearance. The remembrance of such scenes is a joy for ever, in
many instances clouded by the thought that the sight which it is a
happiness to recall will be witnessed no more.

Some years ago the distinguished naturalist and palæontolo-
gist, Mr Richard Lydekker, went out to Buenos Ayres to look over
and arrange the collection of tertiary fossils in the famous La Plata
Museum. He had read my *Naturalist in La Plata* with industrious
zeal, quoting from it in rather a wholesale way when compiling his
Royal Natural History. He had also read Darwin and other naturalists who have described that same region, and had a hundred things
to look at besides the fossils. One thing he desired to see was the
crested screamer – that great spur-winged loud-voiced bird which
has puzzled zoologists to classify, some thinking it ralline others
anserine in its affinities, while Huxley considered it was related to
the archxopteryx. Having established himself on the back of a horse,
Mr Lydekker – a biological Dr Syntax of the twentieth century –
set out in quest of this singular fowl, and eventually in some wild

and lonely spot succeeded in catching sight at a vast distance of
a specimen or two. This did not satisfy him; he wanted to see the
great birds as I had seen them, when I rode among them across a
vast marshy plain and saw them in pairs and parties, and in bunches
of a score or two to a hundred, like an innumerable widely scattered
flock of grazing sheep spread out and extending on every side to the
horizon. And he wanted to hear them as I had heard them, 'counting
the hours', as the gauchos say, when at intervals during the night
they all burst out singing like one bird, and the powerful ringing
voices of the incalculable multitude produce an effect as of thousands and tens of thousands of great chiming bells, and the listener
is shaken by the tempest of sound and the earth itself appears to
tremble beneath him.

All this, our naturalist was informed by persons on the spot, was
pure romance; no such vast congregations of crested screamers were
ever seen, and no such great concerts were ever heard; the bird, as
he had witnessed, was quite rare, and so it had always been.

This vexed him, and he resolved to have it out with me on his
return to England. The castigation was to be made in public and
the *Naturalist in La Plata* to be for ever discredited. Luckily for my
poor little reputation he had made further inquiries before quitting
the country and discovered that I had told the simple truth, that
the screamer, albeit a very big bird, had been excessively abundant
and in dry seasons often formed the stupendous gatherings I had
described; finally, that in about a quarter of a century it had been
practically extirpated on the pampas. All this I had from his own
lips on his return, an almost incredible example of candour, for it is
well known that we naturalists, like the early Christians, love one
another.

Alas! the crested screamer is but one of many noble species which
have met with the same fate in southern Argentina. The rhea, the
great blue heron, the flamingo, the wood ibis, and the great blue ibis

of the marshes and the great black-faced ibis of the uplands with its
resounding cries as of giants beating with hammers on iron plates;
and storks and upland geese, and the white and the black-necked
swans. Then follow others of lesser size – the snowy egrets and
other herons and bitterns, glossy ibis, rails and courlans, big and
little, the beautiful golden-winged jacana, curlews and godwits, and
waders and ducks too numerous to mention. They were in myriads
on the rivers and marshes, they were seen in clouds in the air, like
starlings in England when they congregate at their roosting-places.
They are gone now, or are rapidly going. Their destruction was
proceeding when I left, hating the land of my birth and the Italian
immigration that was blighting it, wishing only that I could escape
from all recollection of the scenes I had witnessed – of the very land
where I first knew and loved birds.

How amazing it seems that the chief destroyers should be the
South Europeans, the Latins, who are supposed to be lovers of the
beautiful and who are undoubtedly the most religious of all people!
They have no symbol for the heavenly beings they worship but a
bird. Their religious canvases, illuminations, and temples, inside
and out, are covered with representations of ibises, cranes, pigeons,
gulls, modified so as to resemble human figures, and these stand
for angels and saints and the third person of the Trinity. Yet all
these people, from popes, cardinals, princes, and nobles down to
the meanest peasant on the land, are eager to slay and devour every
winged creature, from noble crane and bustard even to the swallow
that builds in God's house and the minute cutty wren and fairy-like
firecrest – the originals of those sacred emblematic figures before
which they bow in adoration!

But it is not the Latins only that are concerned in this dreadful
business; our race too – a nobler race as we try to think – at home,
in North America, Africa, and Australasia, have been only too
diligently occupied in exterminating. Let it not be forgotten that

down to 1868, the date of our first Wild Bird Protection Act, the
chief breeding-places of our sea birds were invaded every year at
holiday time by train-loads and ship-loads of trippers with guns to
engage in the wholesale massacre of the birds on the cliffs and the
sea. Nor was it confined to the trippers from London, Manchester,
Birmingham, and other great centres of population; the fascination
of it drew men of all classes, including those who annually shot (and
even owned) the moors and coverts. For in June and July the grouse
and partridge and pheasant were not yet ready for killing, and it
was great fun in the meantime to have a few days with the gannets,
terns, kittiwakes, guillemots, and other auks. It was nothing to
them that the birds were breeding, that the result of this wholesale
slaughter would be the extirpation of the multitudes of sea birds
which people the cliffs before the century was out, since they were
no man's birds – only God's.

Happily there were a few men in England who had the courage
to lift up their voices against this hideous iniquity, who eventually
succeeded in getting an Act for its suppression. Thus it came about
that our sea birds were saved and we have them still, and that we
were given courage to go on and try to save our land birds as well.

And with this business we are still occupied, fighting to save our
country's bird life from destruction – how strange that so long and
strenuous a fight should be necessary to secure such an object! But
that it is a winning fight becomes more evident as the years go on.
There is now a public feeling on our side: we are not a brutish nation
ready to stamp out all beauty from the earth so long as the killing
and stamping out processes minister to our pleasure or profit. On
the contrary, we can affirm that a majority of the inhabitants of
this country are desirous of preserving its beautiful wild bird life.
Those who are on the other side may be classified as the barbarians
of means who are devoted mainly to sport, and would cheerfully
see the destruction of most of our birds above the size of a thrush

for the sake of that disastrous exotic, the semi-domestic pheasant of the preserves; secondly, the private collector, that 'curse of rural England'; and last but not least, the regiment of horrible women who persist in decorating their heads with aigrettes and carcasses of slaughtered birds. In the forty odd years that have passed since a first attempt was made to give some protection to our wild birds much has been done in England; and happily in other lands and continents occupied by men of British race our example is being followed. Would that the Americans had begun to follow it three decades sooner, since owing to their tardiness they have many and great losses to lament. It is not strange that the crested screamer, with many other noble species, has quickly been done to death in a country overrun by Italians, when it is remembered that in the United States of America the passenger pigeon, the most abundant species in all that continent, has been extirpated in very recent times without an effort having been made to save it. Now that it is gone the accounts given by Audubon and Fenimore Cooper of its numbers when its migrating flocks darkened the sun at noon read like the veriest fables – inventions as wild as those of the crested screamer congregations in my *La Plata* book, and of the migration of fishes in the Pacific described by Herman Melville.

To return to the subject which was uppermost in my mind when I sat down to write this chapter, or this digression. It was the peculiar delight produced in us by the sight and sound of birds, especially those of large size, in flocks and multitudes. The bird itself is a thing of beauty, supreme in this respect among living forms, therefore, as we have seen, the symbol in art of all that is highest in the spiritual world. Nevertheless we find that the pleasure of seeing a single bird is as nothing compared to that of seeing a numerous company of birds. Take this case of the wild grey goose – a large, handsome bird, a joy to look at whether flying or standing motionless and statuesque with head raised, on the wide level flats and marshes. But the pleasure is infinitely greater when I see a flock of a thousand or of two or three thousand as I do here where I am writing this on the east coast. They come over me, seen first very far off as a black line, wavering, breaking, and re-forming, increasing like a coming cloud and changing its form, till it resolves itself into the host of great broad-winged birds, now black against the pale immense sky, now · flashing white in the sun. I hear them too, even before they become visible, a distant faint clangour which grows and changes as it comes and is a beautiful noise of many shrill and deep sounds, as of wind and stringed instruments, producing an orchestral effect, as of an orchestra in the clouds.

What is the secret of the delight which possesses me at such a spectacle, which seems at the moment to surpass all other delights, giving me a joy that will last for days? It is not merely that the pleasure in the single bird is intensified, or doubled or increased a hundred-fold. It is not the same old feeling in a greater degree; there is a new element in it which makes it different in character. The sight dwells with pleasure on a pleasant landscape; but if we then ascend a hill and look upon the scene from that higher standpoint a quite different feeling is experienced; the wider horizon is a revelation of vastness, of a greatness which is practically new, since the mind had previously become attuned to earth as viewed from the lower level. Now we get the element of sublimity. So, in the case of the large bird seen in flocks and vast numbers – seen and heard; it is a sudden revelation of wild life in its nobler aspect – of its glorious freedom and power and majesty.

We get this emotion in various degrees at the various breeding stations of our larger birds, notably on the Yorkshire and Northumberland coasts, the Bass Rock, the Orkneys and Shetlands, and 'utmost Kilda's lonely isle'. Those who have experienced it value it above all the delights this spectacular world can afford them, and their keenest desire is for its repetition. It is to taste this feeling that thousands of persons, some with the pretext of bird-study or photography, annually visit these teeming stations within the kingdom, whilst others who are able to go further afield seek out the great bird haunts in other countries.

But the feeling is incommunicable, and is a treasured memory and secret, a joy for ever in the heart. Those who do not know it – who have had no opportunity of finding out for themselves – cannot imagine it. To these it may seem strange that any man should turn his back on the comforts of civilised life to spend long laborious days in dreary desert regions, scorched by tropical suns, devoured by mosquitoes, wading in pestilential swamps; not for sport, the fascination of which is universally known, but just for the sake of seeing a populous rookery or congregation of big birds in their breeding haunts. Those who do know will bear these discomforts, and even greater ones, for the sake of that glorious gladness which the sight will produce in them. This rather than the notes and bundle of photographs which they bring back is what they have gone out to seek.

5 BIRDS IN AUTHORITY

A conversation with a sportsman – Wild geese – A masterful gander –
Stories of pet trumpeters – Singular behaviour of a male sand-martin
– Bird sentinels – Dancing performances of lapwings – Ceremonial
drinking and bathing – Bird sports

I was on my way to the West of England, and from Waterloo for
about a hundred and twenty miles had but one fellow-traveller
in the carriage. A man of a fine presence, about sixty; from his
keen, alert eyes, hard weathered face, and his dress I took him to be
a sportsman. He very soon let me know that he was one, as great
an enthusiast as one could meet; and as he was companionable and
we talked the whole time, I got to know a good deal about him.
Shooting and fishing were his chief pleasures and interest in life: he
had followed both from his early years, in and out of England. For
the last ten or twelve years he had lived at the antipodes, where he
held an important position in one of the colonies; but somehow the
sports he loved best had not the same relish for him in that distant
country as at home, and he was accustomed to take frequent and
long holidays to have a month on the moors and in the coverts and
to go on shooting and fishing excursions to the continent. Wild-
fowling was perhaps the kind of sport he loved best of all, and we
soon got on the subject of wild geese.

That bird was much in my mind at the moment, for I was just
back from the east coast, where I had been staying with the wild
geese, so to speak, at Wells-next-the-Sea, watching them every
day in their great gatherings and listening to their multitudinous

resounding cries, which affect one like bells, 'jangled, out of tune
and harsh' it may be, but the sense of wildness and freedom the
sound imparts is exceedingly grateful. Some of his adventures
among the geese caused me to remark that, even if I had not long
ceased to be a sportsman, I would never again lift a gun against a
wild goose; it was so intelligent a bird that it would be like shooting
at a human being. He had no such feeling – could not understand
it. If geese were more intelligent than other species, that only made
them the better sporting birds, and the pleasure of circumventing
them was so much the greater. There was nothing better to get the
taste of shooting half-tame hand-fed driven birds out of the mouth
than a week or two after wild geese. He had just had a fine time
with them on the coast of Norway. This reminded him of something.
Yes, the wild goose was about as intelligent a bird as you could
find. The friend he had been staying with was the owner of a small
group of islands or islets on the coast of Norway; he had bought
them a good many years ago purely for sporting purposes, as the
geese invariably came there on migration and spent some time on
the islands. There was one island where the geese used to congregate every year on arrival in large numbers, and here one autumn
some years ago a goose was caught by the leg in a steel trap set
for a fox. The keeper from a distance saw the whole vast gathering
of geese rise up and circle round and round in a cloud, making a
tremendous outcry, and going to the spot he found the bird struggling violently in the trap. He took it home to another and larger
island close by where his master, my informant's friend, had a farm.
From that day the wild geese never settled on that islet, which had
been used as a resting-place for very many years. The bird he had
accidentally caught was an old gander, and had its leg smashed; but
the keeper set to work to repair the injury, and after binding it up
he put the bird in an outhouse and eventually it got quite well. He
then pinioned it and put it out with the other birds. A little while

before the old gander had been caught the foxes had become so troublesome at the farm that it was found necessary to secure all the birds every night in enclosures and houses made for the purpose, and as the birds preferred to be out the keeper had to go round and spend a good deal of time every evening in collecting and driving them in. Now before the old wild goose had been able to go about many days with the others it was noticed that he was acquiring a kind of mastery over them, and every day as evening approached he began to try to lead and, failing in that, to drive them to the enclosures and buildings. The keeper, curious to see how far this would go, began to relax his efforts and to go round later and later each evening, and as his efforts slackened the gander's zeal increased, until he was left to do the whole work himself and all the keeper had to do was to go round and shut the doors. This state of things had now continued for some years, and the old wild goose was the acknowledged leader and master of all the birds on the farm.

The story of this wise gander, its readiness in adapting itself to a wholly new way of life and in taking in the situation – the danger by night and need of someone in authority over that heterogeneous crowd of birds who had lost the power of flight, and, from being looked after, had grown careless of their own safety – and, finally, the taking of it all on himself, putting himself in office as it were, may strike us as very strange, but it agrees well enough with the character of the bird as we know it in its domestic condition. It is common to hear of the masterful old gander at farmhouses, the ruler and sometimes tyrant of the farmyard. I have myself observed and have heard of many instances of long-lasting and exceedingly bitter feuds between an imperious gander and some other member of the feathered community, a turkey cock or Muscovy duck or peacock who refused to be governed by a goose. But I was specially pleased to have had this story of the bird in Norway from a sportsman and enthusiastic wild-fowler, one of the class who do not like to think too much about the psychology of the creatures it is their pleasure to follow and destroy.

I have also heard of cases of birds of other species taking on themselves the leadership and guardianship of their fellows. One from South America relates to the trumpeter, the strange and delightful *Psophia leucoptera*, a quaint, beautiful creature, a little ostrich in shape, taller than a fowl, very dark, with white wings, the head and neck glossed with purple and green. A singular bird, too, in its voice and manner, when three or four get together and have a sort of drum and trumpet performance, keeping time to the music with measured steps and bowings and various quaint gestures and motions. Alas! they are delicate birds, and all the beautiful trumpeters we had some time ago in the Zoological Gardens are now dead – to come to life again, let us hope, in their distant home in some Brazilian forest.

About twenty years ago an American naturalist, one Dr Rusby, was in a part of Bolivia where it was common to keep a pet trumpeter, and he says that the Spanish settlers almost worshipped them on account of their amiable and affectionate domestic habits. Early in the morning the trumpeter would go into a sleeper's room and salute him on rising by dancing about the floor, bowing its head and dropping its wings and tail, continuing the performance until its presence was noticed and it was spoken to, whereupon it would depart to visit another bedroom, to repeat the ceremony there, then to another, until the whole household had been visited and bid 'Good-morning'. Afterwards, when all were up, it would attach itself to some one member of the family and follow him or her about most of the day. The trumpeter loved and took an interest in everyone of the house, including the stranger within the gates, but was specially devoted to one or two individuals.

It is right to remember that this beautiful disposition of the trumpeter and all its pretty actions have not been acquired through companionship with human beings: they are mere survivals of its own wild life in the forest with its own fellows, and possibly with birds of other species with which it associates. At all events, I have heard of cases in which a tame trumpeter, in a country house in Brazil or Venezuela, where fowls and birds of various kinds were kept and allowed to roam about at will, placing himself in charge of the others, attending them at their feeding grounds, keeping watch, giving the alarm at the approach of danger, and bringing or hunting them home at roosting-time.

If my reader happens not to be of those who regard a bird merely as a creature to be taken and destroyed for man's pleasure or for the decoration of his women, who like a lovely hat to match the lovely spirit within, I trust that he will not think that these be tall stories about a wise grey goose in grey north lands and a benevolent trumpeter in the tropics, for then he will perhaps say that the story I have got to tell in conclusion is taller still.

It is a common fact in natural history that the males of certain species exhibit a good deal of anxiety about the proper care of the eggs, and exercise supervision and authority over the females, compelling them during the period of incubation to return to the nest when they are inclined to stay out too long. Our swift is a familiar example. But has anyone ever observed an individual of any species, one of a colony, presumably a male, exercising this kind of mastership over a number of females in the absence of their mates? Yet this is exactly what I witnessed on one occasion, and if I were to ask a dozen or fifty naturalists to name the species they would all guess wrong, for the bird in question was the small, delicate, gentle, moth-like sand-martin – the 'mountain butterfly', as it is prettily named in Spain.

Near Yeovil I found a breeding-place of these birds in a vast old sand-pit. It was in May, and no doubt they were incubating. There were about fifty holes in the steepest side of the sand-bank, and when I began watching them there were about fourteen or fifteen birds flying round and round within the basin of the pit, hawking after flies, and perhaps prolonging their play-time after their morning feed. By-and-by I noticed one bird acting in a singular manner; I saw him come out of one hole and go quickly into another, then another still, until he had visited several, remaining about five or six seconds in each, or as long as it would take him to run to the end of the burrow and return. Finally, having finished inspecting the holes, he began pursuing one of the birds flying aimlessly about in the pit; the chase increased in speed and violence until the hunted bird took refuge in one of the burrows. He then started chasing another of the birds flying about, and in due time this one was also driven into one of the holes. Then a third chase began, then a fourth and so on until every bird had been driven into a hole, always after a good deal of rushing about, and he remained alone. After flying up and down a few times he finally flew off, probably to some water-course or moist meadow abounding in flies at a distance from the pit, where he would join the other males of the colony.

I remained for some time on the spot, keeping a close watch on the little black burrows on the orange-coloured sand-bank, but not a bird flew or even peeped out; nor did any of the absent birds return to the pit.

Is it a habit of this swallow in the breeding-time for one male to remain behind when the others go away to feed, and the females, or some of them, are still off their eggs, just as, in other species, when the company settles down to feed or sleep one keeps awake and on guard? The action of the swallow in putting back the others on their eggs strikes one as a development of some such habit or instinct as that of the swift, and it is possible that in the sand-martin the social habit is in a more advanced state and the communities more close-knit than in most species. But there is a good deal to learn yet about the inner life of birds.

Observers of animals are familiar with the fact of a bird of masterful temper making himself head and tyrant of his fellows, albeit it is less common or less noticeable among birds that have the social habit than it is among mammals. It appears to me that the instances given above are not of this kind. The spirit, the motive, is different. Here the bird is seen to take the mastership for the general good, and we can only suppose that, with or without greater strength and intelligence than his fellows, he undoubtedly possesses a keener sense of danger, or superior alertness, and a larger measure of that helpful spirit without which wild animals could not exist in a social state. The action of the gander and of the trumpeter in driving their fellows home in the evening must be regarded as similar in its origin to that of the male swift when he hunts his mate back to the nest and of the sand-martin I observed chasing the females of the colony to their burrows. In a lesser way it may be seen in any flock of birds; they move about in such an orderly manner, springing, as it appears to us, simultaneously into the air, going in a certain direction, settling here or there to feed, presently going away to another distant feeding-ground or alighting to rest or sing on trees and bushes, as to produce the idea of a single mind. But the flock is not a machine; the minds are many; one bird gives the signal – the one who is a little better in his keener senses and quicker intelligence than his companions; his slightest sound, his least movement, is heard and seen and understood and is instantly and simultaneously acted upon. So well and quickly is he understood and obeyed that the fact of his leadership or promptership is difficult to detect. Another manifestation of this same helpful spirit with which observers of wild animals are familiar, is seen in the self-appointed guardian or sentinel of the feeding or sleeping flock. In some mammals it appears in a striking way, as in the guanaco on the Patagonian plains, when one member of the herd ascends a hill or other high spot to keep watch while his fellows are browsing on the bushes or grazing on the plain below. In some birds the watchful spirit is so powerful that the sentinel and alarm-giver is not satisfied to see only those of his own species obey his warning; he would have every feathered creature within hearing escape from danger. The curlew is an example and has been observed by wild-fowlers swooping violently upon and trying to drive up a duck that had remained on the ground after all the other birds in the place had taken flight.

Much more could be said on the subject if there were not so many others to be dealt with in this book: probably every wild-fowler, and in fact every close observer of the actions of birds who reads this chapter will be able to recall some incident he has witnessed which illustrates this helpful spirit. But I cannot conclude before giving one remarkable example of a bird or of birds making themselves masters of a flock not with any important purpose as in the foregoing instances, but purely in play, or for fun. I witnessed this incident many years ago, and told it briefly in *Argentine Ornithology*, but that work is little known and unobtainable, and I am rather pleased at the opportunity of relating it again more fully in this place.

The bird was a *Vanellus*, a lapwing in its shape, crest, and the colour of its plumage closely allied to our familiar bird of the moors and pasture-lands, but a third bigger, with pink beak, crimson eyes, scarlet spurs on its wings, and bright red legs, and these touches of colour, 'angrie and brave', give it a strikingly bold appearance. Our green plover is like a small weak copy of the Argentine bird. The voice of the latter, too, is twice as loud, and its temper more jealous and violent. In its habits it resembles the pewit, but has a greater love of play, which it practises, both when flying and on the ground. This play on the ground, called by the natives the bird's 'dance', is performed by a set of three, and is indulged in every day at intervals all the year round. So fond of it are they that when the birds are distributed in pairs all over the plains, for some time before

and during the breeding season, one bird may frequently be seen
to leave his mate at home and fly away to visit another pair in the
neighbourhood. These, instead of rising up with angry screams to
hunt him furiously away from their sacred ground as they would
any other bird, receive his visit with manifest pleasure, and running
to him where he stands motionless, they place themselves behind
him, standing abreast, their plumage puffed out, and then with loud,
rhythmical, drumming notes uttered by the pair, and loud single
measured notes by the leader, they begin a rapid march, stepping
in time to the music; then, when the march is ended the leader as a
rule lifts his wings and holds them erect, still emitting loud notes,
while the two behind, still standing abreast with slightly opened
wings and puffed-out feathers, lower their heads until the tips of
their beaks touch the ground, at the same time sinking their voices
until the drumming sound dies to a whisper. The performance is
then over, and is repeated, or if the visitor is in a hurry he takes his
departure, to rejoin his mate and receive a visitor himself by-and-by.

One dry summer, long after the breeding season was over, while
out riding I passed by a lagoon, or lakelet, where the birds from all
the plain for some miles round were accustomed to come to drink,
and noticed a gathering of about a hundred lapwings standing
quietly near the water. It was evident they had all had their drink
and bath, and were drying and preening their feathers and resting
before going back to their several feeding-grounds. On seeing
them my attention was instantly arrested by the singular behaviour of two birds, the only restless noisy ones in that quiet, silent
company. It was not a close company; every bird had a good space
to himself, his nearest neighbour standing a foot or more away, and
right in among them the two restless birds were trotting freely
about, uttering loud commanding notes, and apparently greatly
excited about something. I had seen nothing like that before, and it
puzzled me to account for their action. By-and-by there was a fresh

arrival; a lapwing came to drink, and instead of dropping down on the edge of the water, he alighted about thirty feet away, at a distance of two or three yards from the others, and remained there, standing erect and motionless as if waiting. The two busy birds, still crying aloud, now made their way to him, and placing themselves behind him and observing all the attitudes and gestures used in their 'dances' or marches and giving the signal, the three set off at a trot to the sound of drums and the thirsty bird was run down to the water. He at once went in to the depth of his knees and drank, then squatting down, bathed his feathers, the whole process lasting about half a minute. He would, no doubt, have taken much longer over his refreshment but for the two birds who had run him down to the water, and who continued standing on the margin emitting their loud authoritative cries. Coming out, he was again received as at first, and trotted briskly away with drumming sounds to a place with the others. No sooner was this done than the two, smoothing their feathers and changing their notes, resumed their marching about among their fellows, until another lapwing arrived, whereupon the whole ceremony was gone through again.

Without a doubt this performance had nothing but play for a motive, the remarkable thing about it was that it was made to fit so admirably into the serious business which brought them together at that spot. They came, one by one, from all over the plain, at noon on a hot thirsty day, solely for refreshment, yet every bird on arrival instantly fell into the humour of the moment and took his appointed part and place in the game. It struck me at the time as a very strange thing, for well as I knew the bird, I had never witnessed an act precisely like this before. Yet it does not stand alone, except in form; any day and every day we may see acts in other species of social disposition or habits, which are undoubtedly inspired by a similar spirit. Little sham quarrels and flights and chases; we see them squaring up to one another with threatening gestures and language; playing little practical jokes too, as when one approaches another in a friendly way and subtly watches him to snatch a morsel from his beak; or when another pretends to have found something exceptionally good and makes a great fuss about it to deceive a comrade, and when the other carries the joke further by capturing and carrying off the bit of dry stick or whatever it is, and pretending to feast on it with great satisfaction. These and a hundred other little playful acts of the kind are common enough and mingle with and are like a part of the food-getting or other business of the moment.

The strangeness of the plover's performance was due to the singular form which play in them almost invariably takes – the military discipline in all their movements, their drumming sounds and commanding cries, the tremendous formality of it all! The two birds were like little children pretending to be some mighty personages who owned everything and lorded it over the others. They were dispensers of the water of the lake, and were graciously pleased to allow any thirsty bird that came to drink and bathe, but only after the proper ceremonies had been performed; also the drinking and bathing had to be cut rather short on this occasion.

6 A WOOD BY THE SEA

The pine wood at Wells – An extraordinary echo – Crows disturbed
by a barn owl – Pheasant and blackbird feeding together – Friendships
between birds of different species – Account of a pet pheasant

One of my favourite haunts at Wells, in Norfolk, is the pine
wood, a mile or two long, growing on the slope of the
sand-hills and extending from the Wells embankment
to Holkham – a black strip with the yellow-grey dunes and the
sea on one side and the wide level green marsh on the other. It is
the roosting-place of all the crows that winter on that part of the
coast, and I time my visits so as to be there in the evening. Rooks
and daws also resort to that spot, and altogether there is a vast
concourse of birds of the crow family. My habit is to stroll on to
the embankment at about three o'clock to watch and listen to the
geese on their way from their feeding-grounds to the sea, always
flying too high for the poor gunners lying in wait for them. So
poor, indeed, are some of these men that they will shoot at anything
that flies by, even a hooded crow. They do not fire at it for fun – they
can't afford to throw away a cartridge: one of them assured me that a
crow, stewed with any other bird he might have in the larder – pewit,
redshank, curlew, or gull – goes down very well when you are hungry.

Later I go on to the sea, meeting the last of the fishers, or toilers
in the sands, returning before dark; men and boys in big boots and
heavy wet clothes, burdened with spades and forks and baskets of
bait and shell-fish. With slow, heavy feet they trudge past and leave
the world to darkness and to me.

On one of these evenings as I stood on the ridge of the dunes, looking seaward, when the tide was out and the level sands stretched away to the darkening horizon, an elderly woman made her appearance, and had evidently come all that way down to give her dog an evening run. Climbing over the ridge, she went down to the beach, where the dog, a big rough-haired terrier, was so delighted with the smooth sands that he began careering round her in wide circles at his utmost speed, barking the while with furious joy. The sound produced an extraordinary effect; it was repeated and redoubled a hundred-fold from all over the flat sands. It was my first experience of an echo of that sort heard from above – perhaps if I had been below there would have been no echo – but I could not understand how it was produced. It was not like other echoes – exact repetitions of the sounds emitted which come back to us from walls and woods and cliffs – but was fainter and more diffused, the sounds running into each other and all seeming to run over the flat earth, now here, now there, and fading into mysterious whisperings. It was as if the vigorous barkings of the living dog had roused the ghosts of scores and hundreds of perished ones; that they had come out of the earth and, unable to resist the contagion of his example and the 'memory of an ancient joy', were all madly barking their ghost barks and scampering invisible over the sands.

The chief thing to see was the crows coming in to roost from about four to six o'clock, arriving continually in small parties of from two or three to thirty or forty birds, until it was quite dark. The roosting place has been shifted two or three times since I have known the wood, and, by a lucky chance, on the last occasion of their going to a fresh place I witnessed the removal and discovered its cause. For two evenings I had noticed a good deal of unrest among the roosting birds. This would begin at dusk, after they were all quietly settled down, when all at once there would be an outburst of loud angry cawings at one point, as unmistakable in its meaning

as that sudden storm of indignation and protest frequently heard in
one part of our House of Commons when the susceptibilities of the
party or group of persons sitting together at that spot have been
wantonly hurt by the honourable member addressing the House.
It would subside only to break out by-and-by at some other spot,
perhaps fifty yards away; and at some points the birds would rise up
and wheel and hover overhead, cawing loudly for a minute or two
before settling down again.

I concluded that it was some creature dangerous to birds, probably a fox, prowling about among the trees and creating an alarm
whenever they caught sight of him; but though I watched for an
hour I could detect nothing.

On the third evening the disturbance was more widespread and
persistent than usual, until the birds could endure it no longer. The
cawing storms had been breaking out at various spots over an area
of many acres of wood, when at length the whole vast concourse
rose up and continued hovering and flying about for fifteen or
twenty minutes, then settled once more on the topmost branches of
the pines. Seen from the ridge on a level with the top of the wood
the birds presented a strange sight, perched in hundreds, sitting
upright and motionless, looking intensely black on the black treetops against the pale evening sky. By-and-by, as I stood in a green
drive in the midst of the roosting-place, a fresh tempest of alarm
broke out at some distance and travelled towards me, causing the
birds to rise; and suddenly the disturber appeared, gliding noise-
lessly near the ground with many quick doublings among the boles
– a barn owl, looking strangely white among the black trees! A little
later there was a general rising of the entire multitude with a great
uproar; they were unable to stand the appearance of that mysterious
bird-shaped white creature gliding about under their roosting-
trees any longer. For a minute or two they hovered overhead, rising
higher and higher in the darkening sky, then began streaming away

over the wood to settle finally at another spot about half a mile away; and to that new roosting-place they returned on subsequent evenings.

It was a curious thing to have witnessed, for one does not think of this bird – 'Hilarion's servant, the sage Crow' – as a nervous creature, subject to needless alarms; but a few evenings later I was so fortunate as to witness something even more interesting. In this instance a pheasant was the chief actor, a species the field naturalist is apt to look askance at because it is a coddled species and the coddling process has incidentally produced a disastrous effect on our native wild-bird life. Once we rid our minds of these unfortunate associations we recognise that this stranger in our woods is not only of a splendid appearance, but has that which is infinitely more than fine feathers – the intelligent spirit, the mind, that is in a bird.

On a November evening I came out of the wood to a nice sheltered spot by the side of a dyke fringed with sedges and yellow reeds, and the wide green marsh spread out before me. There are many pheasants in the wood, which are accustomed to feed by day on the marsh or meadow lands; now I watched them coming in, flying and running, filling the wood with noise as they settled in their roosting trees, clucking and crowing. In a little while they grew quiet, and I thought that all were at home and abed; but presently, while sweeping the level green expanse with my glasses, I spied a cock pheasant about two hundred yards out, standing bunched up in a dejected attitude at the side of a dyke and wire fence with a few bramble bushes growing by it. He looked sick, perhaps suffering from the effects of a stray pellet of lead in his body if not from some natural disease. I watched him for twenty or twenty-five minutes, during which he made not the slightest motion. Then a blackbird shot out from the wood, passing over my head, and flew straight out over the marsh, and, following it with my glasses, I saw it pitch on the bush near which the pheasant was standing. The

pheasant instantly put up his head; the blackbird then flew down
to him, and immediately both birds began moving about in search
of food, the pheasant stepping quietly over the sward, pecking as
he went; the blackbird making his quick little runs, now to this
side, then to that, then on ahead and at intervals running back to
the other. Presently the sudden near loud cry of a carrion-crow
flying to the wood startled the blackbird, and he rushed away to the
bush, where he remained perched for about a minute; the other was
not startled, but he at once left off feeding and stood motionless,
patiently waiting till his companion returned to him, and they went
on as before. The pheasant now discovered something to his taste,
and for several minutes remained still, pecking rapidly at the same
spot, the other running about in quest of worms until he found and
succeeded in pulling one out and spent some time over it; then came
back again to the pheasant.

During all this time I could not detect any other birds from the
wood, not even a thrush that feeds latest, on all the marsh; they
were all at roost, and it was impossible not to believe that these two
were friends, accustomed to meet at that spot and feed together;
that when I first spied the pheasant, standing in that listless attitude after all his fellows had gone, he was waiting for his little black
comrade and would not have his supper without him.

It was getting dark when the blackbird at length flew off to the
wood, and at once the pheasant, with head up, began walking in the
same direction; then running and soon launching himself on the air
he flew straight into the pines.

My experience is that friendships between bird and bird, if
the preference of two individuals for each other's company, can be
described by that word, is not at all uncommon, though I usually
find that gamekeepers 'don't quite seem to see it'. That is only
natural in their case; it is but a reflex effect of the gun in the hand
on the keeper's mind. Yet one of the keepers on the estate, to whom

I related this incident, although inclined to shake his head, told me
he had observed a ringed dotterel and a redshank keeping company
for a space of two or three months last year. It was impossible not
to see, he said, what close friends they were, as they invariably went
together even when feeding with other shore birds. It is a thing we
notice sometimes when the companionship is between two birds of
different species, but it is probable that it is far more common among
those of the same species, and that among the gregarious and social
kinds the unmated ones as a rule have their chums in the flock.

The friendship I observed between the two birds at Wells
reminded me of the case of a pheasant who had human friends; it
is the only instance I have met with of a pheasant being kept as a
household pet, and was related to me by my old friend the late Dr
Cunninghame Geikie, of Bournemouth, author of religious books.
The bird was a handsome cock, owned by a lady of that place, who
kept it for many years – he said nineteen, but he may have been
mistaken about the time. The main thing was his disposition,
his affection for his people and the fine courage he displayed in
protecting them. His zeal in looking after them was at times inconvenient. He was particularly attached to his mistress, and liked to
attend her on her walks, and made himself her guardian. But he was
distrustful of strangers, and when she was at home he would keep
watch, and if he saw a visitor approaching the house – some person
he did not know – he would boldly sally forth to meet and order
him off the premises with suitable threatening gestures, which if not
quickly obeyed would be followed by a brisk attack, the blows, with
spurs, being aimed at the intruder's legs.

7 FRIENDSHIP IN ANIMALS

The title justified – Position of friendship in the scale of animal qualities – Friendships between horses – A pet wolf – Peter the fox – Friendships among birds – A jackdaw and a small boy – Stories of teal – Birds caring for injured companions – The helping instinct – Partridge and pony – Strange case of a swan and a trout

Some lordly-minded person has said that it is a misuse or an abuse of the word to describe as friendship the distinct preference for each other's company and habitual consorting together of two individuals among the lower animals; because – this wise man continues – being *lower animals,* they cannot rise to the height of that union between two minds, or souls, common among men. Where then does the capacity for this union begin? for who will venture to say that the two-legged upright or man-shaped mammalian of Tierra del Fuego or the Andaman Islands or of the Aruwimi forest is capable of a feeling beyond the power of elephants, dogs, seals, apes, and in fact of all other vertebrates – beasts, birds, reptiles, and fishes? There is no broad line of demarcation between our noble selves and these our poor relations – even the wearers of feathers and scales. We have had to learn, not without reluctance and a secret bitterness, that even our best and highest qualities have their small beginnings in these lowlier beings. That union or feeling of preference and attachment of an individual towards another of its own or of a different species, which I first began to observe in horses during my boyhood, is, like play, unconcerned with the satisfaction of bodily wants and the business of self-preservation and the continuance of the race. It is a manifestation of something higher in the mind, which shows that the lower animals are not wholly immersed in the struggle for existence, that they are capable in a small way, as we are in a large way, of escaping from and rising above it. Friendship is in fact the highest point to which the animal's mind can rise. For whereas play, which has its origin in the purely physical state of well-being and in instinctive impulses universal among sentient beings, does indirectly serve a purpose in the animal's life, friendship can serve no useful purpose whatever and is the isolated act of an individual which clearly shows a perception on his part of differences in the character of other individuals, also the will and power to choose from among them the one with which he finds himself most in harmony. Furthermore, such friendships do not come into existence inevitably, or automatically, as the result of a feeling on the part of an individual: the feeling must be expressed or exhibited and approaches made. These may or may not be accepted, since the animal approached has a will of his own. The result is sometimes a very one-sided friendship, as in the case of an individual who forms an attachment for another which is like an infatuation, and who is happy if his presence is tolerated and who will go on day after day for weeks and months following the indifferent one about. In other cases the advances are resented, and if persisted in will develop a quite savage animosity in their object, resulting in bites and kicks or blows with whatever weapon Nature may have endowed the species.

All these actions may be easily observed in our domestic animals and are common enough, although probably not nearly so common in England as in the pastoral countries where the animals are not housed and fed, but are allowed to lead a semi-independent life. I have said that I first observed friendship in horses. We usually kept fifteen or twenty, and as the country was all open then, our horses did sometimes take advantage of their liberty to clear out altogether; as a rule they kept to their own grazing ground within a mile or so of home, and when a fresh horse or horses were wanted someone was sent to drive the troop in. As a boy who wanted to spend at least half of every day on horseback I went after the troop very often and grew to be very familiar with their little ways. There were always horses in the troop that went in couples, and who were chums and inseparable. After one of a couple had been in use for some hours or for a day, on being liberated he would gallop off in quest of the troop and on catching sight of them neigh aloud to announce his coming. Then his chum would neigh in response and start off at a trot to meet him, and meeting him the two would stand for a few moments, touching noses, which is the horse's way of kissing or expressing affection. They would then go quietly back together to the others and begin grazing side by side.

This book has birds for its subject, and we shall get to something about them by-and-by: just now I want to emphasise the fact of a feeling and union among animals generally, which is in its nature identical with what we call friendship in human beings. The fact is more readily accepted when we treat of mammals, just because they suckle their young and have hair instead of feathers to clothe them. We, evolutionists think, were hairy too in our far past, and some mammals, like ourselves, have lost their hairy covering. That some animals are capable of a strong affection for a human being or master is a fact familiar to everyone; we think instantly of the dog in this connection; the dog is indeed commonly described as the 'Friend of Man', but if the description implies a superiority in this respect it is certainly unjust to other species.

An acquaintance of mine keeps a timber wolf as a pet – the biggest, most powerful, probably the most ferocious of all the numerous varieties of that terrible beast. Yet his owner assures me that his wolf is as much attached to him as any dog could be to a man, that he would trust him as he would the most intelligent,

affectionate, and gentlest-mannered dog. Though so big, this wolf
is privileged to lie on the hearthrug at his feet, and if there are
children about they are permitted to sit on or roll over him, to
pull his ears and open his mighty mouth to look at his fangs. It is
true that the wolf is next door to the dog, but the fox is not quite
so near a neighbour although he lives not far off; he is specialised
in a different direction, and on account of this specialisation, of his
nature, his genius, one would hardly suppose him capable of a very
close friendship with a human master. Let me relate here the story
of Peter the fox, for the truth of which I vouch although I am not at
liberty to give the name and address of its owner.

Peter's mistress is a lady living in a Shropshire village, and
the lady and fox are so much to one another that they are not
happy when apart. When she goes for a walk or to make a call she
takes the fox, just as Mary took her little lamb, and she laughs at
those who say warningly that a fox makes a dangerous pet; that
his temper is uncertain and his teeth sharp; also that he has an
ineradicable weakness for certain things – things with feathers, for
example. Peter, she affirms, never did and never will do anything he
ought not to do, and is moreover the sweetest tempered and most
affectionate pet that any person ever possessed.

After having had Peter for about a year he vanished and his loss
was a great grief to her, and it was no consolation to be told by her
friends that it was just what they had thought would happen, that
sooner or later the call of the wild would come and prove irresistible.

One afternoon, when Peter had been gone several days, she
remembered him and was heavy at heart, and it then first came into
her mind to try an experiment. If her fox still lived, she thought,
where would he be but in the wood a mile or so from the village?
There she would go and seek for him. It was near sunset when she
reached the wood, and after making her way to its innermost part
she stood still and raising her voice to its highest pitch sent forth

a loud shrill call – Peter – Pee-ter – Peee-ter! and then waited.
By-and-by she heard a sound, and looking in the direction it came
from she spied Peter himself coming towards her at his topmost
speed, making the dead leaves fly about him with the wind he
created; but when he got to her there was no touching him, though
she was eager to clasp her dear recovered friend in her arms, for he
was beside himself with joy and could only rush round and round
her in a wide circle and then charging straight at her leaped clear
over her head, and then again, and then a third time! This sounds
incredible, but the lady sticks to it that her fox did accomplish this
feat, and says that she was astonished at the sight of its transports
of joy at finding her. Then, when he had thus worked off his excite-
ment, they went home together, Peter trotting along at her side and
breaking out from time to time into fresh demonstrations of delight
and affection.

Friendship among birds is less remarked than it is in mammals,
simply, I believe, because their inner life is less openly revealed to
us; in other words, because they have wings to fly with, and quicker,
brighter, more variable or volatile minds to match the aerial life.
Numbers of species pair for life, including many that are gregarious;
I take it that in such cases the bond which unites male and female
throughout the year is essentially the same as that between two
horses, or goats, or cows, or llamas, or any other species, wild
or domestic, that become attached to one another. The union is
different in origin, but once the sexual motive is over and done with
the life-partners are no more than friends or chums. Again, birds
being so free and light in their motions do not keep so close together
as mammals do, hence a comradeship between two in a crowd is
not easily detected. We notice and are arrested by it when a friendship exists between two widely different species, as in such cases as
those given in the last chapter of a pheasant and a blackbird, and of
a ringed dotterel and a redshank, and of another I observed in South

America of a lesser yellow shanks and a pectoral sandpiper who
were inseparable, even when mixed in a flock of their own species.

Cases of birds becoming strongly attached to a human being
are quite common – so common indeed that any industrious person
could compile a volume of them. One of a pheasant and a lady has
been given in the last chapter and I had set down several more
to relate in this one, but in view of the multiplicity of subjects, or
adventures, to be treated in the book they must be left out. Or all
but one given here for a special reason. This is the case of a jackdaw
which was found last year, unable to fly, and taken home by a boy
in the village of Tilshead in the South Wiltshire downs. In a very
few days the bird recovered from his weakness and was perfectly
well and able to fly again, but he did not go away; and the reason
of his remaining appeared to be not that he had been well treated,
but because he had formed an extraordinary attachment, not, as one
would naturally suppose, to the boy who had rescued and fed him
but to another, smaller boy, who lived in the next cottage! It was
quite unmistakable; the bird, free to go away if he liked, began to
spend his time hanging about the cottage of his chosen little friend.
He wanted to be always with him, and when the children went to
school in the morning the daw would accompany them, and flying
into the schoolroom after them settle himself on a perch where he
would sit until the release came. But the proceedings were always
too long for his patience, and from time to time he would emit a
loud caw of remonstrance, which would set the children tittering,
and eventually he was turned out and the door shut against him. He
then took to sitting on the roof until school was over, whereupon
he would fly down to the shoulder of his little friend and go home
with him. In the same way he would follow his friend to church on
Sunday morning, but even there he could not repress his loud startling caw, which made the congregation smile and cast up its eyes at
the roof. My friend the vicar, who by-the-by is a lover of birds, could

not tolerate this, and the result was that the daw had to be caught
and confined every day during school and church hours.

There are three or four more jackdaw anecdotes among those I
am compelled to leave out. No doubt some species of birds are much
more capable of these attachments than others: thus the bullfinch,
among caged birds, is noted for his affectionate disposition and
many instances have been recorded of the bird's death from pure
grief after losing its mistress. The daw too is a bird of that character, in spite of his wicked little grey eyes and love of mischief.
Probably he was first called Jack on account of his human qualities;
we might also describe him as the Friendly Daw.

I have told this story just to show that it is not in every case, as
some imagine, mere cupboard love that inspires an attachment of
this kind.

An even more remarkable case than that of the daw remains to
be told. A friend of mine, an Anglo-Argentine residing at Buenos
Ayres, one day when out duck-shooting winged a teal, one of a
common species – *Querquedula flavirostris*. The sight and feel of the
bird when he had it in his hand, its graceful shape and beautiful
plumage and the bright frightened eyes and beating heart, softened
him so that he could not kill it, and putting it in his bag he took it
home; and after bandaging the broken wing the best way he could,
he placed the bird in the large courtyard and supplied it with food
and water. In a short time its wound healed, but it did not recover its
power of flight and made no attempt to escape. It became perfectly
tame and would come at call to be fed or caressed. The strange
thing was that although all the people of the house were interested
in the teal and made it a pet, its whole affection was given to the
man who had shot it. To the others it was indifferent, although they
were always in the house taking notice of and petting it, while this
chosen friend was absent on business in the city every day from
morning to the late afternoon. The teal would keep near him when

he had breakfast, then accompany him to the door opening out
of the courtyard to the street, and having seen him off she would
return to her place and pass her day in a quiet contented manner as
if she had forgotten all about the absent one. But invariably at about
four o'clock in the afternoon she would go to the open street door
to wait for his return, and if he was an hour or so late she would sit
there the whole time on the threshold, her beak turned city-wards,
to the astonishment of the passers-by. On his appearance she was
all joy and would run to his feet, nodding her head and flirting her
wings and emitting all the quacking and other curious little sounds
the bird uses to express its happy emotions. Like most teals it is a
loquacious bird, and very excitable. After that the great happiness
of the teal was to have permission to sit at his feet when he settled
himself in his chair to rest and read. She would actually sit *on* his foot.

It happened that some years ago I told this story of the teal in
an article in a monthly magazine. My belief was that it was a very
strange story, that the experience of my Buenos Ayres friend was
absolutely unique – for who would have imagined that any other
person in the world had found a loved and affectionate pet in a teal,
which he had himself shot with the intention of eating it? But I soon
received a letter from a gentleman residing in South Kensington
who said he had read the incident of the teal with astonishment,
that it had appeared to him just as if I had taken an incident which
occurred in South Africa, transferred it to South America, and
slightly altering the circumstances related the first half of the story.
My informant had been out to the Cape, and while there went to
stay with a friend on his estate. His friend told him that one day
when out shooting he winged a teal, and on picking it up experienced so strong a pang of compassion for it that he took it home and
set to work to bind up the wound, intending if the bird recovered
the use of its wings to restore it to liberty. In a little while the teal
became attached to him, precisely as in the case I had described, and

would trot about after him all over the place just like a little dog. Eventually, when pairing time came round again the teal flew away to the marshes, for it had recovered the full use of its wings, and he never expected to see or at all events to recognise his quacking little friend again. One day when out shooting he had his eye on a bunch of teal flying past at a considerable distance, when all at once one of the birds detached itself from the flock and came swiftly towards him and pitched at his very feet! It was his lost pet, and the teal appeared as delighted at the meeting as he was. After staying with him a few minutes expressing its pleasure and receiving caresses it flew away again in search of its companions. Since that encounter there had been others at long intervals, the teal always recognising its old master and friend at a distance and flying straight to him, but it had never returned to the house.

One imagines that the two persons concerned in these incidents, one in South Africa, the other in South America, cannot now enjoy eating or even shooting teal as much as they did formerly.

Friendships between bird and bird of the same species, if we exclude the companionship of such as pair for life, are exceedingly difficult, almost impossible, to detect for reasons already given. If it were not so we should probably find as many pairs of inseparables in any flock of bachelor chaffinches in winter as in a herd of horses or cattle existing in a semi-feral state.

Another thing to be borne in mind is that it is possible to mistake for friendship an action which, at all events in its origin, is of a different nature. The following cases will serve as illustrations.

One relates to an exotic species, the military starling of the pampas – a bird of a social disposition, like most of its family, the troupials. Breeding over, the birds unite in large flocks and lead a gipsy life on the great plains. They are always on the move, the flock presenting an extended front, the beaks and scarlet breasts all turned one way, the hindmost birds continually flying forward and dropping down in or a little in advance of the front line. It is a pretty spectacle, one I was never tired of seeing. One day I was sitting on my horse watching a flock feeding and travelling in their leisurely manner, when I noticed a little distance behind the others a bird sitting motionless on the ground and two others keeping close to it, one on each side. These two had finished examining the ground and prodding at the roots of the grass at the spot, and were now anxious to go forward and rejoin the company, but were held back by the other one. On my going to them they all flew up and on, and I then saw that the one that had hung back had a broken leg. Perhaps it had not long been broken and he had not yet accommodated himself to the changed conditions in which he had to get about on the ground and find his food. I followed and found that, again and again, after the entire scarlet-breasted army had moved on, the lame bird remained behind, his two impatient but faithful companions still keeping with him. They would not fly until he flew, and when on the wing still kept their places at his side, and on overtaking the flock all three would drop down together.

The next case is from Penzance and was told to me when I was staying there. A lady of that town, a member of one of its oldest and most distinguished families, is a great bird-lover and feeds the birds during the winter on her lawn. She noticed that a blackbird and thrush always came together to the food, and then that the blackbird fed the other, picking up the morsels and placing them in its open mouth. In looking more closely it was discovered that the thrush had lost its beak: this had been cut off close to the head, probably by a steel or a sudden-death spring trap, such as the children in Cornwall commonly use to catch or kill small birds. The bird was incapable of feeding itself.

Another case of a beakless bird with a friend was told to me by Mr E. Selley of Sidmouth, a gardener and local naturalist. His father kept a magpie in a large hutch surrounded by wires through which small birds would pass in to steal the food. Among these was a robin that had lost its beak in a steel trap; and this bird the magpie befriended, though he was at enmity with the others and hunted them out of his house. The robin with no beak to peck with could only pick up small crumbs, and the magpie taking a piece of bread on its perch would pick it into small pieces to feed the robin. 'It sounds like a fairy tale,' said Mr Selley; it is, however, a very credible kind of fairy tale to those who know a bird.

Yet another case told to me recently by a friend who was himself a witness to it. A lark was kept in a cage hanging against the front wall of the house, and it was noticed that some sparrows had formed the habit of clinging to the wires and feeding from the seed-box. To stop this plundering the box was transferred from the front to the back of the cage, where it was well out of their reach. Nevertheless their visits continued and they appeared to be faring as well as ever. With a little closer watching it was discovered that the lark itself was feeding them, not by putting the seed into their beaks but by conveying it from the box to the other side of the cage-floor where the sparrows could get at it.

I take it that in these instances the act does not proceed from friendship but from the *helping* instinct common in animals of social habits. We know it best in the large mammals – cattle, swine, pecca-ries, deer, elephants, and many more. Even the unsocial cat will sometimes feed a fellow-cat. In birds it appears to have its origin in the parental instinct of feeding and protecting the young from danger. A young bird that has lost its parents will sometimes find a response to its hunger-call from a bird stranger, and in some instances the stranger is of a different species. It may be noted here that, in some species, the incubating female when fed by the male reverts to the hunger-cry and gestures of the young. The cry of distress too in an old bird, when captured or injured, which excites its fellows and brings them to its rescue, is like the cry of distress and terror in the young.

Many other cases one meets with of a close companionship between individuals result from the impatience of solitude, in a social species. So intolerable is loneliness to some animals that they will attach themselves to any creature they can scrape acquaintance with, without regard to its kind or habits or of disparity in size. I remember a case of this kind which was recorded many years ago, of a pony confined by itself in a field and a partridge – a solitary bird who was perhaps the only one of its species in that place. They were always to be seen together, the partridge keeping with the pony where he grazed, and when he rested from grazing sitting contentedly at his feet. No doubt this companionship made their lonely lives less irksome.

Another even stranger case must be told in conclusion – the sad case of a lonely swan in search of a friend, and as it is a story of the 'incredible' sort I am glad I have permission to give the names of the persons who witnessed the affair. The place is Little Chelmsford Hall, near Chelmsford, and the witnesses are Lady Pennefather and her friend Miss Guinness who resides with her. Near the house there is an artificial lake of considerable length, fed by a stream which flows into the grounds on one side and out at the other. Lake and stream are stocked with trout. A pair of swans are kept on the lake and three or four years ago they reared a single young one, which after some months when it was fully grown they began to persecute. The young swan, however, could not endure to be alone, and although driven furiously off to a distance a hundred times a day he would still return. Eventually he was punished so mercilessly that he gave it up and went right away to the further end of the lake and made that part his home. About this time Miss Guinness started making a series of water-colour sketches at that end of the lake, and her presence was a happiness to the swan. Invariably on her appearance he would start swimming rapidly towards her, then leaving the water he would follow her about until she sat down to do a sketch,

whereupon the swan would settle itself by her side to stay contentedly with her until she finished. This went on for five or six weeks
till the sketching was done and Miss Guinness went away on a visit.
Again the poor bird was alone and miserable until a man was sent
to work in the shrubbery by the lake, and at once the swan made
a companion of him; each morning it would come from the lake to
meet him, to spend the whole day in his company. In due time the
work was finished and the man went away. Once more the swan
was miserable, and it made the lady of the house unhappy to see
it, so anxious appeared the bird to be with her whenever she went
near the lake, so distressed when she left it. All at once there was a
change in its behaviour; it was no longer waiting and watching for a
visitor to the lake-side and ready to leave the water on her appearance. It now appeared quite contented to be alone and would rest on
the water at the same spot for an hour at a time, floating motionless
or else propelling itself with such a slow and gentle movement of its
oars as to make it appear almost stationary. It was an astonishing
change but a welcome one, as the unhappiness of the swan had
begun to make everybody feel bad, and now it looked as if the poor
bird had become reconciled to a solitary life. A little later the reason
of this change appeared when the extraordinary discovery was made
that the swan was not alone after all, that he had a friend who was
constantly with him – a big trout! The fish had his place at the side
of the bird, just below the surface, and together they would rest and
together move like one being. Those who first saw it could hardly
credit the evidence of their own senses, but in a short time they
became convinced that this amazing thing had come to pass, that these
two ill-assorted beings had actually become companions.

How can we explain it? The swan, we have seen, was in a state
of misery at his isolation and doubtless ready to attach himself to
and find a solace in the company of any living creature on land or
in the water, and a fish happened to be the only creature there. But

how about the trout? I can only suppose that he got some profit
out of the partnership, that the swan when feeding by the margin
accidentally fed the trout by shaking small insects into the water,
and that in this way the swan became associated with food in what
we are pleased to call the trout's mind. The biologist denies that it
– the poor fish – has a mind at all, since it has no cortex to its brain,
but we need not trouble ourselves with this question just now. I also
think it possible that the swan may have touched or stroked the back
of his strange friend with his beak, just as one swan would caress
another swan, and that this contact was grateful to the trout. Fish
have as much delight in being gently stroked as other creatures that
wear a skin or scales. I have picked up many 'wild worms in woods'
and many a wild toad, if wild toads there be, and have quickly over-
come their wildness and made them contented to be in my hands by
gently stroking them on the back.

The sequel remains to be told. There came to the Hall a visitor
from London, who being a keen angler got up very early in the
morning and went to the lake to try and get a trout for breakfast. About eight o'clock he returned and finding his hostess down
proudly exhibited to her a magnificent trout he had caught. He had
not looked for such a big one, and he would never forget catching
this particular trout for another reason. A wonderful thing had
happened when he hooked it. One of the swans was there on the
water, and followed the fish up when it was hooked, and when he
drew it to land the swan came out and dashed at and attacked him
with the greatest fury. He had a good deal of trouble to beat her off!
'Oh, what a pity!' cried the lady. 'You have killed the poor swan's
friend!'

From that time the swan was more unhappy than ever; the sight
of it became positively painful to my compassionate friends, and
by-and-by hearing of an acquaintance in another part of the country
who wanted a swan they sent it to him.

8 THE SACRED BIRD
(*PHASIANUS COLCHICUS*)

The pheasant in Romano-British times – The modern craze for it
– Destruction of bird life by keepers – A heronry depopulated – An
indiscriminate massacre – 'Keeping an eye' on the hawks – Beauty of
the pheasant in autumn woods – Absence of great soaring birds from
English skies

It was hardly necessary to add the scientific name to any British species spoken of as 'sacred'. Certainly it is not the ibis and no mistake is possible seeing that England is not ancient Egypt, or Hindustan, or Samoa, or any remote barbarous land, where certain of the creatures are regarded with a kind of religious veneration. We call our familiar pheasant the sacred bird to express condemnation of the persons who devote themselves with excessive zeal to pheasant-preserving for the sake of sport.

To shoot a pheasant is undoubtedly the best way to kill it, and would still be the best way – certainly better than wringing its neck – even if these semi-domestic birds were wholly domestic, as I am perfectly sure they were in the time of the Romans who first introduced them into these islands. I am sure of it because this Asiatic ground-bird, which in two thousand years has not become wholly native, and, as ornithologists say, is in no sense an English bird, could not have existed and been abundant in the conditions which prevailed in Roman times. The fact that pheasant bones come next in quantity to those of the domestic fowl in the ash and bone pits examined by

experts during the excavations at Silchester shows that the bird was a
common article of food. The country about Silchester was a vast oak
forest at that period, probably very sparsely inhabited; a portion of
the forest exists to this day, and is in fact one of my favourite haunts.
The fox, stoat, and sparrow-hawk were not the only enemies of the
pheasant then: the wolf existed, the wild cat, the marten, and the
foumart; while the list of rapacious birds included the eagle, goshawk,
buzzard, kite, hen-harrier, peregrine falcon, and hobby, as well as all
the species which still survive, only in very much larger numbers.
Then there were the crows: judging from the number of bones of
the raven found at Silchester we can only suppose that this chief and
most destructive of the Corvidæ was a protected species and existed
in a semi-domestic state and was extremely abundant in and round
Calleva – probably at all the Roman stations. It is probable that a
few tame pheasants escaped from time to time into the woods, also
some may have been turned out in the hope that they would become
acclimatised, and we may suppose that a few of the most hardy birds
survived and continued the species until later times; but for hundreds
of years succeeding the Romano-British period the pheasant must
have been a rarity in English woods. And a rarity it remains down to
this day in all places where it is left to itself, in spite of the extermination of most of its natural enemies. Unhappily for England the fashion
or craze for this bird became common among landowners in recent
times – the desire to make it artificially abundant so that an estate
which yielded a dozen or twenty birds a year to the sportsman would
be made to yield a thousand. This necessitated the destruction of all
the wild life supposed in any way and in any degree to be inimical to
the protected species. Worse still, men to police the woods, armed
with guns, traps, and poison, were required. Consider what this
means – men who are hired to provide a big head of game, privileged
to carry a gun day and night all the year round, to shoot just what
they please! For who is to look after them on their own ground to

see that they do not destroy scheduled species? They must be always
shooting something; that is simply a reflex effect of the liberty they
have and of the gun in the hand. Killing becomes a pleasure to them,
and with or without reason or excuse they are always doing it –
always adding to the list of creatures to be extirpated, and when these
fail adding others. 'I know perfectly well,' said a keeper to me, 'that
the nightjar is harmless; I don't believe a word about its swallowing
pheasants' eggs, though many keepers think they do. I shoot them,
it is true, but only for pleasure.' So it has come about that wherever
pheasants are strictly preserved, hawks – including those that prey on
mice, moles, wasps, and small birds; also the owls, and all the birds of
the crow family, saving the rook on account of the landowner's sentiment in its favour; and after them the nightjar and the woodpeckers
and most other species above the size of a chaffinch, are treated as
'vermin'. The case of the keeper who shot all the nightingales because
their singing kept the pheasants awake at night sounds like a fable.
But it is no fable; there are several instances of this having been done,
all well authenticated.

Here is another case which came under my own eyes. It is of an
old heronry in a southern county, in the park of a great estate about
which there was some litigation a few years back. On my last visit
to this heronry at the breeding season I found the nests hanging
empty and desolate in the trees near the great house, and was told
that the new head keeper had persuaded the great nobleman who
had recently come into possession of the estate to allow him to kill
the herons because their cries frightened the pheasants. They were
shot on the nests after breeding began; yet the great nobleman who
allowed this to be done is known to the world as a humane and
enlightened man, and, I hear, boasts that he has never shot a bird in
his life! He allowed it to be done because he wanted pheasants for
his sporting friends to have their shoot in October, and he supposed
that his keeper knew best what should be done.

Another instance, also on a great estate of a great nobleman in
southern England. Throughout a long mid-June day I heard the
sound of firing in the woods, beginning at about eight o'clock in
the morning and lasting until dark. The shooters ranged over the
whole woods; I had never, even in October, heard so much firing on
an estate in one day. I inquired of several persons, some employed
on the estate, as to the meaning of all this firing, and was told that
the keeper was ridding the woods of some of the vermin. More than
that they refused to say; but by-and-by I found a person to tell me
just what had happened. The head keeper had got twenty or thirty
persons, the men with guns and a number of lads with long poles
with hooks to pull nests down, and had set himself to rid the woods
of birds that were not wanted. All the nests found, of whatever
species, were pulled down, and all doves, woodpeckers, nuthatches,
blackbirds, missel- and song-thrushes, shot; also chaffinches and
many other small birds. The keeper said he was not going to have
the place swarming with birds that were no good for anything,
and were always eating the pheasants' food. The odd thing in this
case was that the owner of the estate and his son, a distinguished
member of the House of Commons, are both great bird-lovers, and
at the very time that this hideous massacre in mid-June was going
on they were telling their friends in London that a pair of birds of a
fine species, long extirpated in southern England, had come to their
woods to breed. A little later the head keeper reported that these
same fine birds had mysteriously disappeared!

One more case, again from an estate in a southern county, the
shooting of which was let to a gentleman who is greatly interested
in the preservation of rare birds, especially the hawks. I knew the
ground well, having received permission from the owner to go
where I liked: I also knew the keepers and (like a fool) believed
they would carry out the instructions of their master. I informed
them that a pair of hobby-hawks were breeding in a clump of

trees on the edge of the park, and asked them to be careful not to mistake them for sparrow-hawks. At the same time I told them that a pair of Montagu's harriers were constantly to be seen at a lonely marshy spot in the woods, a mile from the park; I had been watching them for three days at that spot and believed they were nesting. I also told them where a pair of great spotted wood-peckers were breeding in the woods. They promised to 'keep an eye' on the hawks, and I daresay they did, seeing that both hobbies and harriers had vanished in the course of the next few days. But they would not promise to save the woodpeckers: one of the under-keepers had been asked by a lady to get her a few pretty birds to put in a glass case, and the head keeper told him he could have these woodpeckers.

Did I in these cases inform the owner and the shooting-tenant of what had happened? No, and for a very good reason. Nothing ever comes of such telling except a burst of rage on the part of the owner against all keepers and all interfering persons, which lasts for an hour or so, and then all goes on as before. I have never known a keeper to be discharged except for the one offence of dealing in game and eggs on his own account. In everything else he has a free hand; if it is not given him he takes it, and there is nothing he resents so much as being interfered with or advised or instructed as to what species he is to spare. Tell him to spare an owl or a kestrel and he instantly resolves to kill it; and if you are such a faddist as to want to preserve everything he will go so far as to summon his little crowd of humble followers and parasites and set them to make a clean sweep of all the wild life in the woods, as in the instance I have described. No, it is mere waste of energy to inform individual owners of such abuses. The craze exists for a big head of game, or rather of this exotic bird of the woods, called in scorn and disgust the 'sacred bird' by one who was himself a naturalist and sportsman; the owners are themselves responsible for the system and have created the class of men necessary to enable them to follow this degraded form of sport. I use the word advisedly: Mr A. Stuart-Wortley, the best authority I know on the subject, an enthusiast himself, mournfully acknowledges in his book on the pheasant that pheasant shooting as now almost universally conducted in England is not sport at all.

One odd result of this over-protection of an exotic species and consequent degradation of the woodlands is that the bird itself becomes a thing disliked by the lover of nature. No doubt it is an irrational feeling, but a very natural one nevertheless, seeing that whatsoever is prized and cherished by our enemy, or the being who injures us, must come in for something of the feeling he inspires. There is always an overflow. Personally I detest the sight of semi-domestic pheasants in the preserves; the bird itself is hateful, and is the one species I devoutly wish to see exterminated in the land.

But when I find this same bird where he exists comparatively in a state of nature, and takes his chance with the other wild creatures, the sight of him affords me keen pleasure: especially in October and November when the change in the colour of the leaf all at once makes this familiar world seem like an enchanted region. We look each year for the change and know it is near, yet when it comes it will be as though we now first witnessed that marvellous trans-formation – the glory in the high beechen woods on downs and hillsides, of innumerable oaks on the wide level weald, and elms and maples and birches and ancient gnarled thorns, with tangle of vari-coloured brambles and ivy with leaves like dark malachite, and light green and silvery grey of old-man's-beard. In that aspect of nature the pheasant no longer seems an importation from some brighter land, a stranger to our woods, startlingly unlike our wild native ground-birds in their sober protective colouring, and out of harmony with the surroundings. The most brilliant plumage seen in the tropics would not appear excessive then, when the thin dry

leaves on the trees, rendered translucent by the sunbeams, shine
like coloured glass, and when the bird is seen in some glade or
opening on a woodland floor strewn with yellow gold and burnished
red, copper and brightest russet leaves. He is one with it all, a part
of that splendour, and a beautifully decorative figure as he moves
slowly with deliberate jetting gait, or stands at attention, the eared
head and shining neck raised and one foot lifted. Many a writer has
tried to paint him in words; perhaps Ruskin alone succeeds, in a
passage which was intended to be descriptive of the colouring of the
pheasants generally.

> *Their plumage [he said] is for the most part warm brown, deli-*
> *cately and even beautifully spotty; and in the goodliest species the*
> *spots become variegated, or inlaid as in a Byzantine pavement,*
> *deepening into imperial purple and azure, and lighting into lustre*
> *of innumerable eyes.*

But alas! not infrequently when I have seen the pheasant in that
way in the coloured woods in October, when after the annual moult
his own colouring is richest and he is seen at his best, my delight
has vanished when I have lifted my eyes to look through the thinned
foliage at the distant prospect of earth and the blue overarching sky.
For who that has ever looked at nature in other regions, where this
perpetual hideous war of extermination against all noble feathered
life is not carried on, does not miss the great soaring bird in the
scene – eagle, or vulture, or buzzard, or kite, or harrier – floating at
ease on broad vans, or rising heavenwards in vast and ever vaster
circles? That is the one object in nature which has the effect of
widening the prospect, just as if the spectator had himself been
miraculously raised to a greater altitude, while at the same time
the blue dome of the sky appears to be lifted to an immeasurable
height above him. The soaring figure reveals to sight and mind the

immensity and glory of the visible world. Without it the blue sky can never seem sublime.

But the great soaring bird is nowhere in our lonely skies, and missing it we remember the reason of its absence and realise what the modern craze for the artificially reared pheasant has cost us.

9 A TIRED TRAVELLER
(*TURDUS ILIACUS*)

A November day on the east coast – A solitary redwing – Charm of the redwing – Its evening concerts – The redwing soliloquises – Its beauty – A meditation on death

It was fine weather on the morning of the first day of November on the east coast. Coming out, I looked for grey clouds travelling before a biting wind, a grey clammy mist brooding on the flat desolate land, and found, instead, a clear day without a vapour, the sun shining very brightly, the air almost still and deliciously warm. It was, for November, the most perfect day I could have had for a ramble on the grey flat saltings between Wells-next-the-Sea and Stiffkey: they are not as in summer at this time of year, but have the compensating charm of solitariness. I had them all to myself on that morning; there was no sound of human life except the church bells, the chimes coming faintly and musically over the wide marshes. Even the birds were few. From time to time a hooded or carrion crow flew by with his sullen cra-cra, or a ringed dotterel started up from a creek or pool before me and went away with his wild melancholy cry. Only the larks were singing everywhere about me; but it was their winter song – a medley of harsh and guttural sounds, without the clear, piercing, insistent summer note; nor do they rise high at this season, but after fluttering upwards a distance of forty or fifty yards drop again to earth.

Seawards I had for horizon the low ridge of the sand-hills over-grown with coarse grey-green grass, and when on the ridge itself I looked over a vast stretch of yellowish-brown sand; for it was low tide, with the sea visible as a white line of foam and the gleam of water more than a mile away. Here on the sandy ridge there is an old sea-ruined coastguard station, and, coming to it, I sat down on a pile of brushwood at the side of the half-fallen buildings, and after I had been there two or three minutes a bird fluttered up from the grass close to my feet and perched on the wood three or four yards from me. A redwing! A tired traveller from the north, he had no doubt arrived at that spot during the night, and was waiting to recover from his great fatigue before continuing his journey inland. He must have been very tired to remain by himself in such beautiful weather at that spot, when, close by on the further side of the salt grey marsh, the green wooded country, blue in the haze, was so plainly visible. For the redwing is a most sociable bird, and so long as his wings can bear him up he cannot endure to be left behind. Furthermore, he is exceedingly shy of the human form, especially when he first arrives on our shores; yet here was this shy bird, alone and sitting very quietly, within three or four yards of me! Still, it was evident that he was a little troubled at my presence, a little suspicious, from the way he eyed me, flirting his tail and wings; and once or twice, opening wide his beak, he uttered his alarm-note, a sound closely resembling the harsh, prolonged cry of the familiar missel-thrush. But these little signs of alarm were soon over, and he grew quiet, only continuing to emit his low musical chirp a dozen or more times a minute.

To me the meeting was a peculiarly happy one, since if I had been asked to choose a bird, one of our common winter visitors, to be with me in this quiet, lonely place, I think I should have said, 'Let it be a redwing.' He has a special attraction for me for various reasons. He is, I think, the most charming of the thrushes, both in shape and colouring. All of this family, are dear to me, and I perhaps admire

the others more – the fieldfare, for instance, the chattering winter
'blue-bird'; and the missel-thrush, the loud-voiced storm-cock that
sings in wet and blowy weather in February; and, above all, the
blackbird, the big, ebony-black thrush with a golden bill and fluting
voice; but I love the redwing more. There is a wildness, a freshness,
in the feeling he gives me which may be partly due to the fact that
he is not a cage-bird, that, on this account, there are no degrading
images and associations connected with this species. It is true that
he is a sweet singer, the 'Swedish nightingale' of Linnæus, but he
only sings his full song with the louder notes at home, in summer,
in the distant north; and on this account those dreariest Philistines,
the bird-fanciers or 'aviculturists', as they are beginning to call
themselves, who love a bird only when they hold it in the hateful
cage, the most iniquitous of man's many inventions, have so far
neglected this thrush. All the images called up by the redwing, the
sight or sound or thought of him, are of rural winter scenes, and are
pleasing, especially those of the evening gatherings of redwings in
copse or shrubbery; for, like the linnet and starling, they love to hold
a kind of concert, or grand musical confabulation or corroboree,
in which all the birds chirp, twitter and scream together before
settling down to sleep in the evergreens, which look black in the
twilight against the luminous evening sky. In my case there are
still other associations, for it happens that the soft musical chirp of
the redwing reminds me vividly of other birds which have a sound
resembling it, birds that were dear to me in my boyhood and youth;
one a true thrush, another the social military starling of the grassy
pampas and Patagonia. That dark bird with the scarlet breast and
beautiful voice was to me, in winter time in that distant land, what
the redwing is to many an English boy.

Now as I rested there against the pile of brushwood on which he
sat so near me he continued to emit these soft low chirping notes
or little drops of musical sound; and it seemed in part a questioning

note, as if he was asking me what I was? Why I regarded him so
attentively? What were my intentions towards him? And in part it
was a soliloquy, and this was how I interpreted what he appeared
to be saying: 'What has come to me – what ails me that I cannot
continue my journey? The sun is now as high as it will be: the green
country is so near – a few minutes' flight would carry me across
this flat sea-marsh to the woods and thickets where there are safety
and the moist green fields to feed in. Yet I dare not venture. Hark!
that is the hooded crow; he is everywhere roaming about over the
marshland in quest of small crabs and carrion left by the tide in the
creeks. He would detect this weakness I find in me which would
cause me to travel near the surface with a languid flight; and if he
saw and gave chase, knowing me to be a sick straggler, my heart
would fail and there would be no escape. Day and night I have flown
southwards from that distant place where my home and nest was
in the birches, where with my mate and young and all my neighbours we lived happily together, and finally set out together on this
journey. Yesterday when it grew dark we were over the sea, flying
very high; there was little wind, and it was against us, and even at
a great height the air seemed heavy. And it grew black with clouds
that were above us, and we were wetted with heavy rain; it ceased
and the blackness went by, and we found that we had dropped far,
far down and were near the sea. It was a quiet sea, and the sky had
grown very clear, sprinkled with brilliant stars as on a night of
frost, and the stars were reflected below us so that we seemed to be
flying between two starry skies, one above and one beneath. I was
frightened at that moving, black, gleaming sky beneath me, and felt
now that I was tired, and when the flock rose higher and still higher
I laboured to rise with it. At intervals those who were leading
uttered cries to prevent the others from straggling, and from far and
near there were responsive cries; but from the time that the dark,
wetting cloud had come over us I uttered no sound. Sometimes I

opened my beak and tried to cry, but no cry came; and sometimes
as we flew my eyes closed, then my wings, and for a moment all
sensation was lost, and I would wake to find myself dropping, and
would flutter and struggle to rise and overtake the others. At last a
change came, a sudden warmth and sense of land, a solid blackness
instead of the moving, gleaming sea beneath us, and immediately we
dropped earthwards like falling stones, down into the long grass by
the shore. Oh, the relief it was to fold my wings at last, to feel the
ground under me, the close, sheltering stems round and over me, to
shut my tired eyes and feel no more!

'When morning came, the cries of my fellows woke me: they
were calling us up and going away over the marshes to the green
country; but I could not follow nor make any response to their calls.
I closed my eyes again, and knew no more until the sun was high
above the horizon. All were gone then – even my own mate had left
me; nor did they know I was hidden here in the grass, seeing that I
had not answered to the call. They thought perhaps that I had fallen
out a long way back, when the rain oppressed and drove us down
and when probably other members of the flock dropped exhausted
into the sea. They could not remain here in this treeless exposed
place, where the water is salt and there is little food to find. I was
looking for something to eat at the roots of the grasses when this
man appeared and caused me to flutter up to my perch. Had this
strange weakness not been in me I should have rushed away in the
greatest terror on seeing him so near; for we are exceedingly shy
of man, fearing him even more than hawk or hooded crow. But my
weakness would not allow me to fly, and now I have lost my fear, for
though he continues to watch me it is plain that he has no intention
of harming me.'

Having finished this little rambling talk to himself, a review of
his late experiences and present condition, he once more attempted
to fly, but settled again on a stick not twenty yards away, and there

he appeared disposed to stay, his head well drawn in, the beak
raised, his bright eyes commanding a view of the wide sky above. He
would be able to see a flock of passing redwings and call to them,
and if the feeble sound reached them it would perhaps bring them
down to have speech with and cheer him in his loneliness. He would
also be able to catch sight of a prowling crow coming his way; for he
feared the crow, knowing it for an enemy of the weak and ailing, and
would have time to hide himself in the long grass.

There I left him, going away along the shore, but an hour or
two later I returned to the same spot, coming over the wide sands,
and lo! where I had left one redwing there were now two. One flew
wildly away at my approach to a distance of eighty or a hundred
yards before alighting again; the other remained, and when I drew
near it again moved on its perch, a little alarmed as at first, flirting
its wings and tail and once uttering its call note; and then, recovering from its fear, it began uttering little chirps as before. Those
tender little musical sounds, reminiscent of vanished days in distant
lands, were somewhat sad, as if the bird complained at being left
alone. But his mate had not forsaken him after all, or perhaps she
had gone on with the others and then returned to look for him at the
last roosting-place.

Having found my bird, I determined to make the most of our
second meeting. I had never had an opportunity of looking at a
redwing so closely before in such a favourable light, and, seeing it
in that way, I found it a more beautiful bird than I had thought it.
Perched at a height of above five feet, it was seen against the pale
sky in that soft sunlight, pale but crystal clear, and its eyes and
every delicate shade in its colouring were distinctly visible. The
upper parts were olive-brown, as in the throstle, but the cream-
coloured band over the large dark eye made it very unlike that bird;
the dark spotted under-parts were cream-white, tinged with buff,
the flanks bright chestnut-red. I could not have seen it better, nor so

well, if I had held it dead with glazed eyes in my hand; but the dead
bird, however brilliant in its colours it may be, I cannot admire. It
is beautiful nevertheless, it may be said, because of the colour and
the form. Ah yes, but it is dead, and what I see and hold is but the
case, the habit, of the living, intelligent spirit which is no more. This
gold-red hair, which sparkles like gold in the sunlight when I hold
it up, which was exceedingly beautiful when it glorified the head of
one that has vanished – this hair is not now beautiful to me but only
ineffably sad. Yet I would not grieve at the thought that the lovely
children of the air must cease to live, that their warm, palpitating
flesh so beautifully clothed with feathers must be torn and devoured;
or that they must perish of hunger and cold when the frost has its
iron grip on the earth; or fall by the way or on the wide sea, beaten
down by adverse bitter winds and rain and sleet and snow. Indeed,
I would grieve at no natural ending of life, however premature or
painful or tragical it might appear, nor think of death at all; rather
I would rejoice with every breath in all this abounding wonderful
earthly life in which I have a share. It only grieves me and darkens
my mind to think that man should invent and practise every
conceivable form of persecution and cruelty on these loveliest of our
fellow-beings, these which give greatest beauty and lustre to the
world; and, above all cruelties, that they should deprive them of their
liberty, that which sweetens life and without which life is not life.

10 WHITE DUCK

Green grass in March – White ducks in a blue pool – Mental
associations connected with the duck – A legend of the country of
the dead – Beauty and rarity – Sobriquet of an English queen

The green colour of earth is pale in this March month to
what it will be a few weeks hence; nevertheless on this
evening, a fortnight before the first day of spring, after
a long day spent sauntering in quiet places in this Norfolk land, I
seem to have been living in the greenest of worlds. Grass and the
colour of it is so grateful to me, and even necessary to my well-
being, that when removed from the sight of it I am apt to fall into a
languishing state, a dim and despondent mind, like one in prison or
sick and fallen on the days

Which are at best but dull and hoary,
Mere glimmerings and decays.

How good for mind and body, then, to be abroad at this time
when the increasing power of the sun begins to work a percep-
tible change in the colour of earth! How natural that at such a
season, just at the turn of the year, I should take an entire day in
the fields solely to look at the grass, to rejoice in it again after
the long wintry months, nourishing my mind on it even as old
King Nebuchadnezzar nourished his body! The sight of it was all
I went for, all I wanted, and whatever I saw besides pleased me
only because it formed a suitable background, or made it seem

brighter by contrast or served in some way to set it off. Old red-brick farmhouses, seen at a distance, nestling among evergreen and large, leafless trees, in many cases the deep, sloping roofs stained all over with orange-coloured lichen; quiet little hamlets too, half hidden beneath their great elms as under a reddish-purple cloud; the endless grey winding road, with low thorn hedges on either side winding with it, leafless and a deep purple brown in colour except where ivy had grown over and covered them with dark green brown-veined leaves silvered with the sunlight. A hundred things besides – red cows grazing on a green field, a flock of starlings wheeling about overhead and anon dropping to the earth; gulls, too, resting in another field, white and pale grey, their beaks turned to the wind: they were like little bird-shaped drifts of snow lying on the green turf, shining in the sun. For all day long the weather was perfect – a day of soft wind and bright sunshine following a spell of cold, rough weather with flooding rains; a soft blue sky peopled with white and pale grey clouds travelling before the wind.

And seeing these things – seeing and forgetting as one sees whatever comes into the field of vision when eyes and mind are occupied with some other thing – the time went on until a little past noon, when I suddenly came upon a new sight which gave me a thrill and held me, and after I had passed on would not allow me to drop it out of my mind. All the objects I had seen that day, the lichened farmhouses and grey barns, trees and roads and purple hedges, red and black cows in a green field, and gulls and rooks and distant low hills and pine woods, with many more, had appeared to me but as a fringe and small parts of an irregular scattered pattern on the green mantle of earth. This new sight was of a different order, for it took me out of my spring-grass mood, and the green mantle which had seemed the chief thing was now but a suitable setting to this lovely object.

This, then, is what I saw. In the middle of a green pasture I came
on a pool of rain-water, thirty or forty feet long, collected in a depression in the ground, of that blue colour sometimes seen in a shallow
pool in certain states of the atmosphere and sunlight – an indescrib-
able and very wonderful tint, unlike the blue of a lake or of the deep
sea, or of any blue flower or mineral, but you perhaps think it more
beautiful than any of these; and if it must be compared with something else it perhaps comes nearest to deep sapphire blues. When an
artist in search of a subject sees it he looks aside and, going on his
way, tries to forget it, as when he sees the hedges hung with spiders'
lace sparkling with rainbow-coloured dewdrops, knowing that these
effects are beyond the reach of his art. And on this fairy lake in the
midst of the pale green field, its blue surface ruffled by the light wind,
floated three or four white ducks; whiter than the sea-gulls, for they
were all purest white, with no colour except on their yellow beaks.
The light wind ruffled their feathers too, a little, as they turned this
way and that, disturbed at my approach; and just then, when I stood
to gaze, the sun shone full out after the passing of a light cloud, and
flushed the blue pool and floating birds, silvering the ripples and
causing the plumage to shine as if with a light of its own.

'I have never seen a more beautiful thing!' I exclaimed to myself;
and now at the end of the long day it remains in my mind, vividly
as when I looked at it at that moment when the sunbeams fell on it,
and is so persistent that I have no choice but to write it down. The
beauty I saw was undoubtedly due to the peculiar conditions – to
the blue colour of the water, the ruffling wind, the whiteness of the
plumage, and the sudden magic of the sunlight; but the effect would
not have been so entrancing if the floating birds had not also been
beautiful in themselves – in shape and in their surpassing whiteness.

Now I am quite sure the reader will smile and perhaps emit the
sound we usually write *pish* – a little sibilant sound, expressing
contempt. For though he will readily admit that the sun beautifies

many things, he draws the line at a duck – the common domestic
one. Like all of us, he has his prepossessions and can't get away from
them. Every impression, we are told by Professor James, no sooner
enters the consciousness than it is drafted off in some determinate
direction, making connection with the other materials there, and
finally producing a reaction. In this instance the impression is the
story of a duck described as beautiful, the reaction an incredulous
smile. The particular connections it strikes into are determined by
our past experiences and the association of the present impression
with them. The impression arouses its old associates; they go to
meet it; it is received by them, and rearranged by the mind. It is the
fate of every impression thus to fall into a mind preoccupied with
memories, ideas, and interests. This mental escort is drawn from the
mind's ready-made stock. Our philosopher adds: 'In all apperceptive
operations of the mind a certain general law makes itself felt – the
law of economy. In admitting a new experience we instinctively seek
to disturb as little as possible the pre-existing stock of ideas.'

All this is illuminating and helpful, since it enables me to see
into my smiling reader's mind and to indulge in a smile on my part.
For with what in this case will the object described (a white duck)
connect itself? What are the memories, ideas, interests, already in
stock, which will be its associates and form its escort and take it in?
They are of the duck as he has seen, eaten, and known it all his life
– the familiar duck of the farmyard, a heavy bird that waddles in its
walk and is seen dibbling in horse-ponds or in any mud-puddle. It is
the bird which the hen-wife fattens for the market while her husband
is fattening the pigs. If any pleasing memories or associations
connect themselves with it they are not of an aesthetic character:
they refer to the duck without its feathers, to its smell and taste
when eaten with green peas in their season.

If I am asked how I escaped from these inconvenient, not to say
degrading, associations, the only answer would be that associations

of another kind were probably formed at some early period. Perhaps when my infant eyes began to look at the world, when I had no stock of ideas, no prepossessions at all, except with regard to milk, I saw a white duck and was delighted at it. In any case the feeling for its beauty goes far back. I remember some years ago when strolling by the Itchen I stood to admire a white duck floating on the clear current where it is broad and shallow and where the flowering wild musk was abundant. The rich moist green of the plant made the white plumage seem whiter, and the flowers and the duck's beak were both a very beautiful yellow. 'If,' thought I, 'the white duck were as rare in England as the white swallow, or even the white blackbird, half the inhabitants of Winchester would turn out and walk to this spot to see and admire so lovely a thing.'

Many and many a time have I stopped in my walk or ride to admire such a sight, but the white ducks seen today, floating, sunflushed, on a blue pool in a green field, had a higher loveliness, a touch of the extra-natural, and served to recall an old tradition of a primitive people concerning the country of the sky, where the dead inhabit, and all trees and flowers abound as on earth, and all animals and birds, including ducks, but more beautiful than here below. Everyone may know that the country is there because of the blueness; for the air, the void, has no colour, but all matter seen at a distance appears blue – water and trees and mountains; only the sky country is at so vast a distance that we see nothing but the blue colour of it. But there are openings or windows in the great plain, and these are the stars, and through these windows the clear, brilliant light of that country shines down on us when it is dark.

How do the dead get there – flying like soaring birds, up, up, up, until they come to it? They can certainly fly like birds, but no high-soaring bird and no spirit can rise by flying to so immense a height; yet when men die they have no thought and desire but for that country, and have no rest or pleasure here, but roam up and down the earth, flying from the sight of human beings, even of their nearest relations and friends, because they are now invisible to mortal eyes, and to find themselves unrecognised and unheard when they speak and no longer remembered is intolerable to them. Therefore, by day, when people are abroad, they fly to forests and uninhabited places, where they lie, but at night they come forth to range the earth in the form of owls and nightjars and loons and rails and all other wandering night-birds with wild and lamentable voices. Night by night they wander, crying out their misery and asking of those they meet to tell them of some way of escape from earth so that they might come at last to the country of the dead; but none can tell them, for they are all in the same miserable case, seeking a way out. But at last, after months and perhaps years, they come in their wanderings to the end of the earth and the stupendous walls and pillars of stone which hold up the immense plain of the sky; there they eventually discover some way by which to ascend and reach that happy country which is their home.

It was not always so; once the passage from earth to heaven was comparatively an easy one; there was a way then known to every one, dead or living, in the world. It was a tree growing on the river-bank, so high that its topmost branches reached up to heaven. Imagine what a tree that was, its buttressed trunk so big round that a hundred men with arms outspread and hands touching could not have spanned it! There was ample room under the shade of its lower branches for the entire nation to gather and sit at meat, everyone in his place. On higher branches great birds had their nesting-places, and higher still other great birds, eagles and vultures and storks, might be seen soaring skywards, circling upwards until they appeared like black specks in the blue, but beyond these specks the tree rose still until it faded from sight and mixed itself with the universal blue of heaven. By this tree the dead ascended to their future home, climbing

like monkeys, and flitting and flying like birds from branch
to branch, until they came to the topmost branches and to an
opening in the great plain, through which they passed into that
bright and beautiful place.

Unhappily this tree fell a long time ago – oh, a very long time
ago! If you were to range the whole earth in search of the oldest
man in it, and at last discovered him sitting in his cabin, bent down
like a dead man, with his clawlike fingers clasped together on his
knees, his brown face covered with a hundred wrinkles, his hair
white, and his eyes turned white too with blindness, and asked him
of the tree, he would say that it fell before his time, a long time
before, perhaps in his grandfather's or great-grandfather's time,
or even before then. And this is how it fell – it is surely one of the
saddest chapters in the history of the world!

It came to pass that an old and evil-tempered woman died, and,
going to the tree, in due time reached the sky, and was happy to
find herself at last in that bright and beautiful place. She was very
hungry after her long journey and climb, and, making inquiry of
those she met, they told her very pleasantly that the readiest way
to procure food was to catch some fish in one of the lakes close by.
They also gave her a rod and line and directed her to the nearest
lake. Away she went, pleased with herself and everything, her mouth
watering at the thought of those green-and-blue and red-and-yellow
little fishes which were easy to catch and delicious to eat. It was a
small round lake of clear water, about a mile in circumference, to
which she had been directed, and on approaching it she saw that a
good number of persons were there standing, rod in hand, on the
margin. One of the anglers, happening to turn his head, caught sight
of the old woman hurrying down to them, and to have a little fun he
cried out to those near him: 'Look! here comes an old woman, just
arrived, to fish; let's close up and say there is no room for another
here and have a laugh at her expense.'

Here the reader must be told that the part of a man which survives death is in appearance the exact counterpart of the man when alive. To mortal eyes he is invisible, being of so thin a substance; but the dead and immortal see him as he was, young or old and ugly, with his grey hair and wrinkles and every sign of suffering and care and passion on his countenance. And as with the face and the whole body so it is with the mind: if it has been evil, full of spite and malice, it is so still. But he must be told, too, that this state is not permanent, for in that bright and buoyant atmosphere it is impossible for the marks of age and misery to endure; they fade out as the easy, happy exist- ence finds its effect; they grow youthful in appearance once more; and the change is also in the mind. The old woman had, alas! not been long enough in that happy land for any change to have taken place in either her appearance or her spiteful temper.

That was how the people by the lake no sooner beheld the newcomer than they knew her for what she had been, and was still – a spiteful old woman; and being of a merry disposition they were only too ready to take part in the joke. As she drew near they closed up and cried out: 'No room for another fisher here; go further on and find yourself a place.'

On she went; but those who were further up saw what the fun was, and they too in their turn cried: 'No room, no room here, old woman; go a little further on.' And she went on, only to be sent further still, until she had gone all the way round the lake and was back at the spot where she had started, where she was received with a shout of laughter and the cry of 'No room, here, old woman.'

Then in a rage she flung the rod down, and, cursing the people for making a fool of her, she fled from their laughter; and, arrived back at that very opening through which she had climbed into heaven, she cast herself down on the upper branches of the great tree and began her long descent to earth again. She alone of all the dead who had reached that country turned her back on it and returned to this world, to our everlasting sorrow. Arrived at the earth, and mad with rage and the desire of revenge, she turned herself into a huge water-rat, a creature found by that river, a rat as big as a retriever dog, with four great teeth, hard and sharp as steel chisels, two in the upper and two in the lower jaw. Making herself a den at the roots of the mighty tree, she began gnawing the wood, working day and night for many, many days, and for months and years; and if ever she grew tired of her huge task she thought of the indignity she had suffered and of the mocking laughter of the people by the lake, and was roused to fresh fury and continued exertions. In this way the great roots and lower part of the trunk were riddled through and through and hollowed out. Nor was it known to anyone what the malignant old woman was doing, since the vast quantities of wood which she threw out were carried away by floods and the current of the great river. Thus even to the end did her evil spirit sustain her, and the tree bent and swayed in the mighty wind, and at last fell with a noise as of many thunders, shaking the world with its fall, and filling all its inhabitants with terror. Only when they saw the tree which had stood like a vast green pillar reaching to the sky lying prone across the world did they know the dreadful thing which had been done.

So ended that great tree named Caligdawa; and so ends my story, originally taken down from the lips of wise old men who preserved the history and traditions of their race by a missionary priest and read by me in my early youth in the volume in which he relates it.

But I will venture to say that the story has not been dragged in here; I had no thought of using it when I sat down this evening to write about a white duck. That vision of the sunlit, surprisingly white, yellow-billed ducks floating on the wind-rippled blue pool – for it was like a vision – had to be told; but how, unless I said that it was like a glimpse into some unearthly place where all things are as on earth, only more beautiful in the brighter atmosphere? My blue pool with white birds floating on it, in a spring-green field, blown on by the wind and shone on and glorified by the sun, was like a sudden vision, a transcript of that far-up country.

And now, just at the finish, another chance thought comes to help me. The thought has, in fact, been stated already when I said that half the inhabitants of Winchester would turn out to gaze at and admire the white duck seen by the Itchen if white ducks were rare as white swallows in the land. How many things which are beautiful seem not so because of their commonness and of the uses to which they are put! What comes now to help me is the memory of a matter in old English history. Close upon a thousand years ago there lived a very beautiful lady of whom little is known except that she was an earl's daughter, and that the young king, who had a passion for beauty exceeding that of all men, even in those wild and violent times, loved and made her his queen. After bearing him a son, who was king too in his time, she died, to England's lasting sorrow. And she was known throughout the realm as the *White Duck*, on account of her great beauty. We can only suppose that at that distant period the white duck was a rarity in England, therefore that those who saw it looked with concentrated attention at it as we look at any rare and lovely thing – a kingfisher, let us say – and were able to appreciate its perfect loveliness.

11 AN IMPRESSION OF AXE EDGE

Some lucky ornithologists – Compensations that go with limited
opportunities – Axe Edge – Mean farms – The people of the Peak –
Spring on Axe Edge

The ornithologists of today are a somewhat numerous tribe,
including persons of varied tastes, habits, ambitions, and,
above everything, means. Among them are a few fortu-
nate individuals whose object in life is to seek out the least familiar
species, the rarest in the land or the most local in their distribution,
or most difficult to get at and observe closely. Many of us would like
to do our birding in that way, but few are free to take the whole year
for a holiday, to travel long distances, to spend days, weeks, months
in the quest – just to see and study some bird in its haunts – a pine
forest in Rothiemurchus or some such 'vast contiguity of shade', or a
beetling cliff on the coast of Connemara, or a boggy moor or marsh
in the Shetlands or Orkneys, or in 'utmost Kilda's lonely isle'. They
must be young, or, at all events, physically tough, and unless they
can make it pay by procuring specimens for their numerous friends
(dealers and collectors all) they must have money enough to exist
without work. These being the conditions, it is not strange that this
wide-wandering, perpetual-holiday band should, if we exclude the
suspects, be a small one and as enthusiastic in their pursuit as other
open-air men are apt to be about hunting the fox, golfing, fishing,
cricketing, shooting, motoring, and other forms of sport.

Call them sportsmen, ornithologists, or bird-lovers pure and
simple, I envy them their magnificent freedom and could ask for no

happier life than theirs. It is like that of the person whose delight
is in anthropology in passing from land to land, seeing many and
various races of men, visiting remote districts whose inhabitants
through long centuries of isolation have preserved the features and
mental characteristics of their remote progenitors. To pursue wild
birds in that way – to follow knowledge like a sinking star, to be
and to know much until I became a name for always wandering
with a hungry heart – that was my one desire; but alas! it was never
in my power. Compared with the disencumbered ones I am like an
ordinary man, walking on the earth, to men of lighter bodies and
nimbler minds who have found out how to fly and are like birds
chasing birds.

Nevertheless there are compensations. The very restraints which
annoy us may not be without their advantages. The rare experience
of finding myself at last in the presence of some long-wished-for
bird, comparing it with its imaginary mental portrait and with the
mental images of its nearest relations, and finally of being able to
add this one new portrait to the gallery existing in the mind – my
best possession and chief delight – perhaps affords me a keener
pleasure than can be experienced by the man of unlimited opportunities. My humbler triumph is like that of the lover of literature of
small means, who from time to time, by some lucky chance, becomes
the possessor of some long-desired book. For how much greater is
his joy in fingering and in reading it than the wealthy owner of a
great library can know? It is true the poor book-lover dreams of
better things: more leisure to hunt, more money to buy – a legacy
perhaps from some kindly being he knows not of, which will enable
him to grasp greater prizes than have ever come in his way. So
with me: year by year I dream of longer journeys into remoter and
wilder places in search of other charming species not yet seen in
their native haunts. And that was my dream last winter – it always
is my dream – which, when summer came round, found its usual

ending. The longer journey had to be postponed to another year and a shorter one taken; so it came about that I got no further than the Peak district, just to spend a few weeks during the breeding season with half a dozen birds, all familiar enough to most ornithologists, but which are not found, at all events not all together, nearer to London than the Derbyshire hills.

Axe Edge, where I elected to stay, is not the highest hill in that part, being about eighteen hundred feet above the sea, whereas Kinder Scout rises to quite two thousand; but I found it high enough for one who modestly prefers walking and cycling on the level ground. And here I found what I wanted – the bird life peculiar to the district – grouse, curlew, golden plover, snipe and summer snipe, water- and ring-ouzel. The unlovely town of Buxton is close by, set in a hollow in the midst of monstrously ugly lime works. The little town is also much tortured with motor-cars and is blown on with stinging, suffocating white dust. Happily I was soon off the hated limestone, settled in one of the poor little stony farmhouses in a hollow or valley-head on the adjacent hill, the whole central part of which forms a vast moor or tableland, broken at the borders and cut through with ravine-like valleys, or cloughs, with steep rocky sides and rushing burns below, the beginnings of the Wye, the Dove, the Dane, and the Goyt rivers. From Axe Edge on one side you look down on Buxton and the hilly limestone country beyond – a naked ugly land with white patches showing everywhere through the scanty grass covering. From this prospect of scabby or leprous-looking hills one turns with unspeakable relief, to the immense tableland of Axe Edge, where you are off the lime on the gritstone formation, harsh and desolate in aspect, but covered with a dense growth of heather, bilberry, and coarse bog grasses – a habitation of birds.

Few persons live on this high moor; the farms are not visible until you get to the edge of it and can look down on the slopes below and the valleys, where the small cottage-like stone farmhouses are seen sprinkled over the earth, each with its few little green fields walled round with stone. They are the meanest-looking, most unhomelike farms you will find in England, for they have no gardens, few or no shade trees, and there is no sign of cultivation anywhere. From one side, looking towards Leek, I counted twenty-six farms, and at not one of them did they grow a potato or a cabbage or a flower; and if you go all round the hill you could count two or three hundred farms like these. Each one has its stone-fenced fields, on which a few cows feed, and, if the summer is not too cold, a little hay is made for the winter. It is all the cattle get, as there are no roots. The sheep, if any are kept, are up on the moor, a long-woolled, horned animal with black spotted face and looking all black from its habit of lying in the peat holes. They are not in flocks and are not folded, but live on the moor in small parties of two or three to half a dozen. The farmers depend mainly on their lean ill-fed cows for a livelihood; they make butter and feed a pig or two with the skim milk. They live on bacon and buttermilk themselves, and bread which they make or buy, but vegetables and fruit are luxuries. To one from almost any other part of the country it seems a miserable existence, yet the farmers are not less attached to their rude homes and little bleak holdings than others, and though they abuse the landlord or his agent because they cannot have the land for nothing, they appear to be fairly well satisfied with their lot. I sometimes thought they were even too well contented and wanted to know why they did not try to grow a few cabbages or potatoes in some sheltered nook for the house; some said it was useless to attempt it on account of the May and June frosts, and others said that the owners objected to the ground being broken up! I also asked several farmers why they did not cut bracken, which was plentiful enough, to serve as bedding for the cows, since they could not get straw. They answered that occasionally a farmer did so, but it was not the custom and they thought the cows did just as well without any bedding at all!

I pitied the cows; but perhaps they were right; it may well be that the domestic animals, like their masters, have become adapted during many generations to a starvation land, to lie in winter on a hard cold stone floor and to keep alive on the smallest amount of food of the poorest kind, and yet to flourish in a way and yield milk.

But though they appear to be a contented, they are not a happy-looking or a lively people. They have colourless faces and for good looks or brightness or intelligence compare badly with the inhabitants of the adjoining districts and with the people of England generally, north and south. The children are naturally more attractive than the adults; they have the brightness proper to their time of life, which makes their dirty little faces shine; but it is rare to find a pretty one. What has made this people of the Peak what they are, so unlike their neighbours, so wholly absorbed in their own affairs and oblivious of the world outside; mentally isolated, like the inhabitants of a lonely island? It was a depressing experience to converse with youths and young men of an age when if any romance, any enthusiasm, exists it is bound to show itself. They were too serious – they were even solemn, and gave one the idea that they had all been recently converted to Methodism and were afraid to smile or to say a frivolous or unnecessary word lest it should be set down against them by an invisible recording clerk, standing, pen behind his ear, at their elbow, intently listening. There was no trace of that fiery spirit, that intensity of life, that passion for music, sport, drinking and fighting, for something good or bad which distinguishes their very next-door neighbours, the Lancastrians. What is it then – the soil, the altitude and bleak climate, the hard conditions of life, or what? One knows of other districts where life is just as hard, where the people have yet some brightness of mind, some energy, some passion in them. I gave it up; there was no time for brooding over such problems; my quest was birds, not men.

Moreover, now at the end of May the first unmistakable signs
of spring were becoming visible on that lofty moor of a hard and
desolate aspect which I had made my home. Frosts and fogs and
cold winds were not so persistent; there were better intervals;
then came a beautiful warm day the first fine really warm day, the
natives proudly assured me, which they had experienced since the
previous August. The little stone-enclosed fields had taken a livelier
green, and on wet spots and by the burns the shining yellow marsh-
marigolds were in bloom. But the chief change to spring on the high
wintry moor was in the appearance of the bilberry bushes, growing
everywhere in dense patches among the heather. They had now put
on their first leaves and they were like the young leaves of the oak in
spring

Against the sun shene –
Some very red and some a glad light grene.

And this wild place was a habitation of birds, and these were the
people I had come to see and listen to, who were, indeed, more to me
than the human inhabitants.

12 BIRDS OF THE PEAK

Seeking information at Buxton – Cuckoo and meadow pipit on Axe Edge
– A one-sided partnership – Song of the whinchat – Voice of the curlew
– The red grouse – Prologue to Chapter 13

Lunching one day at Buxton, I hobnobbed with a man whose classic features, fine physique and magnificent beard filled me with a great admiration. He was the vicar of a neighbouring parish, a man of the open air, a cultivated mind, and large sympathies – the very person I wanted to meet, for doubtless he would know the birds and be able to tell me all I wanted to learn. By-and-by the subject was introduced, and he replied that he did not know very much about birds, but he had noticed a particularly big crow in his parish – big and black – and he would like to know what it was. There were always some of them about. Perhaps it was a carrion crow or a rook, he couldn't say for certain; but it was exceptionally big – and very black.

One meets with many disappointments when asking for information about the bird life of any locality; one is apt to forget that such knowledge is not common, that it is easier to find a poet or a philosopher in any village than a naturalist. Nevertheless I was singularly fortunate at Buxton in meeting with that same rarity in the person of a tradesman of the town, a Mr Micah Salt, who had studied the birds of the district all his life. But not in books; he did not read about birds, he observed them for his own pleasure and it was a pleasure to him to talk about them, but it went no further. He did not even make a note; bird-watching was

his play – a better outdoor game than golf, as it really does get
you a little forrarder, and does not make you swear and tell lies
and degenerate from a pleasant companionable being to an intolerable bore.

It was through his advice that I went to stay on Axe Edge,
where I would find all the birds I wanted to watch, and where it
seemed to me on first going on to the moor that about five-sixths
of the bird life consisted of two species – cuckoo and meadow pipit.
At the low-roofed stone cabin where I lodged a few wind-torn
beeches had succeeded in growing, and these were a great attraction to the moorland cuckoos and their morning meeting-place.
From half-past three they would call so loudly and persistently and
so many together from trees and roof as to banish sleep from that
hour. And all day long, all over the moor, cuckoos were cuckooing
as they flew hither and thither in their slow, aimless manner, with
rapidly beating wings, looking like spiritless hawks, and when one
flew by a pipit would rise and go after him, just to accompany him,
as it appeared, a little distance on his way. Not in anger like some
of the small birds, even the diminutive furze-jack who cherishes
a spite against the cuckoo, but in pure affection. For the meadow
pipit is like that person, usually a woman, whom we call a 'poor
fool' because of a too tender heart, who is perhaps the mother of a
great hulking brute of a son who gobbled up all he could get out of
her, caring nothing whether she starved or not, and when it suited
his pleasure went off and took no more thought of her – of the poor
devoted fool waiting and pining for her darling's return. The pipit's
memory is just as faithful; she remembers the big greedy son she fed
and warmed with her little breast a year or two ago, who went away,
goodness knows where, a long time back; and in every cuckoo that
flies by she thinks she sees him again and flies after him to tell him
of her undying love and pride in his bigness and fine feathers and
loud voice.

Who that knows it intimately, who sees it creeping about among the grass and heather on its pretty little pink legs, and watches its large dark eyes full of shy curiosity as it returns your look, and who listens to its small delicate tinkling strain on the moor as it flies up and up, then slowly descends singing to earth, can fail to love the meadow pipit – the poor little feathered fool?

Concerning the breeding habits, the friendship and very one-sided partnership between these two species, Mr Salt informed me that all the cuckoos' eggs he had found in fifty-five years, during which he had been observing the birds of the district, were in meadow-pipits' nests. Nor had he ever seen a young cuckoo being tended by the numerous other species supposed to be its foster parents – warblers, wagtails, chats, the robin, redstart, dunnock and wren. Furthermore, he had discussed this subject with numbers of persons living in the district, and their experience agreed with his. His conclusion was that the meadow pipit was the only dupe of the cuckoo, in spite of what was said in the books. The conclusion was wrong, but his facts may be right with regard to this particular district. Doubtless, if this be so, there must be eggs laid from time to time in the nests of other species, but in the long run the instinct of parasitism on dunnock or wagtail or some other species would be swamped by that of the majority of cuckoos, all parasites on the meadow pipit exclusively.

Of all the small musical sounds emitted by birds on moors and other lonely places I think I love the aerial tinkle of the pipit best, unless it be the warble of the whinchat heard in the same situations. Few persons appear to know the whinchat's song, yet it may be heard every day from April to July all over the country wherever the bird has its haunts. The main thing is to know a sound when you hear it. This chat is a shy singer as well as an inconspicuous bird, and as a rule becomes silent when approached. One hears a delicious warble at a considerable distance and does not know whose voice it is; but if on any silent heath or common or grassland, or

any furze-grown brambly waste, you should catch a very delicate
warbled song, a mere drop of sound, yet to all other bird sounds
about it like the drop of dew or rain among many other crystal,
colourless drops, which catches the light at the right angle and
shines with loveliest colour, you may safely say that it was a whinchat. A fugitive sound heard at a distance, of so exquisite a purity
and sweetness, so tender an expression, that you stand still and hold
your breath to listen and think, perhaps, if it is not repeated, that it
was only an imagined sound.

An even more characteristic sound of the high moor than these
small voices which are not listened to is the curlew's voice: not
the beautiful wild pipe nor the harsh scream, the whaup's cry that
frightens the superstitious, but the gentler, lower, varied sounds of
the breeding season when the birds are talking to one another and
singing over their nests and eggs and little ones. Best of all of these
notes is the prolonged trill, which sounds low yet may be heard
distinctly a quarter of a mile away or further, and strongly reminds
me of the trilling spring call of the spotted tinamou, the common
partridge of the Argentine plains – a trill that is like a musical
whisper which grows and dwells on the air and fades into silence. A
mysterious sound which comes out of the earth or is uttered by some
filmy being, half spirit and half bird, floating invisible above the
heath. I liked these invisible curlews, singing their low song, better
than the visible bird, mad with anxiety and crying aloud when the
nest was looked for. But the curlew has one very fine aspect when, at
your approach, he rises up before you at a distance of three or four
hundred yards and comes straight at you, flying rapidly, appearing
almost silver-white in the brilliant sunshine, the size so exagger-
ated by the light and motion as to produce the illusion of a big bird,
the only one left alive by the Philistines and destroyers. But it is a
beautiful illusion which lasts only a few moments. In all this Peak
district you will not find a larger bird than a curlew or mallard or

crow, that very big bird which my clergyman told me about. Not a buzzard, not a harrier, not a raven, or any other species which when soaring would seem an appropriate object and part of the scenery in these high wild places.

What a contrast between all these delicate voices of the moorland, from the faint tinkle of the rising and falling pipit to the curlew's trill, and others I have omitted, the golden plover and water-ouzel, the aerial bleat of the snipe, the wail of the pewit and thin sharp pipe of the sandpiper or 'watersquealer', as the natives call it – between all these and the red grouse. He has no music in him, but great power. On these high moors his habit is to sit or stand on a stone wall to sun himself and keep an eye on his wives and rivals and the world generally. He stands, head erect, motionless, statuesque, the harsh-looking heap of dark gritstone forming an appropriate pedestal. For he is like a figure cut in some hard dark red stone himself – red gritstone, or ironstone, or red granite, or, better still, deep-red serpentine, veined and mottled with black, an exceedingly hard stone which takes a fine polish. And in voice and character the bird is what he looks, hard and brave, both as wooer and fighter. Even near the end of May when many hens are incubating I stumble on a dozen nests a day – he is wooing and fighting all the time, and the fights are not mere shows like those of the ruff, a pretty little feathered French duellist, and other quarrelsome species that fight often without hurting one another. The red grouse that looks like a stone hurls himself like a stone against his adversary, and whether he breaks bones or not he makes the polished feathers fly in clouds. Yet in his wooing this stone-like bird sometimes attains to grace of motion. That is when, carried away by his passion, he mounts into the air, and if there is any wind to help him rises easily to a good height and performs in descending a love flight resembling that of the cushat and turtle-dove. But in his vocal performances there is no grace or beauty, only power. You are astonished at the sounds he emits when he bursts out very suddenly rattling and drumming – rrrrr-rub-a-dub-dub; or you may liken it to a cachinnatory sound as if a gritstone rock standing among the heather had suddenly burst out laughing. Then he changes his tone to a more human sound like a raven's croak prolonged, which breaks up into shorter sounds at the end – ah-ha! come here, come back, go back, go back, quack, quack, or quick, quick, which is probably what he really means.

From the grouse and his rude noises I must now go back to the delicate songsters, to give an impression of the ring-ouzel; for oddly enough I had hitherto had no opportunity of really watching and listening to it during the breeding season. Certain birds at certain times, or on certain rare days, take possession of and hold us to the exclusion of all others. A similar experience is familiar to the lovers of the sublime and beautiful in nature and art, in music and poetry. So (to compare small things with great) we naturalists have our buzzard or raven or wild-geese days, and, better still, our days with this or that fascinating melodist – blackcap or blackbird, or linnet, or wheatear, or nightingale. And when the day is finished and the mood over it is not wholly over even then; we are like the poet who has listened to voices even more unearthly than birds':

> *I thenceforward and long after*
> *Listen to their harp-like laughter,*
> *And carry in my heart for days*
> *Peace that hallows rudest ways.*

Moreover I was here on a special visit to this species; he was more in my mind than the golden plover or any other. I came to be more intimate with him – to have my ring-ouzel day and mood.

13 THE RING-OUZEL AS A SONGSTER

A species unknown to most – A blackbird that is not a blackbird – First sight of the ring-ouzel – Its song – Blackbird and ring-ouzel compared – Nesting ring-ouzels – Thrush-calls of ring-ouzel – A suggested comparative study of thrush languages

From the Peak northwards the ring-ouzel is not an uncommon species in mountainous districts, but in the greater part of England it is unknown, or known only by name like the merlin, crested tit, and phalarope. Indeed to most of us a first sight of it comes as a surprise. The sight of a new species will always produce a shock of pleasure in those who are interested in birds: in the case of the ring-ouzel there is another element in the feeling – something of a mixture of incredulity and even resentment. And all because we find in this until now unknown species a veritable blackbird – black of hue (and comely) with orange-tawny bill; also possessing the chuckle and all the manners and gestures of that familiar being; yet not the real blackbird, not *our* blackbird, the old favourite of wood and orchard and garden. For this real blackbird, the 'garden-ouzel', as our ancients of the seventeenth century called it, is to us so unlike all other feathered beings in figure, colouring, flight, gestures, voice; withal so distinguished among birds, that we have come to look on it as the one and only blackbird in existence. A thrush, it is true, but modified and raised as far above those olive-coloured spotty birds as the lovely and graceful grey wagtail is above the modest little creeping pipits it springs from. That we have been told of other blackbirds in many lands does not matter, since

what we hear about such things does not impress us – we forget and
practically disbelieve it. The sight of a ring-ouzel thus deprives us of
an illusion.

I was not affected in that way at the Peak, having met the bird
a long time before in other parts of the country, but its song had
remained unknown and I had come to hear it. Nor had I long to
wait for that pleasure. On my way to the small hovel of a farmhouse,
on Axe Edge, where I had arranged to stay, while walking in the
old forsaken road, worn very deep and thickly bestrewn with loose
stones like the bed of a dry mountain torrent, I caught the sound
of a bird voice unknown to me, and peeping over the bank at the
roadside, beheld the ring-ouzel within twenty yards of me, sitting
on a stone wall, emitting his brief song at intervals of less than half
a minute.

After listening for about fifteen minutes till he flew off, I went
on my way rejoicing at a new experience and marvelling that this
simple little bird melody, which one would imagine any child could
imitate or describe to you so that when heard afterwards it could
easily be identified, had yet never been described in the orsitho-
logical books. Such a statement may seem incredible considering
the number of books on birds which we possess; but let any reader
take down one from his shelves and try to form a definite idea as to
what this song is like from the author's account. Some naturalists
compare it with the blackbird and missel-thrush. It is unlike both,
being a short set song, as in the chaffinch and chiffchaff, without
any variation and alike in every individual; whereas the blackbird
and missel-thrush vary their phrases with every repetition of the
song, and no two individuals sing quite alike. In the quality of the
sound there is also some difference. Again, it is frequently described
as a warble, or warbled song, which it is not. The word warble, as
Mr Warde Fowler has said, is used of birds' singing in a sense which
may be guessed from Milton's lines:

Fountains, and ye that warble as ye flow
Melodious murmurs, warbling tune his praise.

'The word,' he adds, 'seems to express a kind of singing which is
soft, continuous, and legato.' It is precisely because they sing in this
way that several of our smaller songsters, including the blackcap and
willow-wren, have received the English generic name of Warblers.

The song is also variously characterised as desultory, wild,
monotonous, sweet, plaintive, mellow, fluty, which is all wrong, and
if by chance one word had been right it would have given us no definite idea of the ring-ouzel's song – its shape. It is a whistle, repeated
three and sometimes four times without pause, uttered at short
intervals twenty or thirty or more times. Let the reader think of any
such word as spero, hero, wheero, then whistle, musically, as he is
able, a loud brisk imitation of the word three or four times in quick
succession, and he will reproduce the song well enough to deceive
any person within hearing that it is a ring-ouzel singing. The difference will be that the whistled imitation will never get the expressive bell-like musical character of the bird. The sound has intrinsic
beauty, but its charm is mainly due to the place you hear it in, the
wildness and solitude of the rocky glens or the mountain side.

By going all round the mountain, visiting every clough, I
succeeded in locating about forty or fifty breeding pairs and failed
to detect any individual differences in their singing. As in other
songsters, the ring-ouzel lowers his voice when approached by a
man or when watched; when singing freely the voice carries far, and
may be heard distinctly from the opposite side of a glen three or four
hundred yards wide, and refined by distance it has then a beautiful
bell-like quality.

In May the ring-ouzels were mostly laying their eggs when the
earlier-breeding blackbirds were bringing their young off. One day,
within a ten minutes' walk of the house, I spied a young blackbird

out among the rocks on the glen side, and captured it just to hold
it a minute or so in my hand for the sake of its beauty, also to see
what its parents would do. They came at me in a fury, to flutter
about within two or three yards of me, screaming and scolding their
loudest; and very soon their noise brought a pair of ring-ouzels on
the scene to help them. Here was a fine opportunity of comparing
our two British blackbirds – two pairs, male and female, all
animated by the same passion, and acting together like birds of the
same species, dashing close to my face, as I sat on a stone holding
the richly-coloured young bird in my hand, showing it to them.

The ring-ouzel always looks like a lesser blackbird, even when
they are thus seen side by side, although it is about the same size;
but it is not so black as his cousin, for black, being the most conspicuous colour in nature, exaggerates the size of an object, especially
a living moving one, to the eye. In some lights the ring-ouzel has a
rusty appearance owing to the pale tips of the feathers. The female
is less black than the male and varies in colour according to the
light, sometimes appearing olive-black or brown, and in some lights
a greenish-bronze colour.

On my liberating the young bird the four demonstrators flew
off. On the following day I found the ring-ouzels' nest in a tuft of
bilberry growing on a ledge of rock at the glen side. It contained
four eggs. The male continued to sing at intervals during the day
when the female was sitting, but his favourite time was late in the
evening, when perched on a stone about a hundred yards from his
mate he would repeat his song about twice every minute until it
was dark. He was the latest of the songsters, and would sing on the
coldest evenings, even when it was raining.

My daily visits to this nest were greatly resented by the birds.
It was their misfortune that they had builded their home so near
me and had made it so beautiful. I was also much interested in
the various cries and sounds they emitted when excited by my

presence. The male would flit and fly about at a distance, uttering loud clacking or chacking cries interspersed with a variety of little exclamatory notes, while the female, more anxious, would dash at me, chacking and screaming all the time. But the instant I left the site their rage would vanish; the male would begin his set 'wheero-wheero' whistle, while the female would break out in a sort of song of her own which resembled the first attempts at singing of a young throstle – a medley composed of a variety of guttural and squeaking notes interspersed with more or less musical chirps.

What struck me as most curious was that when troubled with my presence at the nest they uttered two distinct sounds which are not in the blackbird's language but are part of the language of the typical thrushes (*Turdus*); one was the prolonged, tremulous, harsh and guttural alarm cry of the missel-thrush, the other the low, long-drawn, wailing note of the throstle when anxious about its nest or young, a note so high-pitched as to be inaudible to some persons. It can only be supposed that these different sounds, expressing apprehension or anger, have been inherited by thrushes and the ring-ouzel, and have been lost in the blackbird. I have been told that the blackbird does occasionally emit the low robin-like wailing note when its nest is approached, but have never heard it myself.

One would like to listen to and compare the sounds emitted by all the thrushes of the world – the spotted ground thrushes (*Geocichla*), supposed to be the parental form; the typical thrushes (*Turdus*); and the blackbirds (*Merula*). Ornithologists pay little or no attention to the language of birds when considering the question of evolution, but here it might help us to a right conclusion of the question whether the blackbirds are an offshoot of the typical thrushes, or sprang independently from the ground thrushes. In studying the language of the blackbird alone one might spend half a lifetime very pleasantly. In the development of their vocal organs they stand highest among birds, and they have a world-wide distribution, numbering about seventy species. What more fascinating object in life for a wandering Englishman who desires to see all lands, who loves birds and above all others the 'garden-ouzel' of his home? A missionary writes that there is no living thing in Samoa which gives him so much the home feeling as this bird – its blackbird, *Merula samoensis.* The English spring is recalled to another in Ceylon by the ouzel of that country. Yet another wanderer in Somaliland is delightfully reminded of home by the native blackbird. And doubt- less others have had the same feeling produced in them by other blackbirds in other regions – in Siberia; in Cuba, in the Amazonian forests; in the Andes and the Himalayas; and in Burma, Japan, Formosa, the Philippines, New Guinea, Borneo, Java, Fiji, New Hebrides, Norfolk Island, the Louisiades; and other islands and countries too many to name.

14 BIRD MUSIC

Modern indifference to delicate music – Charm due to past associations
– A willow-wren at Harrogate – Intrinsic charm of some bird voices
– Effect of special circumstances – A rainwashed world – Exceptional
songs of chaffinch and whinchat – A wonderful blackbird

To those who delight in bird music it appears strange that there should be many persons who are quite indifferent to it, who will hear you speak of its charm or beauty with impatience and perhaps incredulity. It is probable that in many cases the indifference is the result of a town life and the dulling effect on the sense of hearing of an atmosphere of loud jarring noises, also of the loudness of the instrumental music to which they are accustomed. Our civilisation is a noisy one, and as it increases in noisiness the smaller, more delicate musical instruments which must be heard in a quiet atmosphere lose their ancient charm and finally become obsolete. The tendency is towards louder instruments and masses of sound; the piano is a universal favourite, and the more thunder you get out of it the better it is liked.

In this as in other things our gain is our loss; if in human music the sweetest, most delicate instrumental sounds cease to please, or even to be tolerable, on account of their small volume, how could the very best of the natural music of birds delight us – the small exquisite strains emitted by the wagtails and pipits, the wheatear and whinchat, the willow-wren and wood-wren, the linnet and reed-warbler? The very most that can be said of such minute melodies is that, like the little gurgling and lisping sounds of a pebbly streamlet and of wind in leaves and the patter of rain, it is soothing.

Another cause of indifference is that for some persons the sounds are without expression.

We know that when the occasions of past happiness, and the fact of the happiness itself, have been forgotten, something yet remains to us – a vague, pleasurable emotion which may be evoked by any scene, or object, or melody, or phrase, or any sight or sound in nature once associated with such happiness. It is this halo, this borrowed colour of a thing, which gives the expression. Those who say that they find an indefinable charm or beauty in any sight or sound, do not as a rule know that it is not a quality of the thing itself which moves them, that their pleasure is almost wholly due to association, and that in this case they 'receive but what they give'.

An instance of this charm which any natural object or sound may have for us is given by Gilbert White in his description of an insect. 'The shrilling of the field cricket,' he says, 'though sharp and stridulous, yet marvellously delights some hearers, filling their minds with a train of summer ideas of everything that is rural, verdurous, and joyous.' There can be no such 'train of ideas' nor any vague sense of happiness due to association caused by a bird's voice to one whose life or its early, most happy, and impressible period has been spent apart from rural scenes. The voice may be agreeable if the quality is good, but it is expressionless.

To others, especially to those who have lived with and have been lovers of nature from the cradle, even a slight bird sound may produce a magical effect, and I here recall an experience of the kind which I had two or three summers ago at Harrogate.

I should say, judging from its fine appearance and the numbers of fine people frequenting it, that Harrogate must be highly esteemed by town-loving folk; it is a parasitic town nevertheless, and on that account alone distasteful to me; and to make matters worse I there found myself in a numerous company of the sick – pilgrims from all parts of the land to that pool in which they fondly hoped they would be cured of their ills. Perhaps they did not all hope for a complete cure, as there was a very large proportion of well-nourished, middle-aged, and elderly gentlemen with hard red or port-wine faces and watery eyes who walked or hobbled painfully, some with the aid of two sticks, others with crutches, while many were seen in bath-chairs. I took it that these well-to-do well-fed gentlemen were victims of gout and rheumatism.

In this crowd of sufferers mixed with fashionables I was alone, out of my element, depressed, and should have been miserable but for a small bird, or rather of a small small bird voice. Every day when I went to the well in the gardens to drink a tumbler of magnesia water and sit there for an hour or so I heard the same delicate wandering aerial sound, the thin plaintive note of the same little bird, a willow-wren, which had taken up its summer-end residence at that spot. I do not mean a song; a little bird when moulting, concealed in a thick shrubbery, has no heart to sing: it was only his familiar faint little sorrowful call-note.

People came in numbers at certain hours of the day to the spring and pavilion to drink water and sit in groups chatting, flirting, laughing, or to pace the walks, while the children ran and romped about the green lawns or sailed their little boats on the running water; and by-and-by the crowd would begin to drift away as mealtime approached, until the gardens would be silent and deserted. But the small bird was always there, and though hidden among the bushes where they grew thickest he was not wholly invisible. At intervals his minute shadowy flitting form could be discerned at some spot where there was a slight opening among the dense clustered leaves, seen for a moment or two, then gone. And even when the place was fullest of people and the sound of talk and laughter loudest, still at brief intervals that faint, tenuous, sorrowful little sound would be audible through it all. Listening for it and hearing it, and sometimes catching a glimpse of the small restless creature among the deep green foliage near my seat, a curious mental change would come over me. The sense of dissatisfaction, of disharmony, would pass away; the pavilion, the kiosks, the gravelled walks and offensive flower-beds, the well-dressed invalids and idlers, the artificiality of the scene, with big hotel buildings for background, would be to me something illusory – a mental picture which I could dismiss from my mind at any moment, or an appearance which would vanish at a breath of wind or on the coming of a cloud over the sun. The people sitting and moving about me had no real exist-ence; I alone existed there, with a willow-wren for companion, and was sitting not on an iron chair painted green but on the root of an old oak or beech tree, or on a bed of pine needles, with the smell of pine and bracken in my nostrils, with only that wandering aerial tender voice, that gossamer thread of sound, floating on the silence.

This is doubtless an extreme example of the power of expression, and could perhaps only be experienced by one whose chief pleasure from childhood has been in wild birds and who delights in bird voices above all sounds. But expression is not everything: there is a charm in some sounds so great that we love them from the first time of hearing, when they are without associations with a happy past; and in such cases we can suppose that the emotional expression, if it exists at all, is produced indirectly and forms but a slight element in the aesthetic effect.

There is, besides expression, another thing not often taken into account which makes some bird melodies impress us more than others – the state of mind, or mood, we are in and the conditions in which it is heard. Yet it makes a world of difference even in the songs of species which we love best for their intrinsic beauty. The curious thing is that after hearing a particular bird music in exceptionally favourable circumstances the hearer should become

convinced that *this* musician is the best. It may not be at its best on
the next occasion of hearing it, or ever again, but the image of the
intense pleasure it once produced persists in his mind and the delu-
sion remains.

There are states of the atmosphere when distant objects seem
near and all nature takes on a rare loveliness which makes it like
a new earth. There are states, too, when bird sounds seem purer,
brighter, more resonant than at other times, in some instances
surprising us with new and mysteriously beautiful qualities.

After copious rains in summer there is often a tender silveri-
ness in the sunlit air, the effect of abundant moisture; and on such
occasions we sometimes note a difference in bird songs and cries,
as if they, too, like all else, had been washed and purified; and just
as we inhale the new delicious air into our lungs we take the new
melody into our souls. In this case the exhilarating effect of the
newly washed and brightened air and sight of the blue sky after
the depressing cloud has passed undoubtedly count for much; the
responsive physical change in us acts on the sense organs, and they,
too, appear to have been washed and made clean and able to render
truer and brighter images than before.

Then, too, we have the other cause, in which all natural sounds,
especially bird sounds, produce an unusual effect owing to some
special circumstances or to a conjunction of favourable circumstances. It is pure chance; the effect of today will never be repeated;
it has gone for ever, like the last beautiful sunset we witnessed. But
there will be many more beautiful sunsets to gladden our sight.

On looking on a meadow yellow with buttercups I have seen one
flower, or a single petal, far out, perhaps, in the middle of the field,
which instantly caught and kept my sight – one flower amongst a
thousand thousand flowers, all alike. It was because it had caught
and reflected the light at such an angle that its yellow enamelled
surface shone and sparkled like a piece of burnished gold. By some

such chance a song, a note, may reach the sense with a strange beauty, glorified beyond all other sounds.

One evening, walking in a park near Oxford, I stopped to admire a hawthorn tree covered with its fresh bloom. On a twig on the thorn a female chaffinch was perched, silent and motionless, when presently from the top of an elm tree close by its mate flew down, describing a pretty wavering curve in its descent, and arriving at the bush, and still flying, circling round it, he emitted his song; not the usual loud impetuous song he utters when perched; in form or shape only it was the same, the notes issuing in the same order, but lower, infinitely sweeter, tender, etherealised. The song ended as the bird dropped lightly by the side of its little mate.

I could hardly credit my own senses, so beautiful had seemed this subdued lyric from a songster we regard as very inferior to some of the warblers in delicacy and expressiveness.

On another occasion I was walking across a furze-grown common after dark on a very cold windy evening in early April, when at a distance of about forty yards from me a whinchat warbled the fullest, sweetest song I ever listened to from that bird. After a brief interval the song was repeated, then once again. Whether it was the exceeding purity of the sound, so clear, so wondrously sweet, so unexpected at that hour, or the darkness and silence of that solitary place which gave it an almost preternatural beauty I cannot say, but the effect on me was so great that I have never walked by night in spring in any furzy place without pausing and listening from time to time with the pleased expectation of hearing it again. Probably in these two instances and in a dozen others which I could cite the song was uttered by chance at the precise moment when it would be most impressive – when the conditions and the mood they had induced were most favourable. But the sound too may create the mood, as was the case in the following instance.

I have heard many wonderful blackbirds, for like all songsters, feathered as well as human, they vary greatly in merit, and *pace* Dr A. R. Wallace, there is such a thing as *genius* in nature, but I think the one which most impressed me was just an ordinary blackbird. I was staying at a farmhouse in the New Forest, and on the side of the house where I slept there was a large arbor vitae in which a blackbird roosted every night on a level with my window. Now, every morning at half-past three this bird would begin to sing and go on repeating his song at short intervals for about half an hour. It was very silent at that time; I could hear no other bird; and the sound coming in at the open window from a distance of but five yards had such a marvellous beauty that I could have wished for no more blessed existence than to lie there, head on pillow, with the pale early light and the perfume of night-flowers in the room, listening to that divine sound.

15 IN A GREEN COUNTRY IN QUEST OF RARE SONGSTERS

Green England – An imagined journey to the stars – The silent bicycle – Encounters with blind men – Rambles in Dorset – Wareham – Story of a good little boy – A surprising experience at Poole – The threshold of Hampshire

I can understand the feeling experienced by some visitors from far-distant sunburnt lands – our antipodean 'dependencies', for example – on first coming to England, at a time of year when the country is greenest. The unimagined brilliancy of the hue and its universality affect them powerfully; for though green was known to them in sea and sky and earth and in a parrot's plumage, it is not really the colour of nature in their world as in ours. It is a surprise to all and in some a pure delight, but to others it appears unnatural, and it is degraded by its association in the mind with fresh green paint. But to those who live in England, especially in the southern parts, this verdure is never more delightful and refreshing to the soul than when we come to it straight from some such hilly and moorland district as, say, that of the Peak of Derbyshire, with its brown harsh desolate aspect. All the qualities which go to make our southern landscape what it is to us are then intensified, or 'illustrated by their contraries', as Defoe would have said.

Thus it was that, on coming south from the Peak district at the end of May, it seemed to me that never since I had known England, from that morning in early May when I saw the sun rise behind the white cliffs and green downs of Wight and the Hampshire shore, had it seemed so surpassingly lovely – so like a dream of some heavenly country. There have been days of torment and weariness when the wish has come to me that I might be transported from this ball to the uttermost confines of the universe, to the remotest of all the unnumbered stars, to some rock or outpost beyond the furthest of them all, where I might sit with all matter, all life, for ever behind and with nothing but infinite empty space before me, thinking, feeling, remembering nothing, through all eternity. Now the wish or thought of a journey to the stars came to me again, but with a different motive: in the present instance it was purely for the sake of the long and wholly delightful journey, not for anything at the end. My wish was now to prolong the delight of travelling in such scenes indefinitely. Could anyone imagine a greater bliss than to sit or recline at ease in a railway carriage with that immortal green of earth ever before him, so varied in its shades, so flowery, splashed everywhere with tender, brilliant gold of buttercups, so bathed in sunlight and shaded with great trees – green woods with their roots in the divine blue of the wild hyacinth. Who would not wish to go on for days, months, years even, to the stars if we could travel to them in that way!

I don't know much about the stars, nor am I anxious to visit them; it was only the thought of the long green way that fascinated me. By-and-by it came into my mind that someone had said, just to enable us to grasp the idea of their distance from earth, that it would take a non-stopping express train forty million years to get to a star – which star, if any particular one was meant, I don't remember. The thought of it began to oppress me, for by-and-by, after a few centuries perhaps, I should begin to wish for a break, a stop for half an hour, let us say, at some small wayside station to enable me to lie down for a few minutes on my back in the grass to gaze up into the blue sky with its floating white clouds, and, above all, to listen to the

skylark and to every other sweet singing bird. I began to think that
seeing is not everything, since we have other senses; I wanted to
hear and smell and taste and feel; to wrap myself about with these
sensations, to pierce and dwell in them as some tiny, insect pene-
trates to the hollow chamber of a flower to feed at ease on its secret
sweetness. I recalled the complaint of the spiritual-minded author of
the *Cynthiades* to his Cynthia, that he was not content even in their
moments of supremest bliss – even when she was so close to him
that they knew each other's thought without a whisper:

Yet I desire
To come more close to thee and to be nigher;

still dissatisfied to find that their souls remained distinct and separate when he would have had them touch like two neighbouring
raindrops and become one.

There was no such bar in my case; being one we could not
asunder dwell. For my mistress is more to me than any Cynthia to
any poet; she is immortal and has green hair and green eyes, and
her body and soul are green, and to those who live with and love her
she gives a green soul as a special favour.

With this feeling impelling me I quitted the train and took to the
wheel, which runs without a sound, as a serpent glides or a swallow
skims, and brings you down to a closer intimacy with the earth.

How unspeakably grateful we should be for this gift – we lovers
of the road and of nature's quietude who have a meek and quiet spirit
– to go on our way like the owl by night on its downy silent wings!
So quiet is the wheel that on two separate occasions I have passed
a blind man on a quiet country road, so closely as almost to touch
him, without his knowing it until I spoke. This seemed marvellous to me when I considered the almost preternatural keenness
of the hearing sense in the blind, especially in blind men who are

accustomed to go freely about in country places. In both instances the man, when spoken to, started and wheeling partly round delivered his reply in the direction from which the voice had come, though the speaker was no longer there, having gone twenty or thirty yards past the point.

My second encounter with a blind man was during the ramble in a green country. I alighted, and watched him go on feeling his way along the edge of the road with his stick. He was a mile or more from the village at a spot where the road went by a wood. A little further on by the roadside the benevolent landlord – would that there were more like him! – had placed a garden bench in the shade for tired travellers to rest on. The man was making his way to this seat, and after he had settled down I went back and sat by him. He was a big healthy fine-looking man, a native of the village, a son of a farm labourer. He, more ambitious, left his home as a youth to find other employment, but it was a dangerous trade he took up and as a result of an explosion of powder in his face his vision was destroyed for ever. He came back to his village which, he said, he would never quit again. It was the one place known to him and although it was now covered with darkness he would still see it with his inner eye – the streets and houses, the fields, roads, hedges, woods, and streams – all this area which had been his playground in his early years was so well remembered that he could still find his way about in it.

He told me he made his living by selling tea which he procured in quantities direct from a London merchant and retailed to the cottages in half- and quarter-pound packets. They took their tea from him because he served them at their own doors. On certain days of the week he visited the neighbouring villages, doing a circuit of twenty-five or thirty miles in the day. On these occasions he had a little girl of ten to guide him. Of course she had to attend school on most days, but on Saturdays she was free and she could generally get permission to absent herself from school on another day. Failing her he had to take a larger girl, out of school, who was not half so intelligent as the other and not so well liked by the cottage women.

I noticed that this man, like many other blind persons I have met, though big and strong and in the prime of life, was a very quiet still man who spoke in a low voice and was subdued and gentle in manner. I think it is the habit of always listening that makes them so quiet, and I wondered what his sensations were when a motor cyclist passed us, going by like a whirlwind, a horrible object, shaking the earth, and making it hateful until he was a mile away with a torrent of noise.

In my quieter way on my wheel I rambled on from county to county viewing many towns and villages, conversing with persons of all ages and conditions; yet all this left but slight and quickly fading impressions, for in my flittings about a green land when it was greenest I had an object ever present in my mind – the desire to see and hear certain rare singing birds, found chiefly in the south, whose rarity is in most cases due to the collectors for the cabinet, birdcatchers, and other Philistines, who occupy themselves in the destruction of all loveliest forms of life. Thus, the clear whistle of a golden oriole, when I listened to it in a strictly guarded wood, where it breeds annually and where I was permitted to spend a day, was more to me than the sight of towns, villages, castles, ruins, and cathedrals, and more than adventures among the people.

This, then, is but a hasty and careless itinerary.

Going west I was at Blandford, then at Wimborne, where I found nothing in the town to detain me except the minster, and nothing in that but the whiteness of the stones with which it is built, with here and there one of a surprising red placed at random, giving the structure a harlequin appearance, unlike that of any other church known to me. At Wareham, a small ancient village-like town in a beautiful unspoilt-looking country, I was long in St Mary's Church, absorbed in the contemplation of Edward the Martyr's stone coffin, when a great gloom came over the earth and made the interior almost dark. Coming out I was astonished to find that while I had been in there with the coffin and the poor boy-king's ghost, the streets outside had been turned into muddy, rushing torrents, and going to a group of men standing near, I asked them where all that water came from. 'From above, I imagine,' replied one, smiling at my simplicity, which reply brought back to my mind a story of a good little boy read in my childhood. This little boy had been religiously taught to say about everything painful or unpleasant which befell him, from the loss of a toy or a wetting or a birching, to an attack of measles or mumps or scarlatina, that it 'came from above'. Now one day, during a very high wind, he was knocked down senseless by a tile falling on his head, and, recovering consciousness, found himself surrounded by a number of persons who had come to his assistance. Picking himself up and pointing to the tile at his feet which had knocked him down, he solemnly remarked, 'It comes from above.' At which the crowd laughed, for they were a frivolous people in that town, and they asked him where else it could come from.

That little town of ancient memories and a cloudburst, with the villages round it, is a good place to be in, but it could not keep me since I could not find there what I had gone out to seek; so very soon I turned eastward again, going by way of Poole, which I had not seen for some years. There I met with a surprising experience. There is a fine public park at Poole, with extensive green spaces and a lake for boating – the largest lake in any public park in England. At six o'clock in the evening it was thronged with the townspeople who had gathered at that place to recreate themselves after their day's work, and never have I seen a people enjoy themselves more heartily, or one that seemed more like a naturally joyous people. The greatest crowd was round the bandstand, where hundreds of people were resting on chairs or sitting and lying on the grass, whilst others danced on the green or on the large open-air dancing floors made for the purpose. Further away youths and boys were running races and playing ball on the lawns, whilst numbers of prettily dressed girls flitted up and down the paths on bicycles. So much liberty in a public park was very unusual. Now just when I came on the scene at about six o'clock a big cloud rose up from the south-east and grew and grew until it covered half the entire heavens with its blackness; and as it spread higher and nearer the thunder heard at intervals increased in power and was more frequent, accompanied with vivid flashes of forked lightning which, one would imagine, would have sent the people in terror to their homes. For a very little more and the storm would be directly over us and the whole crowd deluged with rain. But though it remained near us for about an hour and a half, without losing that black, exceedingly threatening aspect, with occasional little tempests of rain, it did not quite reach us, and I then noticed, when strolling about the ground, that there was not the slightest appearance of apprehension or nervousness in the people. The fun and frolic continued without a break through it all until, at nine o'clock, the people dispersed to their homes.

Now I can imagine that the people I had been staying with on those cold, harsh moors in Derbyshire would have stared and gasped with astonishment at such a scene, and would perhaps have refused to believe that it was an everyday scene in that place, that this was how the people spent their summer evening after each day's work. I can imagine, too, that some nonagenarian or centenarian, who had from his youth dreamed of a freer, sweeter, more joyous life for the people of his country, on coming down from some such unchanged district as the one just mentioned and looking upon the scene I have described, would be able to say from his very heart, 'Now lettest Thou Thy servant depart in peace.'

Quitting Poole, I ran for ten miles along a continuous thorough-fare, through Bournemouth to Christchurch, with the ugliness and infernal jar and clang of the electric trams the whole way. Only when I got to the shade of the grey old priory church did I feel that I was safely out of Pandemonium and on the threshold of that county richest of all in wild life which continually calls me back from all others, east, west, and north, to its heaths and forests and rivers.

16 IN A HAMPSHIRE VILLAGE

Rare species and private collectors – An old soldier – Moorhen –
A family of working folk – A talk with my landlady – Her love of
bird music – The story of her lost child

Going further into Hampshire I was by-and-by at a spot which cannot be named owing to the fact that I was there in quest of a rare and elusive little bird. For we who desire to save our birds must keep the private collector in mind; that injurious person who is ever anxious to secure the very last British-killed specimens of any rare species. And should a species be near its end – in other words, should it be rare – then, says the leader and lawgiver of all this rapacious gang, our right and proper course is to finish it off as quickly as may be, seeing that by so doing we furnish our cabinets with a large number of specimens for the benefits of science and of posterity. The law does not protect our birds and country from these robbers; they have too many respected representatives in high places, on the benches of magistrates, in the Houses of Parliament, and among important people generally. For are they not robbers and of the very worst description? Those who break into our houses to steal our gold steal trash in comparison; while these, who are never sent to Portland or Dartmoor, are depriving the country with its millions of inhabitants of one of its best possessions – its lustrous wild life.

Here I came to a village which happened to be one of the very few, certainly not above half a dozen, in all that county never previously visited by me; and as it was within easy distance of the spot I had come to explore I had some idea of settling in it for a few days. I had long known it by name, and it had furthermore been minutely and lovingly described to me by an old soldier, decorated with many medals, who is now a keeper in one of the royal parks. One day last spring he showed me a blackbird's nest in which he took a somewhat anxious interest on account of its unsafe position on a wart or projection on the trunk of a Spanish chestnut tree, a few feet from the ground and plainly visible to mischievous eyes. Our talk about this careless blackbird and other birds led to his telling me of his boyhood in a small out-of-the-world Hampshire village, and I asked him how, with such a feeling as he had revealed about his native place, he had been able to spend his life away from it, and why he did not go back there now. That, he answered, was his desire and intention, not only since he had begun to grow old, but he had cherished the idea even when he was a young man and in his prime, in India, Burma, Afghanistan, Egypt. Now at last the time seemed near when his desire would be fulfilled; two years more in the park and he would retire with a small pension, which, added to his soldier's pension, would enable him to pass the remnant of his life in his native village.

I thought of him now, the tall straight old soldier, with his fine stern face and grey moustache and hair, who had spent his years in defending the empire in many distant lands, and was now anxiously guarding a blackbird's nest in a park from the wild, lawless little Afghans and Soudanese of the London slums. It was nice to think of him here where he would soon be back in his boyhood's haunts, as I sat on the trunk of a sloping tree by the stream, a stone's-throw from the churchyard. I was practically in the village, yet not a sound could be heard but the faint whisper of the wind in the trees near me and the ripple and gurgling of the water at my feet. Then came another sound – the sudden loud sharp note of alarm or challenge of a moorhen a few yards away. There she stood on the edge of the clear water, in a green flowery bed of water-mint and forget-me-not, with a thicket of tall grasses and comfrey behind her, the shapely black head with its brilliant orange and scarlet ornaments visible above the herbage. We watched each other, and it was indeed peaceful at that spot where nature and man lived in such a close companionship, and very sweet to be there; nevertheless, it did not suit me to stay in that village. Its charm consisted mainly in its seclusion, in its being hidden from the world in a hollow among woods and hills, and I love open spaces best, wide prospects from doors and windows, and the winds free to blow on me from all quarters. Accordingly, I went to another village a mile and a half away, where it was more open, and settled there in a cottage with working people – man and wife and one child, a little boy of eleven.

My usual good luck attended me in this place, for seldom have I stayed with people I liked better. The wife was intelligent enough to let me live just as I liked without any fuss, so that I could get up at four o'clock in the morning when they were still sleeping to make tea for myself in the kitchen before going out, and come in when I liked and have what I liked in the way of food. The man, too, was a perfect host; his good qualities and cleverness in his work had raised him to a better position than that of most working men. He was actually earning about three pounds a week, but prosperity had not spoiled him; he might have been making no more than fifteen or eighteen shillings like others of his class, in the village. His manner was singularly engaging, and he was quiet and gentle in the house. One might have thought that he had been subdued by his wife – that she was the ruling spirit; but it was not so: when they were together, and when they sat at table, where I sometimes sat with them, she tuned herself to him and talked with a gentle cheerfulness, watching his face and hanging on his words. Their manner was so unlike that of most persons in their state of life that it was a puzzle to me, and I might have guessed the secret of it from a peculiar pathos in his voice and the inward-gazing dreamy expression in his eyes which haunted me; but I guessed nothing, and only learnt it just before quitting the village.

Then there was the boy, who in the house was just as still, gentle, and low-voiced as his father; a boy who disliked his books and crawled reluctantly to school and took no part in games, but who had an intense love of the wild, a desire to be always out of doors by himself, following and watching the birds.

I was like that myself at his age, but was more happily placed, having no school to crawl to nor miserable books to pore over.

One day, just before leaving, I came in to my six o'clock meal, after a long spell on the heath, to find my landlady as usual ready and even eager to listen to anything I had to tell her. For she, too, at home in her cottage, had been alone all day, except for a few minutes when her boy came in at noon to swallow his dinner and run off to the nearest wood or heath to get as much time as possible before the clanging of the school bell called him in again. Now everything I ever told her about my rambles on the heath had appeared to interest her in an extraordinary way. She would listen to an account of where I had been, to which old ditch, or barrow, or holly clump, also what birds I had found there, and to the most trivial incidents, as if to some wonderful tale of adventure; she would listen in silence until I ended, when she would ask a dozen questions to take me all over the ground again and keep up the talk about the heath. On this occasion she said more, telling me that the heath had been very much to her; then little by little she let out the whole story concerning her feeling for it. It was the story of her life from the time of her marriage up to little over a year ago, when her two children were aged nine and six respectively. For there were two children then, and they lived in a cottage at the side of a pine and oak wood on the border of the heath. Her husband was fond of birds and of all wild animals; he knew them well, and in time she, too,

grew to like them just as much. She loved best to hear their songs
and calls; bird voices were always to be heard, day and night, all the
year round. You couldn't but hear them, even the faintest note of
the tiniest bird, it was so silent at that spot where there was no road
and no house near. Her solace and one pleasure outside the house
was in their singing. She was very much alone there; she read
little and never heard any music – one would have to go miles to
hear a piano; so the songs of birds came to be the sweetest sounds
on earth for her, especially the blackbird, which was more to her
than any other bird. When she first came to live in the village she
could hardly endure the noises – so many cocks crowing, children
shouting, people talking, carts rattling by and all kinds of noises!
It made her head ache at first. Then at night, how they missed the
night birds' sounds – the hooting of the wood owls, especially in
winter, and in summer the reeling of nightjars, and the corncrake
and the nightingale.

Thus for half an hour the poor woman talked and talked about
her old life on the heath, laughing a little now and then at her own
feelings – the absurdity of her home-sickness when she was so near
the old spot – but always with a little break in her voice, avoiding
all the time the one subject uppermost in her mind – the very one
I was waiting for her to come to. And in the end she had to come
to it, and after putting her hand up to hide the tears that could not
be kept back, she was relieved, and began to speak freely of the
lost child. Violet was her name, and everyone who knew her said
that no fitter name could have been given her, she was so beautiful,
so like a flower, with eyes that were like violets. And she had the
greatest love of flowers for a small child. Nobody had seen anything
like it. Dolls and toys she didn't care for – she was all for flowers.
As for sense, she had as much of it as any grown-up person when
she was no more than five. She was a most loving little thing, but
cared most for her father, and every evening when he came home

she would fly to meet him, and would sit on his knee till bedtime. What talks those two had! Now the most curious thing remains to tell, and this was about both the children – the way in which they would spend most of their time. At that distance from the village the boy was allowed, after a good deal of bother about it, to learn his letters at home. If the weather was fine, those two would be up and have breakfast very early, then, taking their dinner in a little basket, would go to the heath, and she would see no more of them till about five o'clock in the afternoon. The boy was always fondest of birds and animals, like his father, and was happy following and watching them all day long. The girl loved the flowers best, and whenever she found a flower that was rare or wholly new to her she would cry out with joy and make as much fuss as if she had found a splendid jewel on the heath. She was a strong child, always the picture of health, so that when she suddenly fell ill of a fever it surprised and alarmed them greatly, and the doctor was sent for. He didn't think it a serious case, but he seemed doubtful about its nature, and in the end he made a fatal mistake – he himself said it was a mistake. The crisis came, and the poor child got so bad that he was sent for, but it was long to wait, and in the meantime something had to be done, and what she did was to give it a hot bath. Then the fit passed, and with it the fever, and the child went off in a quiet sleep with every sign of returning health. Then came the doctor and said the child was getting well – the right thing had been done – but he must wake her up and give her a draught. She begged him not to; he insisted, and roused and made the child drink, and no sooner had the little thing swallowed the medicine than she fell back white as ashes and was dead in a few minutes.

It was going on for two years since their loss; they had been long settled in the village and had grown used to the village life: the boy was gradually becoming more reconciled to school; her husband had a different employment, which suited him better than the former one, and was highly regarded by his master; then, too, they had pleasant relations with their neighbours. But this improvement in their condition brought them no happiness – they could not get over the loss of their child. She, the wife, had her grief when she was alone during long hours every day in the house; but when her man came home in the evening she could, and did, throw it off, and was always cheerful, her whole care being to make him forget his sorrow. But it seemed useless; he was a changed man; all his thoughts, all his heart, were with his lost child. He had always been good-tempered and kind, but he had been merry too, full of fun and laughter; now he was what I had seen – a very quiet, still man who smiled a little at times, but who appeared to have forgotten how to laugh.

17 THE FURZE-WREN OR FURZE-FAIRY

A new locality for the Dartford warbler – A search for it on a heath –
A litter of feathers – First sight of the furze-wren – First hearing of its
song – Its habits and song described – Its originality as a songster

I came to that unnamed little village, as I have said, in quest of
one of our rarest songsters; then the people of the cottage where
I lodged came between me and my subject with their human
sweetness and sorrows, and telling of them I forgot to say whether
or not I had found my bird or even to mention its species.

It happened that about a year or fourteen months before I started
on this quest, a friend wrote to inform me that by chance he had
discovered a new locality for the Dartford warbler, that delicate
birdling of the furze-bushes, our furze-wren, so persistently sought
after for many years past by our collectors. He was cycling in the
south country, and when going by a side-road at the edge of a wide
heath or moor caught sight of a pair flitting among some furze-
bushes. He had never previously seen the bird, but I was satisfied
that he was right in his identification – that he was about the last
man to make a mistake in such a matter. I may add that this same
keen observer is not known to me personally; we correspond, and
having the same feeling about birds are naturally friends. He is one
of those strange but not very uncommon persons who lead a double
life. To some of us he is known as an ornithologist; to the theatre-
going public he is a finished actor, and those who know him only in
his impersonations would, I imagine, hear with surprise, perhaps
incredulity, that, off the boards, he is a haunter of silent, solitary

places where birds inhabit, that in these communings he has a joy
with which the playgoer intermeddleth not.

The heath was a very extensive one, covering an area of several
square miles, and it was not strange that when I searched the spot
he had described I failed to find the birds. I then set patiently and
methodically to work to search the furzy places, especially where
the growth was thickest, in other parts, and after two entire days
spent in this quest I began to fear I was not going to find them after
all. But I had spent so many days and weeks on former occasions in
searching for this same most elusive little creature in eight or nine
other spots where I have found him in the south and west country,
and knew his hiding habits so well, that I still allowed myself to
hope. However, after yet another morning spent in vain I resolved
to give it up that same evening and go back west. It had been labour
in vain, I thought sadly, then smiled and felt a little encouraged to
remember that 'Labour in Vain' was the actual name of a barren
stony piece of ground with a little furze growing on it, where many
years ago I had found my first furze-wren – a spot distant about
thirty miles from the nearest known locality for the bird.

I then went to a high barrow on the heath and sat down to
meditate and cool myself in the wind; there my attention was
attracted to a litter of feathers near my feet of some small bird on
which a sparrow-hawk had recently fed. The body feathers were
red or chestnut brown, the quills black or blackish brown. I began
to speculate as to the species, when it all at once occurred to me
that these were the two colours of the furze-wren. The wind was
blowing strong and carrying the feathers, red and black, fast away
– in two or three minutes there would be few left to judge from. I
quickly gathered those that remained clinging to the stunted heath
on the barrow-top and began examining them. No, the sparrow-
hawk had not struck down and devoured that most unlikely bird, the
furze-wren: there remained one little quill with a white border and

one small pure white feather. They were linnet's feathers – the dark wing feathers and the chestnut-red body feathers from the back.

Now this trivial incident of the barrow-top, where I went to meditate and did not do so, served as a fillip to my flagging energies, and I immediately went off across the heath in quest of my bird again, making for a point about three-quarters of a mile away which I had hunted over two or three days before. I had not proceeded more than about three hundred yards when, in the most unlikely spot in the whole place, I caught sight of a minute, black-looking bird flitting rapidly out of one low ragged furze-bush and vanishing into another. Here was my furze-wren!

Nothing now remained to do but to snuggle down in a cluster of heather and to sit there motionless and watch, and in due time the bird reappeared with his mate, and they came to and scolded me, then, seeing me so still, went away about their business.

In one thing this pair disappointed me. My first object in going to the heath was to make sure that they were still there; I had another, which was not to pull their nesting-bush to pieces, to let in the sunlight, rearrange it, and then photograph the nest 'in its natural surroundings', as our fictionists of the camera have it, but to describe the song immediately, after listening to it, when the impression would be fresh in the mind. This bird, from dawn to dark, declined to sing or say anything except that he objected to my presence. His girding note is like that of a refined whitethroat – he chides you like a fairy. The songlessness was no doubt due to the fact that there was no other pair, or no cock bird, to provoke him, in that part.

One evening, three days later, I was in another part of the heath, about half a mile from the breeding-place of the first pair, when a small bird flitted up from the furze and perched for a few moments on the topmost twig of a bush; another furze-wren, his dainty figure silhouetted, black as jet, against the pale evening sky, on the summit of his black and gold furze-bush! It was a joyful moment, a discovery

wholly unexpected, as I had previously explored that part and found
nothing. It was in a spot where the furze grew in a dense thicket,
four to six or seven feet high, and covering three to four acres of
ground. As a rule the bird prefers a sparser growth with open
spaces among the bushes.

My bird soon vanished and refused to come out again.
Something better followed; fifty yards further on a second bird
appeared and perched on a bush began to sing, allowing me to
approach to within twenty yards of him. He too then dived down
into the thicket and was seen no more. I went home with that small
song in me, but did not attempt to describe it, as I wished first to
hear it again more freely and fully uttered.

Next day I found no fewer than nine pairs, all living and breeding
near together, at that one point in the vast dense thicket. Outside it
was all empty and barren; just there the little living gems sparkled in
profusion. But how melancholy to think that any cunning scoundrel
hired by a private collector, or the keeper of a bird-stuffer's shop who
calls himself 'Naturalist', might appear any moment with an air-gun
and extirpate the whole colony in the course of a morning!

I found that my best time to observe these birds was about five
o'clock in the morning, when they are most excitable and vocal. I
would then sometimes have two, at times three, pairs about me,
flitting hither and thither, vanishing and reappearing, scolding
and by-and-by fighting; for any spot in which I stationed myself
to observe them would be within the territory of a particular pair,
and when other pairs came in to assist in the demonstration against
me, they were regarded as intruders. The cock in possession of the
ground would resent their presence and sing defiantly, the other
would reply, but was never able to stand against the furious onset
which would follow; in every case he was chased ignominiously back
to his own ground. The victor would then return to pour out his
triumph and challenge to all outsiders.

The song, albeit so passionate, does not carry far, so that to hear it well the listener must be as near as he can possibly get to the bird. It is short, lasting only a few seconds at each repetition, but when in the singing spirit the little vocalist will sometimes continue the performance for several minutes at a stretch. As to the character of the song, Montagu, who was the first man in England to write about it, said that it resembled the song of the stonechat. That is true, since the little chat's song is composed of a few low and guttural notes interspersed with others bright and clear; but Montagu omitted to say that he spoke only of the chat's song uttered from a perch and not the song the same bird emits when he rises high in the air and, falling and rising, pours out his little rhythmical melody – his better song. But the song, or rather songs, of the stonechat are known to few persons, owing to the fact that this bird is intolerant of the presence of a human being near him. Heard at a considerable distance, the lower notes in the song of the furze-wren are lost, and the sound that reaches the ear might be taken for a stonechat; or linnet, or dunnock, or even a pipit. The white throat, heard in the same localities, has a louder, coarser song, which is not much softened or etherealised by distance. The whitethroat's girding or chiding note is familiar to everyone; the chiding note of the furze-wren is like the same note subdued and softened. It is this same chiding or scolding note which is used in singing, only louder and more musical and uttered with such extraordinary rapidity that the note may be repeated eighteen or twenty times in three seconds of time. The most hurried singing of the sedge-warbler seems an almost languid performance in comparison. This rapid utterance produces the effect of a continuous or sustained sound, like the reeling of the grasshopper-warbler; the character of the sound is, however, not the same; it is rather like a buzzing or droning, as of a stag beetle or cockchafer in flight, only with a slightly metallic and musical quality added. This buzzing stream of sound is interspersed with small, fine, bright, clear notes, both shrill and mellow. Some of these are very pure and beautiful.

Meredith says of the lark's song that it is a

silver chain of sound
Of many links, without a break.

The same may be said of many other songsters all the world over
– all, in fact, that do not sing in a leisurely manner, or, like the
throstle and nightingale, with frequent pauses. But chains differ in
form; so with these chains of sound of the rapid singers: in some
the links (otherwise, the notes) may be seen and distinguished as
separate parts of the piece. In the furze-wren it is not so; the excessive rapidity with which the notes are emitted and repeated makes
the performance more like a close-woven cord than a chain, and,
to continue the metaphor, we may see it as a black or grey cord, set
and sparkling with loose thread-ends of silver, gold and scarlet. The
black or sombre cord represents the low chiding or buzzing sound,
the brilliant threads the bright, shrill and delicate sounds.

The furze-wren is one of our minor songsters, ranking with the
stonechat, dunnock, redstart, and lesser whitethroat. Its chief interest
is its originality – its unlikeness to that of any other singer. This makes
it difficult to describe, since we cannot convey an impression of a bird
sound or song except by likening it to other well-known sounds or
songs. Our ornithologists, who have written about the bird for the last
century and a half, have not attempted to describe its song. I remember
that I once asked the late Howard Saunders why this was so, and his
reply was that the furze-wren has such a curious little jiggy song that
you couldn't describe it. Of course one can describe the song of any
unhuman being, from a shrill insect to an angel, but the sad truth of the
matter is that the impression cannot be properly conveyed by words to
another. Nevertheless the description may be a help to the bird-seeker. It
does not give him a perfect image of the song – only the bird itself can
do that – but it helps him to identify the singer when he first hears it.

18 BACK TO THE WEST COUNTRY

A procession of white cows – Revisiting old friends – Montacute
House – Ham Hill stone – A nightingale and a commercial traveller
– A north-countryman at Salisbury – Poetic feeling of northerners
– The commercial traveller's disappointment – Between Yeovil and
Glastonbury – The people of Somerset

My object gained, I quitted the little Hampshire village the richer for three prized memories: first and best was that of the people I had been staying with in their cottage; next in order of merit, the image of those little feathered fairies in a vocal rage; and last, that of five white or cream-coloured cows issuing from some small or cottage farm at the side of the heath, driven or followed by a young woman to their daily grazing-place on some distant part of the moor. Every morning they appeared from among the green foliage of trees and shrubs, behind which the homestead was hidden, to take their slow way over the wide brown heath in a scattered procession, always followed by that young woman, tall and straight, her head uncovered, her limp gown of a whity-grey colour almost like the white of the cows. A beautiful strange spectacle, seen from afar, as they moved across the moor in the dewy shimmering light of the early sun. They had a misty appearance, and there was something, too, of mystery in it, due perhaps to association – to some dim suggestion of ancient human happenings, in a time when there were gods who heeded man and white cows that were sacred to them.

I had seen and heard and made these precious things mine; now I wanted to turn back to the west again, to be in other green flowery places before the bloom was gone. It was nearing mid-June and by making haste now I might yet find some other feathered rarity and listen to some new song before the silent time. The golden oriole and furze-wren were but two of half a dozen species I had come out to find.

At Yeovil I delayed two or three days with a double motive. One of the most delightful experiences of a rambler about the land is, when the day's end has brought him to some strange or long-unvisited place, to remember all at once that this is the spot, the very parish, to which old friends came to settle two or three or more years ago. He missed their dear familiar faccs sadly in that part of the country where he had known them, but he has never wholly forgotten or ceased to love them, and now how delightful to find and drop in by surprise on them, to take pot luck as in the old days, to talk of those same dear old days and the old home, of every person in it from the squire to the village idiot.

It is hardly necessary to add that these lost friends one goes about to recover are not persons of importance who keep a motor-car, but simple people who live and for long generations have lived the simple life, who are on the soil with some of the soil on them, who see few visitors from a distance – from the great world, and whose glad welcome is one of the sweetest things in life.

This then was motive the first, and when I discovered my lost friends not far from the town I found them unchanged, still in the old mind, the feeling that I was one of them, of their very kin, and though rarely seen and perhaps regarded as the vagabond of the family, not less well loved on that account.

My second object was to look at Montacute House and park which had been missed on previous visits. The park held me for several hours, for it is like a wilderness or a place in a dispeopled land that was once a park, but I found no feathered rarity there or anywhere in the country round.

As to the famous Montacute House, it is built of Ham Hill stone – the one building stone I cannot abide. By others it is greatly admired, and it is perhaps worth explaining why I, loving colour as I do, yellows as much as any, have this feeling about our famous yellow stone. It is, I take it, an associate feeling due to the disagreeable effect which yellow as an interior colour produces in me. Sherborne Abbey is without a doubt one of our noblest ecclesiastical buildings, more beautiful in the stone sculpture enriching its roof than any cathedral or church in the land. Yet I cannot appreciate it, since the effect of the colour is a severe headache, a profound depression. After an hour inside I feel that I am yellow all through, that my very bones are dyed yellow, that if I were to drop down among the furze-bushes on some neighbouring common and rest there undiscovered for several years, those who found me would not believe that my remains were human, but only a skeleton cunningly carved out of Ham Hill stone. This sensation, or its memory, or the feeling which remains in the mind when the memory and images have vanished, enters in and gives an expression to all buildings of this same yellow material. This feeling was in me when I spent a couple of hours in full sight of Montacute House; otherwise I should probably have thought, as no doubt most persons do, that the colour of the stone added greatly to the beauty of the building, that it harmonised with its surroundings, the green spaces and ancient noble trees, bathed in a brilliant sunlight, and the wide blue sky above.

On my first evening in the town I went out into the neighbouring wood on the steep slope above the little river Yeo, and listened to a nightingale for half an hour, the only one I could find in the place. On the following afternoon I had sitting opposite to me at the table when taking tea at the hotel a commercial traveller whose appearance and speech amused and interested me. A tall bony uncouth-looking young man with lantern jaws and sunburned skin, in a rough suit of tweeds and thick boots; he was more like a working farmer than a 'commercial', who as a rule is a towny, dapper person. I ventured the remark that he came from the north. Oh yes, he replied, from a manufacturing town in Yorkshire; he had been visiting the West of England for the last two or three years, and this was the first time he had elected to spend the night at Yeovil. He had nothing more to do in the place, having finished his business early in the afternoon. He could have got to Bristol or gone on to Exeter; he was staying only to hear the nightingale. He had never heard it, and he didn't want to finish his rounds on this occasion and go back north without that long-desired experience.

These rough fellows from the north, especially from Yorkshire and Lancashire, are always surprising us with their enthusiasm, their aesthetic feeling! One Sunday morning not long ago I was on the cathedral green at Salisbury watching the pigeons and daws on the vast pile, when I noticed a young working man with his wife and child sitting on the grass by the elm trees. They had a luncheon basket with them, and were evidently out for the day. By-and-by the young man got up and strolled over to where I was standing, looking up at the birds soaring round the spire, and, entering into conversation with me, he told me that he was a zinc-worker from Sheffield, that he had been sent south to work at Tidworth in the erection of zinc and iron buildings for the army. When he saw Salisbury Cathedral and heard the choir he was so delighted that he resolved to spend his Sundays and any day he had off at the cathe-dral. He was musical himself, and belonged to some musical society in his own town. He talked of his love of music with sparkling eyes, and while he talked he continued watching the birds, the daws sweeping round and round, mounting higher and higher until they were above the cross; and then from that vast height they would hurl themselves suddenly downwards towards the great building and the earth. All at once, as we watched a bird coming down, he threw his arms up and cried excitedly, 'Oh, to fly like that!'

And you, said I to myself, born in a hideous grimy manufacturing town, breathing iron dust, a worker in an ugly material engaged in making ugly things, have yet more poetry and romance, more joy in all that is beautiful, than one could find in any native of this soft lovely green south country!

Does not this fact strike every observer of his fellows who knows both north and south intimately? How strange then to think that well-nigh all that is best in our poetic literature has been produced by southerners – by Englishmen in the southern half of the country! Undoubtedly the poetic feeling is stronger and more general in the north, and we can only conclude that from this seemingly most favourable soil the divine flower of genius springeth not.

To return to my commercial traveller. I told him where to go in search of the nightingale, and meeting him later that evening asked him if he had succeeded. Yes, he replied, he had found and listened for some time to its song. It was a fine song, unlike that of any other bird known to him, but it did not come up to his expectations, and he had formed the idea that this bird was probably not a very good specimen of its kind. It consoled him to be told that he was absolutely right, that Yeovil's one nightingale was a rather poor performer.

From Yeovil to Glastonbury is but a few miles, some fifteen as the crow flies – no distance at all to the person of importance in a motor-car and nothing to detain him by the way. To me – to all whose desire in travelling is not to arrive at their destination – it was as far as I liked to make it. It was in fact a vast green country where I discovered several small ancient towns and more villages than I can remember; churches in the shadow of whose grey old towers one would like to spend the slow last years of life; inns too where bread and cheese and beer, if nothing else, can be obtained for refreshment, and the cottage homes of the people one loves best. They are never wildly enthusiastic like the Lancastrians about anything, but they are sweeter, more engaging in temper and manner, whether on account of their softer climate or the larger infusion of Celtic blood in their Anglo-Saxon veins I know not. They are perhaps a perfect amalgam, like their Welsh neighbours on the other side of the Severn with the harsh lines of the Welsh features subdued, and like their Saxon neighbours on the east side without their stolidity. Moreover, they are not without a spark of that spirit which is in the northerner – the romance, the inner bright life which is not wholly concerned with material things.

19 AVALON AND A BLACKBIRD

Excavations and restorations at Glastonbury – Blackbird music –
Its relation to human music: C. A. Witchell's theory – A blackbird of
genius – Intrinsic beauty of the blackbird's voice – Our favourite singer –
The blackbird in early Irish poetry

At Glastonbury I spent some hours at the abbey, somewhat
disturbed at the huge diggings and a little saddened at
the sight of the repairs and restorations; yet they were
necessary if this loveliest ruin in England is to be kept standing a
few centuries longer. Unfortunately, however skilfully the restoring
work is done, the new portions will insist on looking outrageously
new. Time will doubtless restore the lost harmony, the ancient
venerable appearance, but it will be long before these staring fresh
parts will cease to have the effect of patches of a new cloth on the
frayed and faded garment. Fifty years of sun and rain will prepare
the fresh, hard surfaces for the vegetation that makes a ruin beautiful – valerian, ivy-toadflax, wallflower, and grey and green lichens
and mosses.

In the course of a conversation I had with some of those engaged
in these works at the abbey, during which the subject of birds came
up, Mr Blythe Bond, the gentleman who has charge of the excavations, informed me that a blackbird in his garden whistled a perfect
musical phrase.

He took me to hear it at his house in the High Street, which
had a large garden at the back; there we seated ourselves in the
summer-house and in a very few minutes the bird began fluting

his little human roundelay for our benefit. My host whistled and hummed it after him, then took me to his drawing-room and touched it off on his piano, and finally when I told him that after all it would perhaps escape my memory he noted it down for me, and here it is:

It is not a rare thing to hear phrases in the blackbird's singing which are like human music and speech and may be taken down in our musical notation. I will give a quotation here on this subject from one of C. A. Johns' pleasant but forgotten little books – *Home Walks and Holiday Rambles* (1863).

> *A blackbird had stationed himself on the top of a tree hard by, and seemed resolved to sing on until fine weather returned. The burden of his song was the following passage, which was repeated so often that if one could tire of natural music I should have been tired then:*

> *All the other strains were unmetrical, and there seemed to be in them no melodious arrangement of notes; so that the general effect was nearly what could be produced by a person talking in his natural tone of voice, and repeatedly introducing a snatch of an old song by which his memory was haunted, though he was unable to recall either the words or the melody of the remainder.*

This is interesting because it is so common – the perfect musical phrase occurring in a song which is for the rest of a quite different character.

The question arises, Are these phrases imitations or natural to the bird? Human music in bird-song is a subject an American naturalist, Mr Henry Oldys, has made peculiarly his own, and he will be welcomed by all lovers of bird music when he carries out his intention of coming over to us to make a study of the British songsters. Meanwhile we have the late C. A. Witchell's *Evolution of Bird-Song* to go on with. He has recorded in musical notation no fewer than seventy-six blackbird strains in his book, and his views as to the origin of this kind of singing, in which the phrases of the bird are identical with our musical intervals, are of very great interest, as he is the only person in this country who has made a special study of the subject. There is, he writes, nothing surprising in these phrases when we consider the imitative powers of the best singers, and the frequency of human music in their haunts. The field-labourer whistles; from villages issue louder, though not always sweeter, musical sounds; throughout the year music is heard in country towns. It appears also that our musical scale is of remote origin, and that for thousands of years the intervals which we now employ have been wafted from musical instruments used by men to the ears of listening birds.

This is far from convincing. Some of our songbirds are imitative in a much higher degree than the blackbird, yet never come near to human music in their songs. The cuckoo with us and numerous other species all the world over, many of them in wild lands where human-made music is never wafted to their ears, do yet observe the same intervals as in our own scale in their calls and songs. My belief is that the blackbird sings in this way naturally, that he approaches nearer to us in his musical scale just as the grasshopper-warbler, the red night-reeler, and the furze-wren go further from us and are like insects in their music, simply because it is his nature to. Blackbirds, we have seen, are distributed pretty well all over the globe and are of many species, ranging in size from those no bigger than a throstle to others large as or larger than jays, but all have beautiful voices which remind English travellers in tropical forests and distant temperate regions of the home bird, and in some instances it is said to sing better than our bird. I think that if these travellers had been specially interested in this subject and had listened attentively to the exotic species, they would have found that these too have phrases that sound like fragments and snatches of human melodies.

The blackbird often reminds me of the common Patagonian mocking-bird, *Mimus patachonicus*, not in the quality of the sounds emitted, nor in the shape of the song, nor in any resemblance to human melody, but in the way the bird throws out his notes anyhow, until in this haphazard way he hits on a sequence of notes, or phrase, that pleases him, and practises it with variations. Finally, he may get fond of it and go on repeating it for days or weeks. Every individual singer is, so to speak, his own composer.

In listening to a blackbird, even where there is no resemblance to a man-made melody, it always appears to me to come nearer to human music than any other bird songs; that the bird is practising, or composing, and by-and-by will rise to a melody in which the musical intervals will be identical with those of our scale. I recall the case of a blackbird of genius I once heard near Fawley in the New Forest. This bird did not repeat a strain with some slight variation as is usually the case, but sang differently each time, or varied the strain so greatly as to make it appear like a new melody on each repetition, yet every one of its strains could have been set down in musical notation. A musical shorthand-writer could in a few days have filled a volume with records of its melodies, and they would, I think, have been far more interesting than the seventy odd recorded by Witchell. No person who had listened for half an hour to this bird could believe that these strains were borrowed. They were too many and they came as spontaneously as water gushing from a rock. The bird was in a thorn hedge dividing two grass fields, and there I stood for a long time, how long I do not know, in the fading light, my astonishment and admiration growing all the time, and I was like one in a trance, or like the monk in the legend, only my wonderful bird was black instead of white. By-and-by he flew away and that was the last of him, for on other days I searched and listened for him in vain. Perhaps on the very morning after that evening he fell to the gun of some person anxious about the safety of his reddening strawberries – some farmer or cottager who did not know that he was killing an angel. However, a worse fate would have befallen him if one of those who prefer to have their birds in cages had chanced to hear his wonderful song and had proceeded to capture him for exhibition about the country, winning great glory from the 'fancy' and perhaps making a thousand pounds out of his prisoner for life.

This character of the blackbird's music, which I have been discussing – its resemblance to human-made music – is not the whole nor the principal cause of its charm. The charm is chiefly due to the intrinsic beauty of the sound; it is a fluty sound and has that quality of the flute suggestive of the human voice, the voice in the case of the blackbird of an exquisitely pure and beautiful contralto. The effect is greatly increased by the manner in which the notes are emitted – trolled out leisurely, as if by a being at peace and supremely happy, and able to give the feeling its most perfect expression.

It is this delicious song of the blackbird – a voice of the love-liest quality, with an expression derived from its resemblance to melodious, brightened human voice, uttered in a leisurely and careless manner, as of a person talking sweetly and mingling talk with snatches of song – it is all this combined which has served to make the blackbird a favourite and more to most of us as a songster than any other, not excepting the nightingale. If the editor of some widely circulating newspaper would put the question to the vote, the

blackbird would probably come first, in spite of the myths and traditions which have endeared certain other species to us from childhood – the cuckoo the messenger of spring, the dove that mourns for
its love, and Philomel leaning her breast upon a thorn; the temple-
building martlet, and robin redbreast who in winter comes to us
for crumbs and has so great an affection for our kind that in woods
and desert places he will strew leaves over the friendless bodies of
unburied men.

But, it may be said, we have always had the blackbird in Britain,
a resident species, very common and universally distributed – why
does it not figure more prominently in our old literature? If this
can be taken as a test undoubtedly the blackbird comes a long way
after the nightingale, though this species is known only in a portion
of England, actually less than a fourth part of the British area over
which the black ouzel with orange-tawny bill is a familiar songster. It is, however, not a good test. The fact that our older poets,
including those of Scotland and Wales, make much of the nightingale merely serves to show that they were following a convention of
the continental poets, ancient and modern.

Ireland is an exception, to judge from the translations of the very
early Irish poetry made by Professor Kuno Meyer. Here, one is glad
to find, are no old imported bird myths and conventions, but a native
bird life and a feeling for birds which amaze us in those remote and
barbarous times. Many species are mentioned in these poems, from
the largest – eagle and raven and wild goose – down to the little
kitty wren, but the blackbird is first on account of its lovely voice –
'sweet and soft and peaceful is his note,' one has it.

There is one blackbird poem in the collection which might have
been written by a poet of today. For we are apt to think that to love
birds as we love them, not merely as feathered angels, beautiful to
see and hear, but with human tenderness and sympathy as beings
that are kin to us, is a feeling peculiar to our own times. The poet

laments the bird's loss when it has seen its nest and fledglings
destroyed or taken by ruthless cowboy lads. He can understand the
bird's grief 'for the ruin of its home', because a like calamity has
been his: his wife and little ones are dead, and though their taking
off was bloodless it is terrible to him as slaughter by the sword. He
cries out against the injustice of heaven, for even as that one nest
was singled out among many for destruction so were his home and
loved ones:

> *O Thou, the Shaper of the world!*
> *Uneven hands Thou layest on us;*
> *Our fellows at our side are spared,*
> *Their wives and children are alive.*

There is another remarkable poem conceived in the spirit of
that time of wild passions and the shedding of blood, in which the
first early note of the blackbird with its message to the 'faithful' is
introduced in a wonderfully impressive way. This tells how Fothad
Canann carried off the wife of Alill with her consent, and was hotly
pursued by Alill, and how they met and fought until both were
slain. Now Fothad had arranged with the woman to meet her in the
evening after the fight, and true to his word he kept the tryst. As
he comes to her she flies to meet him, to clasp him with her arms
and pour out all her passion on his breast. But he will not have it, he
waves her back imperiously and will not allow her to utter a word.
He must do all the talking himself, for he is overflowing with great
matters, great news, and the time for telling them is short. He tells
her how they fought; how well they were matched, what a glorious
battle it was! One can see it – the deadly meeting of those two long-
haired men, their blue-grey eyes glinting with rage and the joy of
battle; the shouts of defiance and insult; the furious onset and the
swift movements of their lithe and powerful frames, as of tigers; the

ringing blows on shield and steel, and the end when they are down, their shields shattered and weapons broken, their bodies hacked and pierced, their spilt blood spreading and mingling in one pool!

To such a fighter, slain in such a fight, what else was there in the world to talk about! She, and her passion and everlasting grief for her slain lover – it was not worth a thought! The fight was the thing, and she must listen in silence to the story of it – she, the last human listener he would ever have.

Suddenly the torrent of speech is arrested; the voice of the blackbird, 'sweet and soft and peaceful', comes to them out of the darkness. Hark! he cries to her before vanishing for ever from her sight,

I hear the dusky ouzel send a joyous greeting to the faithful,
My speech, my shape, are spectral – hush, woman, do not speak to me!

20 THE LAKE VILLAGE

An enthusiastic excavator – Inhabiting two worlds at once – The
wind in the bulrushes – Drayton on bird life in the fens – A visionary
multitude of wild birds – Crossbills in the Mendips – Among the bells
in St Cuthbert's tower

From the abbey to the prehistoric Lake Village is but a step
of two miles, and here I spent agreeable hours with Dr
Bulleid, the discoverer and excavator of this little centre
of British life of the dawn, turning over his finds dug out of the
black, peaty soil. Here is an enthusiast if you like – there are some
in the south! – a busy doctor who works every day of the year in
his practice, excepting when he takes an annual summer holiday
of a few weeks and spends every day of it, from morn to dewy eve,
at the excavations, studying every spadeful of earth thrown up by
his dozen diggers. My chief interest was in the bones of the large
water-birds on which the lake-dweller subsisted, and the weapons
with which he slew them – the round, hard clay balls which were
hurled from slings.

From the village I rambled on over the bed of the ancient lake
to its deeper part, which is still a wet marsh, though partly drained
and intersected with hedges and dykes. Here there are large areas
of boggy ground so thickly grown over with cotton-grass that at a
little distance it looks like an earth covered with snow. Straying in
this place, revelling in that wind-waved feathery fairy whiteness all
round me, I finally sat down by the water-side to watch and listen.
Mallard, moorhen, and water-rail, the last heard though not seen,

and little grebe were there, but no unfamiliar sound came to me from the songsters in the sedges and bulrushes or from the osiers and alders.

I was perhaps inattentive; mine on this occasion was a wandering mind; I was still suffering from the effect of my interview with Dr Bulleid; for even the dullest person among us cannot very well spend an hour with an enthusiast without catching something from him – a slight rise in his tepid temperature, a little rose-coloured rash on his skin, which will presently vanish and leave him well again – as sane and healthy a person as he ever was and ever will be to the end of his comfortable, humdrum existence. But just then, with the infection still in me, I was inhabiting two worlds at one and the same time – that dank green marshy world, whitened with cotton-grass, once a great inland lake and before that an estuary which was eventually cut off from the Severn Sea through the silting up of the sand at its mouth. And I was also in that same shallow inland sea or lake, unmoved by tides, which had been growing shallower year by year for centuries with a rank aquatic vegetation spreading over it as far as the eye could see – a green watery world. I could hear the wind in the bulrushes – miles on miles of dark polished stems, tufted with ruddy brown: that low, mysterious sound is to me the most fascinating of all the many voices of the wind. The feeling is partly due to early associations, to boyhood, when I used to ride into the vast marshes of the pampas in places where, sitting on my horse, the tufted tops of the bulrushes were on a level with my face. I sought for birds' nests; above all for that of the strange little bittern. It was a great prize, that small platform of yellow sedge leaves, a foot or two above the water, with three oval eggs no bigger than pigeon's eggs resting on it, of a green so soft, brilliant, indescribably lovely, that the sight of them would thrill me like some shining supernatural thing or some heavenly melody.

Or on a windy day when I would sit by the margin to listen to the sound unlike any other made by the wind in the green world. It was not continuous, nor one, like the sea-like sound of the pines, but in

gusts from this part or that all round you, now startlingly loud, then
quickly falling to low murmurings, always with something human in
it, but wilder, sadder, more airy than a human voice, as of ghost-like
beings, invisible to me, haunting the bulrushes, conversing together
and calling to one another in their unearthly tones.

And the birds! Ah, to be back in the Somerset of that far time —
the paradise of birds in its reedy inland sea, its lake of Athelney!

I have often wished to be back in the old undrained Lincolnshire
for the sake of its multitudinous wildbird life in far more recent times,
as described by eye-witnesses — Michael Drayton, for example, no
longer ago than the time of Elizabeth. Does any bird-loving reader
know the passage? I doubt it, for is there anyone in England, including
the student of the poetry of that period, who can say with his hand on
his heart that he has read the whole of *Polyolbion* — every twelve-foot
line of its many thousands, each line laboriously dragging its slow
length along. It is hard to read even the hundred lines descriptive of
the fens except for the picture conjured up of those marvellous bird
gatherings. It was Lincolnshire's boast, according to Drayton, that
no such abundance could be seen in any other part of the kingdom.
I imagine that there was an even greater abundance and variety in
the Somerset lake of prehistoric times. It was a better climate, a more
sheltered district, and birds must have been far more numerous in the
ages before man found out how to slay them at long distances with guns
and to frighten them with smoke and flame and a noise like thunder.

Now, with Drayton's picture in my mind and many old memories of immense congregations of wild fowl in the lakes and marshes
of a distant region, witnessed in my early years but nevermore to be
seen, I could reconstruct the past. Indeed, for a little space, while the
infection lasted, I was there afloat on that endless watery wilderness
as it appeared to the lake dweller of, say, twenty-five centuries ago.
The lake dweller himself was with me, poling and paddling his long
canoe by devious ways over the still waters, by miles and leagues of

grey rushes and sedges vivid green, and cat's-tail and flowering rush and vast dark bulrush beds and islets covered with thickets of willow and alder and trees of larger growth. It was early morning in early spring: at all events the geese had not gone yet, but were continually flying by overhead, flock succeeding flock, filling the world with their clangour. I watched the sky rather than the earth, feasting my eyes on the long-unseen spectacle of great soaring birds. Buzzard and kite and marsh harrier soared in wide circles above me, raining down their wild shrill cries. Other and greater birds were there as well, and greatest of all the pelican, one of the large birds on which the marsh-men lived, but doomed to vanish and be forgotten as a British species long ages before Drayton lived. But his familiar osprey was here too, a king among the hawks, sweeping round in wide circles, to pause by-and-by in mid career and closing his wings fall like a stone upon the water with a mighty splash. We floated in a world of birds; herons everywhere standing motionless in the water, and flocks of spoonbills busily at feed, and in the shallower places and by the margins innumerable shore-birds — curlews, godwits, and loquacious black and white avocets. Sheldrakes too in flocks rose up before us, with deep *honking* goose-like cries, their white wings glistening like silver in the early morning sunlight. Other sounds came from a great way off, faintly heard, a shrill confused buzzing clangour as of a swarm of bees passing over-head, and looking that way we saw a cloud rising out of the reeds and water, then another and another still — clouds of birds, each its own colour, white, black, and brown, according to the species — gulls, black terns, and wild duck. Seen at that distance they appeared like clouds of starlings in the evening at their winter roosting haunts. Presently the clouds dispersed or settled on the water again, and for a little space it seemed a silent world. Then a new sound was heard from some distant spot perhaps a mile away — a great chorus of wild ringing jubilant cries, echoing and re-echoing all over that illimitable watery expanse; and I knew it was the crane — the giant crane that hath a trumpet sound!

These birds were all very real to me, seen very vividly, their voices so loud and clear that they startled and thrilled me; but the long-haired brown-skinned marsh-man who was my boatman was seen less distinctly. The anthropological reader will be disappointed to learn that no clear image was retained of his height, build, features, and the colour of his eyes and hair, and that the sense of all his wild jabber and gestures has quite gone out of my memory.

From all this greatness of wild-bird life seen in a vision, I returned to reality and to very small things; one of which came as a pleasant surprise. I went on to the Cheddar valley and near Winscombe I dropped in on an old friend, a writer and a lover of birds, who had built himself a charming bungalow among the Mendips. We had tea on the terrace, a nice cool rose- and creeper-shaded place after my long hot ramble, a green lawn beneath us, with a row of large pine trees on its other side. My friend was telling me of a flock of crossbills which to his delight had been haunting the place for some days past, when lo! down came the very birds, and there for half an hour we had them right before us while we drank tea and ate strawberries, and watched them working at the cones – our quaint pretty little parrots of the north, so diversely coloured – one red like a red cardinal, one or two yellow, others green or mixed.

On the following day I was at Wells; it was Sunday, and in the morning, happening to see the bell-ringers hurrying into St Cuthbert's Church, I was reminded of an old wish of mine to be in a belfry during the bell-ringing. This wish and intention was formed some years ago on reading an article in the *Saturday Review* by Walter Herries Pollock, describing his sensations in a belfry. Here then was my opportunity – a better could not have been found if I had sought for it. St Cuthbert's is one of the greatest of the great Wells church towers, with a peal of eight big bells. I had often listened to them with pleasure from a respectable distance, and now I felt a slight twinge of apprehension at the prospect of a close acquaintance. The bell-ringers

were amused at my request: nobody ever wanted to be among the
bells when they were being rung, they assured me; however, they did
not object, and so to the belfry I climbed, and waited, a little nerv-
ously, as some musical enthusiast might wait to hear a symphony
from the days of the giants, composed (when insane) by a giant
Tschaikovsky, to be performed on 'instruments of unknown form'
and gigantic size. I was not disappointed; the effect was too awful for
words and was less musical than I had thought it would be. In less
than three minutes it became unendurable, and I then slipped out on
to the roof to save myself from some tremendous disaster. In a minute
I was back again, and with intervals of escape to the roof I remained
till the ringing finished. I could not have stood it otherwise, and as it
was, I feared every moment that it would deafen me permanently so
that I would no more hear birds sing. That, to me, would be the end of
all things. Pollock, in the article mentioned above, has described the
sensations I experienced in a sentence or two. 'It is not like the voice
of any single singer nor like the voices of a trained choir,' he wrote.
'It is more the speech, resolved into musical sound, of a vast crowd
half perhaps rather than wholly human, whose accents vary from the
highest joyousness to the deepest melancholy, from notes of solemn
warning to cries of terrifying denunciation and all that of course with
an infinity of half and quarter shades of expression.'

Probably the St Cuthbert bells were larger than those he heard,
and perhaps I was closer to them – I was in fact in the belfry with
them – as I found no joyous expression in the sound at all; it was all
terrible, and the worst thing in it, which he does not mention, was
a continuous note, a single loud metallic sound, persisting through
all the shrieking, crashing, and roaring, like the hum of a threshing-
machine so loud and sharp that it seemed to pierce the brain like
a steel weapon. It was this unbroken sound which was hardest to
endure and would, I imagined, send me out of my senses altogether
if I stayed too long in the belfry.

21 THE MARSH WARBLER'S MUSIC

Two remarkable trees at Chepstow – Birds at the abbey – A colony of
marsh warblers – Distribution of the marsh warbler – Its high rank as
a songster – Its artistic borrowings – Species whose notes are imitated
– The delight of bird-watching – Varying behaviour of birds under
observation – A lucky accident

From Wells I went on to Bristol and thence to Chepstow,
where, a few miles out, I hoped to find one of my rare birds,
but on inquiry discovered that it had long vanished from
this haunt. There was nothing for me but to extract what pleasure
I could from the castle, the valley of the Wye, and Tintern Abbey.
At Chepstow, a small parasitic town much given to drink, I saw two
wonderful things, which the guide-book writers probably do not
notice – a walnut tree and an ivy tree, both growing in the castle.
The first must be one of the finest walnut trees in the country: one
of its enormous horizontal branches measured eighteen yards from
the trunk to the end; the branch on the opposite side of the trunk
measured, fifteen yards, giving the tree a breadth of ninety-nine
feet! The other, the ivy, was a tree in the ordinary sense of the word,
that is to say, a plant above the size of a bush which is not a parasite
supported by another tree but wholly self-sustained. It grows near
but not touching the wall, with a round straight bole three feet in
circumference and fifteen feet in height, with a rough elm-tree-like
bark, crowned with a dense round mass of branches and leaves.
Doubtless it once grew on a tree and had a strong straight bole of
its own when the tree died, and during the slow dying and gradual

decay of the support it added to its wood and grew harder to meet
the changing situation, until when the old trunk it grew against had
crumbled to dust it was able to stand erect, a perfect independent tree.

At the too famous abbey the chief interest was in the birds.
Starlings, sparrows, and daws were there in numbers, and many
blue and ox-eye tits, flycatchers, and redstarts, all feeding their
young or bringing them off. The starlings were most abundant, and
the young were being spilt from the walls all over the place. I talked
with a slow old labourer who was lazily sweeping the dead leaves
and straws from the smooth turf which forms the floor of the roof-
less ruin, when one of the young birds, more stupid than the others,
began following us about, clamouring to be fed. The old sweeper,
using his broom, gently pushed the poor fool away. 'There, there, go
away, or you'll be getting hurt,' he said, and the bird went.

'No more rare birds *this* season!' I said and turned homewards;
but in Gloucestershire I found a man who told me of a colony of
the marsh warbler, a rarity I had not counted on meeting; better
still, he took me to it, although he wished me to understand that it
was *his* colony, his own discovery, also that he had been making a
good thing out of it. He left me on the spot to experience that rarest
delight of the bird-seeker, the making the acquaintance of, and
growing hourly and daily more intimate with, a new species. In this
instance it was nothing but a plain little brown bird, plainer than
the nightingale and hardly to be distinguished, even in the hand,
from the familiar reed warbler, but in virtue of its melody of a lustre
surpassing our blue kingfisher or indeed any shining bird of the tropics.

The colony was in a withy bed of a year's growth, the plants
being three or four feet high, the whole ground being covered with
a dense growth of tall grasses and sedges, meadow-sweet, comfrey,
and nettles. It was moist and boggy in places but without water,
except in one small pool which served as a drinking and bathing
place to all the small birds in the vicinity.

Sitting on a mound a few feet above the surface I could survey
the whole field of seven to eight acres enclosed by high hedges
and old hedgerow elm and oak trees on three sides, with a row of
pollarded willows on the other, and I was able to make out about
nine pairs of marsh warblers in the colony. It was easy to count
them, as each couple had its own territory, and the males were
conspicuous as they were constantly flying about in pursuit of the
females or chasing away rival cocks, then singing from the topmost
twigs of the withy-bushes. This, I found, was but one of a group of
colonies, the birds in all of which numbered about seventy pairs.
Yet it only became known in quite recent years that the marsh
warbler is a British breeding species! It had been regarded previously as a chance or occasional visitor from the Continent, until Mr
Warde Fowler discovered that it was a regular summer visitant to
Oxfordshire, also that it was the latest of our migrants to arrive and
a later breeder by several weeks. It is curious that in a small country
so infested with ornithologists as ours this species should have been
overlooked. They, the ornithologists and collectors, say that it is not
so, that a bird with so beautiful a song, so unlike that of his nearest
relations the reed and sedge warblers, could not have been overlooked. Undoubtedly it was overlooked, and this colony, or group of
colonies, numbering seventy or more pairs, must be quite an ancient
one. There are others too in Somerset, and no doubt many besides in
the west country and Midlands. The species has not diffused itself
more in the country, I imagine, on account of its habit of nesting
almost exclusively in the withy beds, where their nests are as much
exposed to destruction as those of the skylark and landrail in the
corn. The moist grounds where the willows are planted are covered
annually with a luxuriant growth of grasses and herbage which
must be cut down to give air and life to the willows. The cutting
usually takes place about mid-June when the eggs are being laid and
incubation is already in progress in many nests. The nests, whether

attached to the withies or to the tall sterns of the meadow-sweet and other plants, are mostly destroyed.

I have gone into these details just to show that it would be easy to give this bird a better chance of increasing its numbers by inducing the owners of withy beds where they are known to breed to do the mowing at the end of May instead of in the middle of June or later. This could be best done by local bird-protecting societies in Gloucestershire and Somerset and in other counties where colonies may be found.

Certainly no sweet songster in Britain is better worth preserving than the marsh warbler. I should class it as one of our four greatest – blackbird, nightingale, skylark, marsh warbler. The blackbird is first because of the beautiful quality of its voice and its *expression*, due to its human associations. The marsh warbler compared with lark and nightingale has a small voice, which does not carry far, but in sweetness he is the equal of any and in variety excels them all. It could not be otherwise, since he is able to borrow the songs of the others, even of the best. He is

> *That cheerful one who knoweth all*
> *The songs of all the winged choristers,*
> *And in one sequence of melodious sound*
> *Pours all their music.*

Thus wrote Southey of the American bird in one of the very few quotable passages in the vast volume of his numerous epics: his three or four happy lines are worth more, as giving the bird its characteristic expression, than all the verses of the transatlantic poets on the subject.

The mocking-bird, I may say here, is a powerful singer, and I noticed that in listening to the white-winged mocking-bird of Patagonia, which I believe to be the greatest of the genus, he subdued or *smalled* his voice when imitating the small or weak-voiced songsters, but in spite of the subduing, the song, coming from his larger organ, had gained in power and penetration. With the marsh warbler it is just the reverse: the low songs are reproduced with fidelity, the loud strains while retaining their exact form are emitted in a lower tone. Thus, he can copy the phrases of the thrush, but the notes do not carry much further than his imitation of the willow-wren. One is reminded of Sir John Davies' lines:

All things received do such proportions take
As those things have wherein they are received;
So little glasses little faces make,
And narrow webs on narrow frames be weaved.

On the other hand he makes many of the songs he copies sweeter and more beautiful than their originals. We may say that he is a perfect artist in his borrowings, and brings the songs of all the others into harmony with his own native notes and with one another. This was observed by Warde Fowler, who was the first in England to describe the song. He wrote: 'In spite of many imitations in which the bird indulges there is always a very sweet silvery individuality about the song, which makes it quite unmistakable.' In that native quality of the voice, its silvery sweetness, it comes nearest, I think, to the reed warbler's song. Its silvery-sweet quality is indeed the principal merit of this warbler's strains, which can only be properly appreciated when the listener stands or sits on a level with the reeds within a very few yards of the singer.

Listening to the marsh warbler at some distance it seemed to me at first that he sang his own song interspersed with imitations, that the borrowed songs and phrases were selections which accorded best with his own notes, so that the whole performance was like one ever-varying melody. On a closer acquaintance I found

that the performance was mainly or nearly all imitations in which
the loud, harsh, and guttural sounds were subdued and softened –
that the mocker's native silvery sweetness had in some degree been
imparted to all of them. The species whose songs, detached phrases,
and calls I recognised were the swallow, sparrow, goldfinch, green-
finch, chaffinch, redpoll, linnet, reed-bunting, blackbird (its chuckle
only), throstle, missel-thrush (its alarm or anger cry), blackcap,
willow-wren, robin, redstart, whinchat, yellow wagtail, tree-pipit,
skylark, and partridge – its unmistakable call, but subdued and
made musical. There were also some notes and phrases that seemed
perfect copies from the nightingale, but I would not say that they
were imitations as there were no nightingales at that spot, and
I came to the listening in a sceptical spirit, quite resolved not to
believe that any note or phrase or song could be an imitation unless
the bird supposed to be imitated could be found in the vicinity.
Another bird I could not find in the place was the grasshopper-
warbler, yet one day one of the birds I listened to produced what
seemed to me a most perfect imitation of its reeling performance.

But how, the reader will ask, could the marsh warbler have
acquired the redpoll's song seeing that the redpoll would be far
away in its breeding haunts in the pine forests of the north when
the warbler was in the west country? Strange to say, there was a
small colony of half a dozen redpoll pairs breeding in the hedgerow
elms at the side of the withy bed. My guide to the spot had told
me of these birds, and it was a rare pleasure to listen in southern
England to their slight pretty song in the elm tops, with its curious
little breezy trill like a dry leaf rapidly fluttered by the wind against
another leaf.

I did not hear an imitation of the blackbird's song, although its
chuckling notes were sometimes given, and it struck me that the
marsh warbler, good artist that he is, does not attempt, like the
bungling starling, to reproduce sounds that are outside of his register.

Other listeners, however, have said that he does mimic the blackbird's song. Then, as to the whinchat, in two days' listening I heard
no imitation of its song, although the bird was present and building
in the withy bed. I thought that that little delicious tender song too
was beyond the warbler's power; but I was mistaken, and by-and-by
I heard it reproduced so perfectly that I could hardly believe my ears.
The wren's song I did not hear and concluded that the warbler refused
to copy it on account of its peculiar distinctive sharp quality which
some persons associate in their minds with an acid flavour.

I think the imitation which pleased and surprised me most was
that of the willow-wren's exquisite joyous yet tender melody. Until
I heard it I could not have believed that any feathered mocker could
reproduce that falling strain so perfectly.

One of the greatest pleasures in life – *my* life I mean – is to be
present, in a sense invisible, in the midst of the domestic circle of
beings of a different order, another world, than ours. Yet it is one
which may be had by any person who desires it. Some of the smaller
birds lend themselves easily to this innocent prying. And one is
more in sympathy with them than with the smaller, more easily
observed insects. The absolute indifference of these to our presence
only accentuates the fact of their unlikeness to us in their senses
and faculties. There is a perpetual fascination in some social insects,
ants especially, but it disquiets as well as delights us to mark their
ways. They baffle our curiosity, and if we be of animistic mind we
become when watching them uncomfortably conscious of a spirit, an
entity, in or behind nature that watches us and our watching with an
unfathomable look in its eyes and a challenging and mocking smile
on its lips.

One of our most distinguished biologists, who has written books
on some lower forms of life which are classics, has never included
insects in his studies just because he has never been able to free

himself from a sense of uncanniness they give him. In me, too, they produce this feeling at times: – these myriads of creatures that float like motes in the sunbeam; minute, gem-like, winged bodies of strange shapes and gem-like minds to match, they come upon us like a living glittering dust shaken from the tail of some comet in our summer skies – a dust that will settle down by-and-by and vanish when the air grows cool at the approach of winter.

But little birds – dear little birds or darlings as we may call them without rebuke – are vertebrates and relations, with knowing, emotional, thinking brains like ours in their heads, and with senses like ours, only brighter. Their beauty and grace, so much beyond ours, and their faculty of flight which enables them to return to us each year from such remote outlandish places, their winged swift souls in winged bodies, do not make them uncanny but only fairy-like. Thus we love and know them, and our more highly developed minds are capable of bridging the gulf which divides us from them, and divides bird from mammal. Small as they are bodily, in some cases no bigger than one of a man's ten toes, we know they are, on the same tree of life as ourselves, grown from the same root, with the same warm red blood in their veins, and red blood is thicker than water – certainly it is – thicker than the colourless fluid which is the life of the insect.

To come back to particulars, and the subject of this chapter, there are very great differences in the temper and behaviour of even the smallest birds of different species in the presence of their human fellow-beings. Some are strangely, unaccountably shy, and so suspicious that they will not comport themselves as they do immediately we are out of sight and mind. What a contrast in this respect is there between such species as the stonechat and goldcrest! One is always watching us, always anxious, and refuses not only to go on with his love-making or nest-building but even refuses to sing if we are there; while to the other our presence is no more than that of a rock or tree. I was delighted to find that the marsh warbler was more like the last than the first, that he went on with his feeding, wooing, nest-building, his feud with his rivals, or with the neighbouring cock who from time to time ventured to intrude on his little dominion, and above all with his beautiful singing, just as though I had not been there at all. My greatest pleasure was to mark a spot which a pair of the birds had selected as their own and to go and settle myself down in the very middle of the sacred ground. There the cock would quickly come to me, evidently recognising in me a living creature of some kind – a big animal with the faculty of locomotion – and at first he would appear to be a little anxious about the safety of his nest, but after a few minutes the trouble would vanish from his little volatile mind and he would be all freedom and gladness and melody, with transitory fits of rage and other emotions, as before. On these occasions I sometimes had one singing almost continuously for several minutes to half an hour within a dozen yards of where I sat. At such times his strains sounded louder but no less sweet than when heard at a distance of forty or fifty yards. On one occasion I had him even nearer, owing to a mishap. I was walking along the dry bottom of a wide old ditch under a hedge at the side of the withy bed, when I came to a deep pool or hole full of mud and slimy water, and to save myself the trouble of going round it I took hold of an overhanging willow branch and swung myself across to the other side, but failed to get quite clear and was plunged deep into the slime. After scraping off the fetid mud and slime which covered me I went back to the deep pool of clear water in the withy bed and taking off my tweed suit and boots spent an hour in washing them, then spread them out in the sun. The drying I thought would take five or six hours, and as I could not roam about in my stockings and underclothing, which had not got wet, or return to the town and civilised life to get a meal or tea, I thought my best plan was to spend the rest of the day lying down close to one of the marsh warbler's favourite singing-bushes. There I made myself a nice bed of dry sedges in a sunny spot within two yards of the singing-bush, and presently the cock bird came and flew round and perched here and there on the stems, scolding and singing. He went and came a good many times, but at last gave up being troubled at my presence and eventually began coming to his own withy-plant and to sing there fully and freely for long intervals at that short distance of two yards from my head.

I thought I had never listened to sweeter music than this bird's, and that my fall into the mud-hole had proved an exceedingly happy accident.

22 GOLDFINCHES AT RYME INTRINSECA

Yetminster – Ryme Intrinseca – Mobbed by goldfinches – Recent
increase of goldfinches in Dorset – Effect of bird-protection orders –
Abundance of the goldfinch in Cobbett's days – Goldfinches and thistles:
a misleading statement – Recollections of the Argentine goldfinch
– Caged birds – A Spanish poem about a goldfinch – The translator's
difficulties – A prose rendering of *El Colorín de Filos*

There is much in a name, and when I left Yeovil to run to
Dorchester by that lonely beautiful road which takes you
by the clear swift Cerne and past the ancient figure of a
giant with a club on the down side over against Cerne Abbas, I went
a little distance out of my way to look at a small village solely on
account of its singular and pretty name. Or rather two villages –
Yetminster and Ryme Intrinseca. Who would not go a dozen miles
out of his road for the pleasure of seeing places with such names! At
the first I was unlucky, since the only inhabitant I made acquaintance with was an unprepossessing voluble old woman with greedy
eyes who, though not too poor, at once set herself to conjure a shil-
ling out of my pocket. In the end we quarrelled and I went away
regretting I had met her, seeing that her unpleasing image would
be associated in my mind with the picture of Yetminster – its noble,
ancient church standing in its wide green space, surrounded by old
stone-built thatched houses with valerian and ivy-leaved toad-flax
and wallflower growing on the crumbling walls.

At Ryme Intrinseca I was more fortunate. It was a charming
village with stone cottages, as is usual in that stone country,

and a pretty little church standing in the middle of a green and
flowery churchyard. Here there were several small yew trees, and
no sooner had I got inside the gate than out fluttered a goldfinch
in brilliant feather, emitting his sharpest alarm note. Then from
trees and bushes all round where they had been concealed, more
goldfinches fluttered forth, until there were twelve, all loudly
protesting against my presence at that spot, flitting from tree
to tree and perching on the terminal twigs within three or four
yards of my head. Never had I seen goldfinches so excited, so bold
in mobbing a man: I could only suppose that very few visitors
came into that secluded churchyard, where they were breeding,
and doubtless a stranger in the place was a much more alarming
figure to them than the parson or any of the native villagers would
have been. But it was a new and delightful, experience to find so
many pairs breeding together, making their nests within reach of a
man's hand.

Now as I stood there watching the birds I by chance noticed that
a man and his wife and little girl standing at their cottage door
hard by were intently and suspiciously watching me. On coming
out I went over to them and asked the man how long they had had
goldfinches breeding so abundantly in their churchyard. A very
few years ago I had been told that the goldfinch had almost ceased
to exist in Dorset. He replied that it was true, that goldfinches had
begun to increase only during the last three or four years since they
had been protected by law all the year round.

He could not have given me more agreeable news. I remembered
with a keen sense of satisfaction that the late Mr Mansel Pleydell-
Bouverie, of Whatcombe in Dorset, had written to me asking my
advice in drawing up a new bird-protection order for the county,
and that in replying I had strongly urged him to secure the fullest
protection the law can afford to this most charming and most persecuted of all small birds.

Two or three years before that date I spent several weeks in Somerset, walking a good deal, without once seeing or hearing a goldfinch, yet if I had come within fifty yards of a copse or orchard inhabited by a pair, their sharp, unmistakable whit-whit would have advertised their presence. At Wells I made the acquaintance of a man past middle age who had taken to bird-catching as a boy and still followed that fascinating vocation. 'Have you never had goldfinches in these parts?' I asked him; to which he replied that he remembered the time when they were abundant, but for the last thirty years or longer they had been steadily decreasing and were now practically gone. They had gone because they were too much sought after; then he added: 'I daresay they would come again if there was a law made to stop us from catching them.' I expressed the hope that such a law would come in time, at which he shook his head and grunted. Now Somerset has such a law and I hear that goldfinches are again to be seen in the Wells district. In fact, county after county has taken up the cause of this pretty and useful little bird, and in a small map of the country lying before me, in which the counties where the goldfinch receives protection throughout the year are coloured red, I find that on more than three-fourths of the entire area of England and Wales the bird is now safeguarded. As a result it is increasing all over the country, but it will be many years before we have it in its former numbers. How abundant it was about eighty years ago, before its long decline began, may be gathered from the following passage in Cobbett's *Rural Rides* describing his journey from Highworth to Malmesbury in Wiltshire:

> *Between Somerford and Ocksey, I saw, on the side of the*
> *road, more* goldfinches *than I had ever seen together; I think*
> *fifty times as many as I had ever seen at one time in my life.*
> *The favourite food of the goldfinch is the seed of the* thistle.
> *The seed is just now dead ripe. The thistles all cut and carried*

away from the fields by the harvest; but they grow alongside
the roads, and in this place in great quantities. So that the
goldfinches were got here in flocks, and, as they continued to
fly before me for nearly half a mile and still sticking to the
roads and brakes, I do believe I had, at last, a flock of 10,000
flying before me.

Cobbett rightly says that the seed of the thistle is the favourite
food of the bird; and once upon a time an ornithologist made the
statement that the improved methods of agriculture in England had
killed the thistle, thus depriving the goldfinch of its natural food,
the result being that the bird had declined in numbers to the verge
of extinction. The statement has been copied into pretty well every
book on British birds since it was made. O wise ornithologists, what
does the goldfinch live on during nine months of the year? How
does he exist without his natural food? How does he live even in the
unnatural conditions of a cage without thistle-seed? I know of one
case in which the poor prisoner lived shut up in his little wire box
for eighteen years. Besides, the museum or closet naturalist is very
much out of it when he talks about the extirpation of the thistle. The
good old plant is doing very well. Long before the Act of 1894–5
which empowers the local authorities to protect their birds, I had
been a frequent visitor to, and a haunter of, many extensive thistle-
grown places in southern England – chalk downs that were once
wheatfields, gone out of cultivation for half a century or longer,
ruined sheep-walks, where in July and August I could look over
hundreds of acres of rust-brown thistles, covered with their glistening down, the seed 'dead ripe', and never a goldfinch in sight!

And now I must go back to Ryme Intrinseca – the pretty name
of that village makes me reluctant to leave it – and to its goldfinches,
the little company of twelve fluttering with anxious cries about my
head, a very charming spectacle, and to an even more brilliant picture

or vision of the past which was all at once restored to my mental
eye. We are familiar with the powerful emotional effect of certain
odours, associated with our early life, in this connection; occasionally effects equally strong are produced by sights and sounds, and
this was one. As I stood in the churchyard watching the small flut-
terers in their black and gold and crimson liveries, listening to their
excited cries, a vision of my boyhood was brought before me, so vivid
as to seem like reality. After many years I was a boy once more, in
my own distant home, and the time was October, when the brilliant
spring merges into hot summer. I was among the wind-rustled tall
Lombardy poplars, inhaling their delicious smell, at that spot where a
colony of a couple of dozen black-headed siskins were breeding. They
are without the crimson on their faces; their plumage is black and
gold, but to all English-speaking people in that far country they are
known as goldfinches, and in flight and habits and love of thistle-seed
and in melody and in their anxious piping notes they are like our
English bird. They are now fluttering about me, like these of Ryme
Intrinseca, displaying their golden feathers in the brilliant sunshine,
uttering their agitated cries, while I climb tree after tree to find two
or three or four nests in each – dainty little mossy down-lined cups
placed between the slender branches and trunk, each with its comple-
ment of shining pearly eggs – a beautiful sight to a boy!

   Then another picture follows. We are now in the burning days
of November and December, the vast open treeless plains as far
as one can see parched to a rust-brown, and cattle and horses and
sheep in thousands to be watered at the great well. I see the native
boy on his big horse drawing up the canvas bucket; the man by the
well catching the hoop as it comes to the surface and directing the
stream of clear cold water into the long wooden troughs. But the
thing to see is the crowd of beasts, the flocks and herds gathering
before noon at the accustomed spot, first seen coming in troops and
lines, walking, trotting, galloping from all that shadeless illimitable

expanse where the last liquid mud in the dried pools has been sucked up. What a violent crowd! What a struggling and what an uproar of bellowings, whinnyings and multitudinous bleatings! And what dreadful blows of horns and hoofs rained on each other's tough hides! For they are all mad at the sight and smell of water, and only a few at a time have room to drink at the trough.

But the crowding and fighting and drinking are now ended; even the sheep, the last to get to the water, have had their fill and streamed away over the plain once more, and the spilt water lying in pools at the side of the long wooden troughs is visited by crowds on crowds of little birds – small crested song-sparrows, glossy purple cow-birds, with other-coloured troupials, the 'starlings' of the New World; and tyrant-birds of divers colours – olive-green, yellow, chestnut, black and white and grey and many more; doves, too, and finches in great variety. The best of these were the goldfinches, in close little flocks and in families, the young birds clamouring for food and drink with incessant shrill tremulous reedy cries.

What a contrast between this dainty bright-coloured crowd of feathered drinkers and that of the pushing, fighting, bellowing beasts! And what a sight for a boy's eyes! There I would stay in the hot sun to watch them when all the others, the work of watering over, would hurry away to the shade of the house and trees, and my desire to see them more closely, to look at them as one can look at a flower, was so insistent and so intense as to be almost a pain. But I had no binocular and didn't even know that such an instrument existed; and at last to satisfy the craving I took it into my head to catch them – to fill my hands with goldfinches and have them in numbers. It was easily done. I put an old deal box or packing-case over a pool of water, one side propped up with a stick, to which a long string was attached. With the end of the string in my hand I sat and waited, while birds of many kinds came and took their half-dozen sips and flew away, but when a flock of goldfinches appeared and gathered to drink under the box, I pulled the string and made them prisoners. Then I transferred them to a big cage, and, placing it on a stand under the trees, sat down to feast my eyes on the sight – to look at a goldfinch as I would look at a flower. And I had my reward and was supremely happy, but it was a short-lived happiness, for very soon the terror and distress of my little captives, and their senseless frantic efforts to get out of their prison, began to annoy and make me miserable. I say 'senseless' because I had no intention of keeping them in captivity, and to my small boy brain it seemed that they might have restrained themselves a little and allowed me to enjoy seeing them for an hour or two. But as their flutterings and strainings and distressing cries continued I opened the cage and allowed them to fly away.

Looking back on that incident now, it strikes me as rather an inhuman thing to have done; but to the boy, whose imagination has not yet dawned, who does not know what he is doing, much has to be forgiven. He has a monkey-like, prying curiosity about things, especially about living things, but little love for them. A bird in a cage is more to him as a rule than many birds in a bush, and some grow up without ever getting beyond this lower stage. Love or fondness of or kindness to animals, with other expressions of the kind, are too common in our mouths, especially in the mouths of those who keep larks, linnets, siskins, and goldfinches in cages. But what a strange 'love' and 'kindness' which deprive its object of liberty and its wonderful faculty of flight! It is very like that of the London east-end fancier who sears the eye-balls of his chaffinch with a red-hot needle to cherish it ever after and grieve bitterly when its little darkened life is finished. 'You'll think me a soft-hearted chap, but 'pon my soul when I got up and went to say good-morning to my bird, and give him a bit of something to peck at, and found poor Chaffie lying there dead and cold at the bottom of his cage, it made the tears come into my eyes.'

It is love of a kind, no doubt.

The east-ender is 'devoted' to his chaffinch, but for the generality the first favourite is undoubtedly the goldfinch, and if few are
seen in cages compared with larks and linnets it is because they
are much rarer and cost more. Our 'devotion' to it, as we have seen,
nearly caused its extermination in Britain, and we now import large
numbers from Spain to supply the demand. One doubts that the bird
will stand this drain very long, as the Spanish are just as fond of it
(in a cage) as we are.

Here I am reminded of a very charming little poem about a
caged goldfinch by one of my favourite authors – *El Colorín de
Filis*, by Melendez, an eighteenth-century poet. I do not think that
anyone who reads this poem and others of equal merit to be found
in the literature of Spain, would deny that the sentiment of admiration and tenderness for birds is sometimes better and more beautifully expressed in Spanish poetry than in ours. Not only in the
old, which is best, but occasionally in reading modern verse I have
been surprised into the exclamation, Would that we could have this
poem, or this passage, suitably translated! This may seem strange,
since we cannot allow that the Spanish generally, wedded as they
are to their ancient barbarous pastimes, and killers of all small
birds for the pot as they are now becoming in imitation of their
French neighbours, can surpass or even equal us in sympathy for
the inferior creatures. It is the language which makes the difference:
the Spanish is better suited to the expression of tender sentiments
of that kind. The verse flows more freely, with a more natural music
than ours; it is less mechanical and monotonous in sound, and as
it is less distinct from prose and speech in form we are never so
conscious of the artistry. The feeling appears more genuine, more
from the heart, because of the seeming artlessness. We see it all
in this little goldfinch poem and say at once that it is untranslat-
able, or that it would be impossible to render its spirit, because in
English verse the tender feeling, even if it could be expressed so

delicately and beautifully, would not convey the same air of sincerity. Swinburne could not do it, which may seem a bold thing to say, seeing that he has given a music to our language it never knew before. It is a music which in certain supreme passages makes one wonder, as if it did not consist in the mere cunning collocation of words but in a magic power to alter their very sound, producing something of a strange, exotic effect, incomparably beautiful and altogether new in our poetry. But great as it is, it never allows us to escape from the sense of the art in it, and is unlike the natural music of Melendez as the finest operatic singing is unlike the spontaneous speech, intermingled with rippling laughter, of a young girl with a beautiful fresh sparkling voice.

From Swinburne to Adelaide Anne Procter is a long drop, but in this lady's works there is a little poem entitled *The Child and the Bird*, which, if not precisely a translation, strikes me as a very close imitation of the *Phyllis and her Goldfinch* of Melendez, or of some other continental poet, probably Spanish, who has treated the same subject. At all events, the incident related is the same, except that a little girl has been substituted for the girl wife of the original. Here is the first stanza:

Wherefore pinest thou, my bird?
Thy sweet song is never heard.
All the bird's best joys surround thee,
Ever since the day I found thee.
Once thy voice was free and glad,
Tell me why thou art so sad?
If this coarse thread cause thee pain,
Thou shalt have a silken chain.

What poor, artificial stuff it is! How it bumps you, each line ending with the dull, hard, wooden thud of the rhyme! Doubtless if a better poet had written it the result would not have been so bad; my sole reason for quoting it is that I can find no other translation or version in our literature. We abound in bird poems, some of them among the most beautiful lyrics in the language; but I confess that, for the reasons already given, even the best, such as those of Wordsworth, Hogg, Shelley, Meredith, and Swinburne himself, particularly in his splendid ode to the seamew, fail to give me entire satisfaction.

I am bad at translating, or paraphrasing, anything, and the subject of the Spanish poem is one peculiarly suited to verse; if taken out of that sublimated emotional language, I fear it must seem flat, if not ridiculous. Nevertheless, I will venture to give here a simple prose translation of the anecdote, and will ask the reader to retranslate it in imagination into swift-flowing verse, in a language perhaps unknown to him which reproduces to the eye and ear of the mind the sights and sounds described – the disordered motions, the flutterings and piercing cries of the agitated bird, and the responsive emotions of its tender-hearted mistress, which come, too, in gusts, like those of her captive, and have, too, their own natural rhythm.

The poem tells that one day Phyllis finds her pet goldfinch in a strangely excited state, in revolt against its destiny, at war with the wires of its cage.

Phyllis of the tender heart, the simple tastes, the lover of little birds from a child, who, though now a wife, finds in them still her dearest, most intimate happiness.

What ails her bird? He strikes his little beak on the wires, then strikes again; he clings to the side of his cage; he flits, above, below, to this side and to that, then grasping a wire with his small mandibles, tugs and tugs as if he hoped by putting forth all his little strength to break it. He cannot break nor bend it, nor can he rest, but tired of tugging he thrusts his head through the close bars and strives and strains to force his way out, beating on them with his wings. Then, after a brief pause, renews and redoubles his puny efforts; and at last, taken out of himself, dashes from side to side, until the suspended cage is shaken with his passion.

Ah, my birdling, cries lovely Phyllis, astonished and grieved at the spectacle, what a poor return you are making me! How badly this temper fits you! – how unlike your gentle twittering this new sharpness in your voice which wounds me! But I know the cause too well! Fear not, dear bird, to alienate my love – that I shall forget in this your rebellious moment the charm that made you precious, and charge you with ingratitude and in anger and disdain thrust you from my sight. For what avails my solicitude and affection – what does it matter that with my own hands I supply you with food and drink and a hundred delicate morsels besides; that with my fingers I tenderly caress you; that I kiss you with my lips? It is nothing that you are dear to me, that my chief delight is in listening to your sweet lively trills and twitterings, since I am but your gaoler who holds you from that free air which is your home and the sweet mate you would be with! No, you cannot be glad; nor is it possible you should not fear the hand that ministers to your wants, since it is the same hand that has cruelly hurt you and may hurt you again with a yet closer, more barbarous confinement.

Alas, I know your pain, for I too am a captive and lament my destiny, and though the bonds that hold me are woven with flowers I feel their weight and they wound me none the less. Left an orphan early in life, it was my fate to leave my home before completing my seventeenth year, at the will of others, to be a wife. He who took me was amiable and more than kind to me. Like a brother, a friend, a passionate lover, he protects, he honours, he worships me, and in his house my will is law. But I have no pleasure in it. His devotion, his gifts, are like mine to you, when I am carried away by the charm of your beauty and melody, when I call you my sweet little one, and you come to my call to bite me caressingly with your little beak and flutter your black and yellow wings as if to embrace me; when in my ardour I take you tenderly in my hands to hold you to my heaving breast and wish and wish that in kissing you I could breathe into you my very life!

Even so does my owner with me: when in the delirium of passion he strains me to him, when he showers gold and gems and all beautiful gifts on me, and seeks after every imaginable pleasure for my delight, and would give his very life for me – his mistress, bride and queen, who is more than all the world to him. In vain – in vain! Here in my heart there is a voice which asks me: Does it delight you? Does it sweeten your captivity? Oh, no, no, his benefits do but increase this secret eternal bitterness! Even so do you, oh, my little bird, reward me for all my love and tenderness and blame me with those painfully sharp notes for this tasteless life to which you are doomed; even so do you cry for your lost liberty, and open and flutter your wings with the desire to fly.

You shall not open them in vain – your pleadings have pierced my heart. You shall go, my beloved bird – you shall go in peace. My love can no longer deny you the boon desired so ardently – so easily bestowed! Go, and know the happiness which freedom gives, which is now yours, but can nevermore, alas! be mine.

So saying, Phyllis opens the cage and sets it free. Away it flies; tears burst forth at the sight; with misty eyes she watches it winging its way through the air till its little form is lost in the distance; and gazing still, for one sweet moment has the illusion that she, too, has flown, following it, that she too has recovered her lost liberty.

23 THE IMMORTAL NIGHTINGALE

The barren days of early March – On the track of the absent
nightingale – The mystery of its return – The immortal bird of the
poets – Its puzzling distribution – The parish nightingale – A rector's
story of a nightingale – Birds striking against window-panes – The
nightingale a home-keeping bird – Its human enemies – The fight to
save our wild birds – Educating the country children

Never is earth more empty of life than during the early days
of March before the first of the migrants have returned
to us. The brighter sun serves only to show the naked-
ness of nature and make us conscious of its silence. For since the
autumn, through all the cold, hungry winter months, the destroyer
has been busy among the creatures that stayed behind when half
the bird population forsook the land; the survivors now seem but a
remnant. Today, with a bleak wind blowing from the north-east, the
sun shining from a hard pale grey sky, the wide grass and ploughed
fields seem emptier and more desolate than ever, and tired of my
vain search for living things I am glad to get to the shelter of a
small isolated copse, by a tiny stream, at the lower end of a long
sloping field. It can hardly be called a copse since it is composed
of no more than about a dozen, or twenty old wide-branching oak
trees growing in a thicket of thorn, hazel, holly, and bramble bushes.
It is the best place on such a day, and finding a nice spot to stand in,
well sheltered from the wind, I set myself to watch the open space
before me. It is shut in by huge disordered brambles, and might
very well tempt any living creature with spring in its blood, moving

uneasily among the roots, to come forth to sun itself. The ground
is scantily clothed with pale dead grass mixed with old fallen leaves
and here and there a few tufts of dead ragwort and thistle. But in
a long hour's watching I see nothing; – not a rabbit, nor even a
wood mouse, or a field or bank vole, where at other seasons I have
seen them come out, two or three at a time, and scamper over the
rustling leaves in pursuit of each other. Nor do I hear anything;
not a bird nor an insect, and no sound but the whish and murmur
of the wind in the stiff holly leaves and the naked grey and brown
and purple branches. I remember that on my very last visit this
same small thicket teemed with life, visible and audible; it was in its
spring foliage, exquisitely fresh and green, sparkling with dewdrops
and bright with flowers about the roots – ground ivy, anemone,
primrose, and violet. I listened to the birds until the nightingale
burst into song and I could thereafter attend to no other. For he was
newly arrived, and although we have him with us every year, invariably on the first occasion of hearing him in spring, the strain affects
us as something wholly new in our experience, a fresh revelation of
nature's infinite richness and beauty.

I know that in a few weeks' time he will be back at the same
spot; in this case we do not say 'barring accidents'; they are not
impossible, but are too rare to be taken into consideration. Yet it
is a strange thing! He ceased singing about June 20, nearly nine
months ago; he vanished about the end of September; yet we may
confidently look and listen for him in about six weeks from today!
When he left us, so far as we know, he travelled, by day or night,
but in any case unseen by even the sharpest human eyes, south to
the Channel and France; then on through the whole length of that
dangerous country where men are killers and eaters of little birds;
then across Spain to another sea; then across Algeria and Tripoli to
the Sahara and Egypt, and, whether by the Nile or along the shores
of the Red Sea, on to more southern countries still. He travels his

four thousand miles or more, not by a direct route, but now west and now south, with many changes of direction until he finds his winter home. We cannot say just where our bird is; for it is probable that in that distant region where his six months' absence is spent the area occupied by the nightingales of British race may be larger than this island. The nightingale that was singing in this thicket eleven months ago may now be in Abyssinia, or in British East Africa, or in the Congo State.

And even now at that distance from his true home – this very clump where the sap is beginning to move in the grey naked oaks and brambles and thorns – something stirs in him too: not memory nor passion perhaps, yet there may be something of both in it – an inherited memory and the unrest and passion of migration, the imperishable and overmastering ache and desire which will in due time bring him safely back through innumerable dangers over that immense distance of barren deserts and of forests, of mountain and seas, and savage and civilised lands.

It is not strange to find that down to the age of science, when the human mind had grown accustomed to look for the explanation of all phenomena in matter itself, an exception was made of the annual migration of birds, and the belief remained (even in Sir Isaac Newton's mind) that the impelling and guiding force was a supernatural one. The ancients did not know what became of their nightingale when he left them, for in Greece, too, he is a strict migrant, but his reappearance year after year, at the identical spot, was itself a marvel and mystery, as it still is, and they came inevitably to think it was the same bird which they listened to. We have it in the epitaph of Callimachus, in Cory's translation:

They told me, Heraclitus, they told me you were dead;
They brought me bitter news to hear and bitter tears to shed;
I wept when I remembered how often you and I

Had tired the sun with talking and sent him down the sky.
And now that you are lying, my dear old Carian guest,
A handful of grey ashes, long, long ago at rest,
Still are thy pleasant voices, thy nightingales, awake,
For Death he taketh all away, but these he cannot take.

It is possible to read the thought in the original differently, that immortality is given to the song, not the bird. As one of my friends who have made literal translations for me has it: 'Yet thy nightingale's notes live, whereon Hades, ravisher of all things, shall not lay a hand,' or 'But thy nightingales (or nightingales' songs) live; over these Hades, the all-destroyer, throws not a hand.'

Keats, too, plays with the thought in his famous ode:

Thou wast not born for death, immortal Bird!
No hungry generations tread thee down;
The voice I hear this passing night was heard
In ancient days by emperor and clown:
Perhaps the self-same song that found a path
Through the sad heart of Ruth, when sick for home
She stood in tears amid the alien corn;
The same that oft-times hath
Charmed magic casements, opening on the foam
Of perilous seas, in faery lands forlorn.

His imagination carries him too far, since the 'self-same song', or the song by the same bird, could never be heard in more than one spot – at Hampstead, let us say; for though he may travel far and spend six months of every year in Abyssinia or some other remote region, he sings at home only. Of all the British poets who have attempted it, George Meredith is greatest in describing the song which has so strong an effect on us; but how much greater is Keats

who makes no such attempt, but in impassioned stanza after stanza
of the supremest beauty, renders its effect on the soul. And so with
prose descriptions; we turn wearily from all such vain efforts to find
an ever-fresh pleasure in the familiar passage in Izaak Walton; his
simple expressions of delight in the singer 'breathing such sweet
loud music out of her little instrumental throat, that it might make
mankind to think that miracles are not ceased'.

The subject of the nightingale's superiority as a singer does not,
however, now concern us so much as its distribution in England, and
its return each year to the same spot. To this small isolated thicket,
let us say, the very bird known here in past years, now away perhaps
in Abyssinia, will be here again about April 8 – alone, for he will
not brook the presence of another of one of his species in his small
dominion, and the female with which he will mate will not appear
until about a week or ten days later.

How natural, then, for the listener to its song to imagine it the
same bird he has heard at the same place in previous years! Even
the oldest rustic, whose life has been passed in the neighbourhood,
who as a small boy robbed the five olive-coloured eggs every season
to make a 'necklace' of them with other coloured eggs as an orna- -
ment for the cottage parlour; whose sons took them in their childhood for the same purpose, and whose grandchildren perhaps rob
them now – even he will think the bird he will listen to by-and-by
the same nightingale of all these years. But this notion is, no doubt,
strongest in those parts of the country where the bird is more thinly
distributed. Here, on the borders of Surrey and Hampshire, we are
in the very heart of the nightingale country, and in these localities
where two birds are frequently heard singing against each other
and are sometimes seen fighting, it might be supposed that when
the bird inhabiting a particular copse or thicket comes to an end,
another will quickly take the vacant place. The three counties of
Hampshire, Surrey, and Kent abound most in nightingales; they are

a little less numerous in Sussex and Berkshire; but these five counties (or six if we add Buckinghamshire) undoubtedly contain more
nightingales than all the rest of England together. The bird, coming
to us by way of France, travels north, each to his ancestral place, the
majority finding their homes in the south of England, on its south-
eastern side; the others going north and west are distributed more
thinly. On a map coloured red to show the distribution, the counties
named above would show the deepest colour over a greater part of
the entire area; while north and west there would be a progressive
decrease in the depth over the south-western counties, the home
counties north of the Thames, the Midlands, East Anglia, and north
to Shropshire and South Yorkshire, where it would disappear. And
on the west side of England it would finish on the Welsh border and
in East Devon. In all of Devonshire west of the valley of the Exe,
with Cornwall; in practically all Wales and Scotland and Ireland,
there are no nightingales.

It is a singular distribution, a puzzling one; for why is it that the
blackcap, garden warbler, wood-wren, and other delicate migrants
who come to us by the same route, extend their range so much
further north and west? We can only say that the nightingale's
range is more restricted, but not by climatic conditions, and that he
is more *local*; in other words, that we don't know. Some have imagined that he is a delicate feeder and goes only where he can find
the food that pleases him; others, that he inhabits where cowslips
grow kindly; still others, that he seeks a spot where there is an echo.
These are but a few of many fancies and fables about the nightingale.

Not only is it a singular distribution, but in a way unfortunate,
since everyone would like to hear the nightingale – the summer
voice which has, over and above the pleasing associations of the
swallow and cuckoo and turtle-dove, an intrinsic beauty surpassing
that of all other bird voices. As it is, a large majority of the population of these islands never hear it. In districts where it is thinly

distributed, as in Somerset and East Devon, there will be perhaps only one nightingale in an entire parish, and the villagers will be proud of it and perhaps boast that they are better off than their neighbours for miles around.

I was staying late in April at a village near the Severn when one Sunday morning the working man I was lodging with informed me that he had heard of the arrival of their nightingale (there was but one), and together we set out to find it. He led me through a wood and over a hill, then down to a small thicket by a running stream, about two miles from home. This was, he said, the exact spot where he had heard it in previous years; and before we had stood there five minutes, silently listening, we were rewarded by the sound we had come for issuing from a thorny tangle not more than a dozen yards away – a preclusive sound almost startling in its suddenness and power, as of vigorous, rapidly repeated strokes on a great golden wire.

And as in this one, so it is in hundreds of parishes all over the country where the nightingale is thinly scattered. Each home of the bird is known to every man in the parish; he can find it easily as, when thirsty, he can find the spring of clear water hidden away somewhere among the rocks and trees of his native place; and the song, too, is a fountain of beautiful sound, crystal pure and sparkling, as it gushes from the mysterious inexhaustible reservoir, refreshing to the soul and a joy for ever.

The loss of one of these nightingales where there is but one is a sorrow to the villagers, especially to the young lovers, who are great admirers of the bird and take a peculiar delight in listening to its evening performance. For it does sometimes happen that the nightingale whose 'solitary song' is the delight of a village, disappears from his place and returns no more. The only explanation is that the faithful bird has at length met with his end, after a dozen or twenty years, or as many years as any old man can remember.

The most singular case of the loss of a bird I have come across was in East Anglia, in a place where there were very few nightingales. In my rambles I came to a little rustic village, remote from railroads and towns, which has a small, ancient, curious-looking church standing by itself in a green meadow half a mile away. I was told that the rector kept the key himself, and that he was something of a recluse, a studious learned man, Doctor of Divinity, and so on.

Accordingly I went to the rectory, a charming house standing in its own extensive grounds with lawns, shrubbery, large garden and shade trees, and a wood or grove of ancient oaks separating it from the village. I found the rector digging in his garden and could not help seeing that he was not too well pleased at my request; but when I begged him not to leave his task and promised to bring back the key, if he would let me have it, he threw down his spade and said that he must accompany me to the church himself, as there were points about it which would require to be explained.

There were no monuments, and when we had looked at the interior and he had pointed out the most interesting features, he came out and sat down in the porch.

'Are you an archaeologist or what?' he said.

I replied that I was nothing so important, that I merely took an ordinary interest in old churches. I was mainly interested in living things – a sort of naturalist.

Then he got up and we walked back. 'In birds?' he asked presently. 'Yes, especially in birds.'

'And what do you think about omens – do you believe in them?'

The question made me curious, and I replied with caution that I would tell him if he would first tell me the particular case he had in his mind just then.

He was silent; then when we had got back to the rectory he took me round the house to where a large French window opened on the lawn and a shrubbery beyond. 'This,' he said, 'is the drawing-room, and my wife, who was very delicate, used always to sit there behind the window on account of the aspect. We had a nightingale then; we had always had him since I came to this parish many years ago. He was a most beautiful singer, and every morning, as long as the singing time lasted, he would perch on that small tree on the edge of the lawn, directly before the window, and sing for an hour or two at a stretch. We were very proud of our bird and thought him better than any nightingale we had ever heard. And he was the only one in the neighbourhood; you would have had to go a mile to find another.

'One morning about eleven o'clock I was writing in my study at the other side of the house, when my wife came in to me looking pale and distressed, and said a strange thing had happened. She was sitting at her work behind the closed window when a little bird had dashed violently against the glass; then it had flown a little distance away and, turning, dashed back against the glass as at first; and again it flew off, only to turn and strike the glass even more violently than before; then she saw it fall fluttering down and feared it had injured itself badly. I went quickly out to look, and found the bird, our nightingale, lying gasping and shivering on the stone step beneath the window. I picked it up and held it to the air in my open hand; but in two or three seconds it was dead.

'I lost my wife shortly afterwards. That was five years ago, and from that time we have had no nightingale here.'

It was not strange that the tragedy of the little bird had made a very deep impression on him; that the death of his wife coming shortly afterwards had actually caused him to think there was something out of the natural in it. But I could not say that I was of his opinion, though I could believe that the acute distress she had suffered at witnessing such a thing, and possibly the effect of thinking too much about it, had aggravated her malady and perhaps even hastened her end.

For the rest, the accident to the nightingale, which deprived the rectory and the village of its singer, is not an uncommon one among birds; our windows as well as our overhead wires are a danger to them. I have seen a small bird on a good many occasions dash itself against a window-pane; and, in one instance, at a country house in Ireland, the bird, a chiffchaff, came violently against my bedroom window twice when I stood in the room watching it. The attraction was a fly crawling up the pane inside. But this explanation does not fit the case of the nightingale with other cases I have observed; he is not like the warblers and the pied wagtail (a frequent striker against window-glass) a pursuer of flies. No doubt birds are sometimes dazzled and confused or hypnotised by the glitter of the glass with the sun on it, and in this case the singing-bush of the bird was directly before the window, at a distance of twenty-five to thirty feet. The singer, motionless on his perch, had looked too long on it, and the effect was such that even after two hurting blows on the glass his little brain had not recovered from its twist. Then came its third and fatal blow.

To return to the subject of the nightingale's curious distribution in England. The facts appear to show that practically the species is stationary with us; that it remains strictly within the old limits and in about the same numbers. Bird-catchers, birds'-nesting boys, and cats extirpate them round the towns; but, taking the whole country, we do not observe any great changes such as we note in some other migrants – the swallow and martin, for example, and among warblers, to name only one, the lesser whitethroat. The conclusion would seem to be that each season's increase is just sufficient to make good the annual losses from all natural causes and from man's persecution; that every bird returns to the exact spot where it was hatched, and that no new colonies are formed or the range extended.

The practical question arises: Would it not make a difference if the annual destruction through human agency could be done away with? I believe it would. Each cock nightingale, we find, takes possession of his own little domain on arrival, and, like his relation, the robin, will not allow another to share it with him; so that if two or more males of a brood, or family, survive to return to the same spot, one presently makes himself master, and the other or others, driven away, settle where they can, as near by as possible. It is probably harder for the nightingale to go a mile away from his true home, the very spot where he was hatched and reared, than to fly away thousands of miles to his wintering-place in the autumn. The bird is exceedingly reluctant to leave his home, but if the annual increase was greater, a third greater let us say, more and more birds would be compelled to go further afield. They would go slowly, clinging to unsuitable places near their cradle-home rather than go far, but the continual pressure would tell in the end; the best places within the nightingale country, the ten thousand oak and hazel copses and thickets which are now untenanted, would be gradually occupied, and eventually the limits would be enlarged. That they cannot be extended artificially we know from the experiments in Scotland of Sir John Sinclair and of others in the north of England, who procured nightingales' eggs and had them placed in robins' nests. The young were hatched and safely reared, and, as was expected, disappeared in the autumn, but they never returned. We can only assume that the 'inherited memory' of its true home, which was not Scotland nor Yorkshire, but where the egg was laid, was in every bird's brain from the shell, that if it ever survived to return from its far journey it came faithfully back to the very spot where the egg had been taken.

That man's persecution tells seriously on the species may be seen from what has happened on the Continent, even in countries where the hateful custom of eating nightingales with all small birds is unknown, but where it is greatly sought after as a cage bird. Thus, in southern Germany the nightingales have been decreasing for very

many years and are now generally rare and have been wholly extirpated in many parts. With us, too, the drain on the species has been
too heavy; it is, or has been, a double drain – that of birds'-nesting
boys and of the bird-catchers.

With regard to the first, there is unfortunately no sentiment of
superstition concerning the nightingale as in the case of his cousin,
the redbreast – 'yellow autumn's nightingale', as it was beautifully
called by one of the Elizabethan poets. How effective such a sentiment can be I have witnessed scores of times when I have found that
even the most thoroughpaced nest-takers among the village children are accustomed to spare the robin, because as they say something bad will happen to them, or their hand will wither up, if they
harry its nest. The nightingale's eggs, like those of the throstle and
shuffle-wing and Peggie whitethroat, are taken without a qualm;
they are, indeed, more sought after than others on account of their
beauty and unusual colouring and because they are less common.

I believe that the increase of the birds each summer would be
about a third more than it is but for the loss from this cause alone.

The destruction caused by the bird-catcher is not nearly so
serious now as it has been, even down to the sixties of the last
century, when a single London bird-catcher would trap his hundred
or two hundred cock nightingales on the birds' arrival. And this
drain had gone on for centuries; at all events we find that as far back
as Elizabethan times the nightingale was eagerly sought after as
a cage bird. Willughby, the 'Father of British Ornithology', in his
account of the bird, gives eight times as much space to the subject of
its treatment in a cage as to its habits in a state of nature.

The cost to a species of caging is probably greater in the case of
the nightingale than of any other songster. It is well known that if
the bird is taken after it has paired – that is, immediately after the
appearance of the females, a week or ten days later than the males
– it will quickly die of grief in captivity. Those taken before the

females appear on the scene may live on to the moulting time, which almost always proves fatal. Scarcely one in ten survives the first year of captivity.

We may congratulate ourselves that it is no longer possible for nightingales to be taken in numbers in this country, thanks to the legislation of the last fifteen years, chiefly to Sir Herbert Maxwell's wise Act empowering the local authorities to give additional protection to wild birds and their eggs in counties and boroughs. It has been a long fight to save our wild birds, and is far from finished yet, seeing that the law is broken every day; that bird-dealers and their supporters the bird-fanciers, and their servants the bird-catchers, who take the chief risk, are in league to defeat the law. Also that very many country magistrates deal tenderly with offenders so long as they respect 'game'. A partridge, and probably a rabbit, is of more consequence to the sportsman on the bench than a small, plain brown bird, or than many linnets and goldfinches. The law, we know, is effectual when it has a strong public feeling on its side; the feeling is not yet universal and nowhere strong enough, or as strong as bird-lovers would wish it to be, but it exists and has been growing during the last half a century, and that feeling, supported by the improved laws which it has called into being, is having its effect. This we know from the increase during recent years in several of the greatly persecuted species. The goldfinch is a striking example. The excessive drain on this species, one of the favourites of the lover of birds in cages, had made it exceedingly rare throughout the country twenty years ago, and in many counties it was, if not extinct, on the verge of extinction. Then a turn came and a steady increase until it had ceased to be an uncommon bird, and if the increase continues at the same rate for another decade it will again be as common as it was fifty years ago. This change has come about as a direct result of the Orders giving it all-the-year-round protection, obtained by the county and borough councils throughout the country.

The nightingale has not so increased, nor has it increased at
all; it is not so hardy a species, and albeit an 'immortal bird', and a
'creature of ebullient heart', it probably does not live nearly as long
as our brilliant little finch. Nor is it so prolific; moreover it nests
upon or near the ground at the same spot year after year, so that its
breeding-place is known to every human being in the neighbourhood, and on this account it is more exposed to the depredations
of the nest-robber than most small birds. The increase of such a
species, which must in any cage be exceedingly slow, can only come
about by the fullest protection during the breeding time. That is to
say, protection from human destroyers; from wild animals and other
destructive agencies we cannot safeguard it.

This infers a considerable change in the nature or habits of the
country boy, or the growth of a new sentiment with regard to this
species which would be as great a protection to it as the sentiment
about our tame, familiar, universal robin has been to that bird. But
it is not a dream. I believe this change is being wrought now in
our 'young barbarians' of the countryside; that it is being brought
about in many ways by means of various agencies – by an increased
and increasing number of lovers of animals and of nature, who in
towns and villages form centres of personal influence; by associations of men and women, such as the Bird Protection, the Selborne,
and kindred societies; by nature study in the schools throughout the
rural districts, and by an abundant supply of cheap nature literature for children. So cheaply are these books now produced that the
very poorest children may have them, and though so cheap they are
exceedingly good of their kind – well written, well printed, well and
often very beautifully illustrated. I turn over a heap of these publi-
cations every year and sigh to recall the time when I was a young
barbarian myself and had no such books to instruct and delight me.

But I have another and better reason than the fact of the existence of all these activities for my belief that a change is taking

place in the country boy's mind, that his interest and pleasure in
the wild bird is growing, and that as it grows he becomes less
destructive. A good deal of my time is passed in the villages in
different parts of the country; I make the acquaintance of the
children and get into the confidence of many small boys and find
out what they do and think and feel about the birds, and it is my
experience that in recent years something new has come into their
minds – a sweeter, humaner feeling about their feathered fellow-
creatures. I also take into account the spirit which is revealed in
the village school children's essays written for the Bird and Tree
competitions established by the Royal Society for the Protection of
Birds. During the last four or five years I have had to read many
hundreds of these essays, each dealing with one species from the
child's own personal observation, and it has proved a very pleasing
task to me because so many of the young essayists had put their
whole heart in theirs. Their enthusiasm shines even in the weakest
of these compositions, considered merely as essays, and we may
imagine that the country boy or girl of ten or twelve or thirteen
finds the task assigned him not a very simple one, to be placed at
a table with sheets of foolscap paper before him and given an hour
in which to compose an essay on the bird selected – the gist of his
observations; to be reminded at the same time that he is one of the
team of nine chosen for the work, that the eyes of the village are
on him, that he must do his best to win the county shield for the
school. The conditions are not too favourable; nevertheless, the
children are doing remarkably well, because, as I have said, their
heart is in it, and one is delighted to find that this study of a bird
has not only quickened the child's interest in nature but has taught
him to think of the bird in a new way, with the feeling which seeks
to protect. We may safely say that these children will not forget
this new lesson they are being taught, whatever else may drop out
of their memories when they leave school; that in coming time,

when they are fathers and mothers themselves, they will instil the same feeling into their own children.

This then of all the various efforts we have made and are making to save the wild-bird life of our country is to my mind the most promising for the future, and makes it possible to believe that the bird of greatest lustre we possess, our nightingale, will not only maintain its own ground in undiminished numbers, but in due time will increase and extend its range.

24 THE CLERK AND THE LAST RAVENS

The parish clerk at Itchen Abbas – William Neave's epitaph – The
parish clerk's reminiscences – A ghost story – Fascination of the raven –
The last ravens at Avington – Tree-climbing feats – Persecution of tame
young ravens by the old birds

The old parish clerk is almost as obsolete as the village
church band or orchestra, but you do come upon him occasionally 'still lingering here' in remote districts, and until
a few years ago there existed one at Itchen Abbas, a pretty little
village on the Itchen, a few miles above Winchester. Let me hasten
to say, lest anyone's susceptibilities should be hurt, that this same
village in everything except its parish clerk appeared to be quite up
to date. At the Sunday morning service he sat near me where I could
see and hear him very well. His quaint appearance and manner first
attracted my attention: it was out of date, out of keeping, or, shall we
say, *harmony*; yet the harmony being what it was in that spiritless
mechanical service, the little discord came as a rather pleasing relief.

He was a small thin old man with black alert hawk-like eyes,
white beard, and a black skull-cap on his grey head. His high-pitched voice and speech were those of a Hampshire peasant,
and it happened to be the one clear articulate voice amidst the
confused gabble of the others, all apparently anxious to get on
and finish the tedious business of public worship as quickly as
possible. When the Psalms were read I tried, as an experiment,
by beginning the instant the minister ceased and rattling off the
words as fast as I could to keep up with the others, but invariably

I finished some words behind. They had practised the trick too long for an outsider accustomed to a different method. But he, the old parish clerk, had never allowed himself to be carried away by the torrent: his father had taught him to go slowly, and slowly he would go to the end of the chapter, in the old ancient way: in a clear high but quavering voice, he distinctly enunciated each word, each syllable, in a measured way, finishing solemnly a good many words after the congregation. The congregation had, so to speak, thrown him off, or run away from him, but he would not give in and gabble or slur anything; he plodded religiously on, unregarded but doing his own part of the service decently and in order, under great difficulties.

For me, a stranger and hater of gabblers, his presence had made the service endurable, and I was glad to make his acquaintance. It was easily made on a week day: dressed in his frayed and discoloured old clothes that hung like sacks about him and rusty shapeless hat, he was the most familiar figure in the village, in appearance an animated scarecrow. He was also the busiest man there. He kept fowls and grew fruit and vegetables in his cottage garden and an allotment a little distance away. Twice a week, on market day, he loaded his little cart with his produce and went off to sell it at the neighbouring town. His spare time was filled up with odd jobs – hedge-trimming, lawn-mowing, gardening generally, repairing thatched roofs, and forty things besides. I never found him sitting down, nor could get him to sit down for more than five minutes at a stretch; but he would rest on his spade sometimes and give me scraps of his ancient history. Yet he was a small weak-looking man, aged seventy-four! He had been parish clerk over forty-five years, and his father before him had held the office for upwards of fifty.

I was reminded of his case afterwards on two occasions in Hampshire churchyards by epitaphs on parish clerks. One was at Heckfield, near Eversley. The inscription reads:

Beneath this stone lies William Neave, who on the 10th
January, 1821, ended a blameless and inoffensive life of 79
years during 45 of which he was Clerk of the Parish. His
father, Thomas Neave, and his grandfather, William Neave,
had previously filled this office, which (dedicated as it is to
uphold in its degree the order and decency of the Established
Church) was here uninterruptedly held by three generations of
the Neaves through a series of 136 years. In this period how
many for whom they had prepared the Font and whose giddy
childhood they had effectually chastised were by them finally
conducted to the spots around, where now they rest in humble
hope of resurrection to life eternal.

Let us return to the old clerk of Itchen Abbas, whose life had
been spent in the village and whose bright memory retained the
story of its life during the whole of that long period. Squire, parsons,
farmers, labourers, he remembered them all – the old-style farmers
who sat at meat with their men before the division of classes, and
before the piano came in and the church organ to kill the villagers'
music. Also the fairies and ghosts. The tricksy little people were not
seen but were known to be about in a field close by; 'Fairy Field' it
was called because when it was being ploughed the horses invariably stopped short at a certain spot and refused to go on. Eventually,
during the late owner Sir Charles Shelley's time a well-preserved
Roman pavement was discovered by chance at a depth of three to
four feet, just on the spot over which the horses had always refused
to draw the plough! The other supernatural story relates to an old
house adjoining the village and overlooking the quiet valley of the
Itchen. Here, tradition says, a crime was committed by a former
owner, and from the time of his death the place was haunted, but
in a singular way; at all events I have never heard any ghost story
quite like it. At night when the air was perfectly still, a sound as of a

sudden high wind could be heard among the trees, travelling like a whirlwind in the direction of the house, but invariably on coming to the house it would die away into silence.

The old clerk introduced me to one of his life-long pals and asked him to tell me his story of the ghost. The story was that when he was a young man about fifty years ago, he went to the house one still dark night about midnight to get some apples. There was a large apple orchard between the woods and the gardens and lawns surrounding the house and divided from them by a high stone wall. It was in October and the trees were laden with tempting ripe apples. Getting over the wall he began hastily plucking the fruit and stowing them in his smock-frock after fastening it round his waist with his belt. When he had got as many apples as he could carry and began to reflect that with such a burden it would be difficult to climb the wall, a sudden rushing sound of wind rose in the wood outside the orchard and appeared to be coming swiftly towards him and the house. He knew from all he had heard from others that it was the ghost-wind. In a moment it rose to the sound of a furious tempest though not a leaf trembled, and in terror he fled before it and in spite of the huge burden was on the top of the wall in a moment. A cat, he said, couldn't have got up quicker and he wondered how he had done it! But on the top of the wall he slipped and came down on the other side; his belt parted at the same time and the apples were sent rolling all over the smooth lawn. He didn't stay to pick them up; he made a dash for the gate and cleared it with a flying leap which landed him in the road, and never stayed till he was back in his cottage. These and other tales of the past were good to hear, but I was more interested to know the story of the last ravens of Avington, and the old clerk was better able to tell it than any other person in the village.

The raven, whether we love it or no, is the most fascinating of feathered beings. Its powerful character impresses the imagination.

Certainly it has an intelligence almost uncanny in a bird; a savage spirit too, and power; a deep human-like voice; and a very long life. These qualities affect the mind and have been the cause of the raven's strange reputation in former ages – the idea that he was something more than a bird, a messenger of doom, an evil spirit, or the spirit of some great dead man revisiting the scenes of his earthly career.

Common all over the country down to the early years of the nineteenth century, he has now been pretty well exterminated as an inland bird. On the iron-bound coasts in a few spots where his eggs are comparatively safe, and in a few wild mountainous districts in the interior, he still exists. But it does not seem long since he was lost, for his memory still lives: 'raven trees' are common all over the country – trees in which the vanished birds built their big nests and reared their young each year. Tales of 'last ravens' are also told in numberless places all over the country. Everyone who knows his *Selborne* will remember the pathetic history of the last ravens in his neighbourhood told by Gilbert White. That is a long time back, and it is known that ravens continued to breed in Hampshire for over a century after White's death. I am here speaking of the *inland-breeding* birds; for up till now one pair of ravens still breed on the Isle of Wight cliffs. The last pair of birds that bred inland, on trees, were the Avington ravens. How long they inhabited that ancient noble domain I do not know, but it is certain that they continued to breed annually in the park until about the year 1885. The 'ravens' clump' where the birds had their nest still flourishes, but the more famous, immeasurably older Gospel Oak, which was an ancient tree when the cathedral at Winchester was built and is believed to be the tree under which St Augustine stood when he preached to the heathen in these parts, is, alas! dead for ever, and its hollow ruinous trunk is slowly crumbling to dust.

These Avington ravens were a good deal persecuted, but invariably when one lost its life the other would disappear for a

few days to find and bring home a new mate. At last some scoundrel got both birds, and that was the end, for of course no others
came to fill their place. The old clerk related that when he was
a young man he worked for some years as under-woodman on
the estate, and he had many exciting stories to tell of his tree-
climbing feats. In those distant days – about 1850 – climbing
contests were common among the men who worked in the woods
and parks, and he was the champion tree-climber in the place.
One day, when coming from work with the other men, a squirrel
was seen to run up an exceedingly tall isolated fir tree, and he, in
a moment of madness, undertook to catch and bring it down. Up
after the squirrel he went until he could go no further, and the
little thing was still above him, afraid to jump down and give him
a chance to capture it, clinging to a slender branch directly over
his head and out of reach. He then thought to knock it down into
his hands, and having selected a small branch for the purpose was
engaged in wrenching it off when the squirrel made its jump, and
as it came flying down past his head he attempted to capture it,
using both hands, but missed it, and at the same time his legs lost
their grip on the branch he was on; and down after the squirrel
he came, crashing through the higher branches and coming at last
with a thud to the earth. He had fallen on his back, and was taken
up senseless and terribly injured and sent away to the hospital
at Winchester. For twelve long months he was kept there, on his
back, and when sent home was told that he would never be fit to do
any outdoor work, although he might perhaps live for some years.
They were wrong; he did get perfectly well, and when I knew him,
half a century or more after this terrible accident, he was still hard
at work mowing, digging, and wood-cutting.

Two or three years before this terrible fall put an end to his
tree-climbing exploits, a member of the ducal family who were then
the owners of Avington thought it would be interesting to have

some tame ravens as pets, and the young champion climber was instructed to take the fledglings from the nest in the park.

When he got up to the nest he was surprised to find six birds, half fledged; and he took them all, and all were safely reared at the house. These birds when grown remained perfectly tame although they were never pinioned; they spent most of their time flying about the park and outside of it, but invariably came to the house to be fed and to roost.

As time went on it was observed that the old birds became more and more jealous of their presence in their territory and from day to day they persecuted them with increasing fury. The young accustomed to be fed at the house refused to leave the place, as the young reared annually in the nest are invariably compelled to do; and the result was that one by one they were killed by their savage parents. My informant actually witnessed the killing of one of them: the young bird tried to escape by flying to the house, but was buffeted with such fury that in the end it was borne down to the earth in the park and was then quickly done to death by the savage blows of the two powerful beaks.

There are other birds just as intolerant of the presence of their full-grown young as the raven. This is the case with our robin redbreast, but in the case of this species it is the cock bird only that fights, and the fight is thus a more equal one. The young bird sometimes conquers the old one. In the raven, the mother bird hates her children as much as the father does, and as they fight in company, playing into each other's hands, and take their young one by one, they are invariably the victors.

25 THE TEMPLES OF THE HILLS

History of the chalk hills – Hill-top groves – Their best aspect –
Abundance of wild life in them – Carrion-crows – Nesting sparrow-
hawks – The fascinating spectacle of the chase – Long-eared owls
– The owl as a practical joker – A keeper's gibbet – The great woods of
Wiltshire – What is lacking in them

The groves were God's first temples,' says the poet; and viewed from the outside no groves are so like the temples made with hands, Christian or pagan, as the 'clumps', as they are commonly called, growing on the chalk hills in Sussex, Hampshire, Wilts, and Dorset. Nature's way is to grow her larger trees on the lower levels, and it is doubtful that the downs have ever had a forest growth other than the kind which we find on them now, composed mainly of the lesser native trees – hawthorn, blackthorn, holly, juniper, and yews of no great size, mixed with furze, bramble, and wild clematis. All these plants are perpetually springing into existence everywhere on the downs, and are persistently fed down and killed by the sheep; take the sheep away from any down, and in a few years, as I have seen, it becomes an almost continuous thicket, and that, one imagines, must have been its original condition. We must suppose that man in early times, or during the Neolithic period when he had domestic animals and agriculture, found the chalk hills a better place than the lowlands, covered as they must then have been with a dense forest growth, the habitation of wolves and other rapacious beasts. On the hills where the thin soil produced only a dwarfish tree vegetation, it was easier to make a clearing and pasture for his cattle. No doubt it was also easier for him to defend himself and his possessions against wild beasts and savage human enemies in such situations. The hills were without water, but the discovery and invention of the dewpond, probably by some genius of the later Stone Age, made the hill-people independent of natural springs and rivers. In later times, when the country was everywhere colonised and more settled, the hill-people probably emigrated to the lower lands, where the ground was better suited for cattle-grazing and for growing crops. The hills were abandoned to the shepherd and the hunter; and doubtless as the ages went on they became more and more a sheep-walk; for it must have been observed from early times that the effect of the sheep on the land was to change its character and to make it more and more suited to the animal's requirements. Thus, the very aspect of the downs, as we know them, was first imparted and is maintained in them by the sheep – the thousands on thousands of busy close-nibbling mouths keeping the grass and herbage close down to the ground, and killing year by year every forest seedling. And how wonderful they are – that great sea of vast pale green billowy hills, extending bare against the wide sky to the horizon, clothed with that elastic fragrant turf which it is a joy to walk on, and has nothing like it in the world!

It must have been in quite recent times, probably, during the last half of the eighteenth century, that the idea first came into the mind of a landowner here and there that a grove on the top of a high bare chalk down would have a noble appearance, and form a striking landmark for all the country round. The result is our hill-top clumps: and one would have imagined that the effect would be altogether bad; for how could a tall dark grove on a hill in a country of such an aspect, of smooth rounded pale-green downs, be anything but inharmonious? Either it is not so, or long custom has reconciled us to this ornament invented by man, and has even made it pleasing

to the eye. Association comes in, too: I notice that the clumps which
please me best are those which are most temple-like in their forms.
Thus, a grove of trees of various kinds growing in a dense mass, as
in the case of the famous Chanctonbury Ring on the South Downs,
gives me no pleasure at all: while a grove of Scotch firs, the trunks
sufficiently far apart as to appear like pillars upholding the dark
dense foliage, has a singular attraction. In some instances the effect
on the hill itself of its crown of trees is to give it the appearance of a
vast mound artificially raised by man on which to build or plant his
temple. This is most striking when, as at Badbury Rings, in Dorset,
the hill is round and low, with a grove of old, very large trees. In
this case the effect is heightened by the huge prehistoric earth-
works, ring within ring, enclosing the grove on the space inside.
Indeed, the sublimest of these temple-groves are not those which
stand on the highest hills; in many cases they stand but a little
above the surrounding level, as in the case of Badbury Rings and of
Hollywater Clump in Wolmer Forest, where the soil is sand.

To my mind the best appearance presented by the higher hill-top
groves is on a hot, windless summer day, during the phenomenon of
'visible air', or 'heat', when the atmosphere near the surface appears
as a silvery mist, or as thinnest white and crystalline flames,
ascending, wavering, dancing, and producing an illusion of motion
in all distant solid objects, such as houses, fences, trees, and cattle.
If the sun had greater power, this silvery flame-like appearance
would become more visible still and take the appearance of water of
a marvellous brilliancy, as of molten silver, flowing over the earth,
with cattle standing knee-deep in it, and distant buildings and
groves rising like islands out of it. This effect of mirage is occasionally visible in England in hot, dry summers, but is very rare. It is on
these burning silvery days, when air and sunlight have a new magic,
that I like best to see the hill-top grove; when at a distance of a
mile or two the tall columnar trunks of the pines, showing the light

between, seem to have a wavering motion, and, with the high dense
roof of branches, look absolutely black against the brilliant whiteness of the air and the pale hot sky beyond.

The downland groves are, however, less to me in their aesthetic
aspect, and as features in the landscape, than as haunts of wild life.
It is indeed as small islands of animal life that I view them, scattered
over the sea-like smooth green waste, vacant as the sea. To others it
may not be so – to the artist, for example, in search of something to
draw. We have each our distinct interests, aims, trades, or what you
like: that which I seek adds nothing to, and takes nothing from his
picture, and is consequently negligible. We cannot escape the reflex
effect of our own little vocations – our pre-occupations with one side
of things, one aspect of nature. Their life is to me their beauty, or the
chief element in it, without which they would indeed be melancholy
places. It refreshes me more than the shade of the great leafy roof on
a burning day. On this account, because of the life in them, I prefer
the clumps on the lower hills. They grow more luxuriantly, often
with much undergrowth, sometimes surrounded with dense thickets
of thorn, furze, and bramble. These are attractive spots to wild birds,
and when not guarded by a gamekeeper form little refuges where even
the shy persecuted species may breed in comparative security. It is
with a sense of positive relief that I often turn my back on some great
wood or forest where one naturally goes in quest of woodland species,
even after many disappointments, to spend a day, or many days, with
the feathered inhabitants of one of these isolated groves.

The birds, too, may be better observed in these places; they are
less terrified at the appearance of the human form than in woods
and forests where the pheasant is preserved, and man means (to
the bird's mind) a gamekeeper with a gun in his hand. For, in many
cases, especially in Wiltshire, the hill-groves are on land owned by
the farmers themselves, who keep their own shootings and do not
employ a gamekeeper.

One day I was standing under a low oak tree at the highest
point in an immense wood, where the sight could range for a long
distance over the treetops, when I was astonished at the sight of a
carrion crow flying low over the trees and coming straight towards
me. It was a wonderful thing to see in that place where I had spent
several days, and had seen no crow and no bird of any kind banned
by the keepers. Yet this was one of the largest woods in Wiltshire, in
appearance an absolutely wild forest, covering many miles without
a village or house within a mile of its borders on any side, and with
no human occupants except the four or five keepers who ranged it to
look after its millionaire owner's pheasants. The crow did not catch
sight of me until within about forty yards from the tree under which I
stood, whereupon, with a loud croak of terror, he turned instantly, and
dashed away at right-angles to his original course at his utmost speed.

Leaving the great wood, I went a few miles away to visit one
of the large unprotected clumps, and found there a family of four
carrion crows – two adults and two young; at my approach they
flapped heavily from the tree in which they were resting, and flew
slowly to another about fifty yards away, and sat there peering at me
and uttering loud caws as if protesting against the intrusion.

At another unprotected clump on a low down I discovered a
varied colony of birds – some breeding, others with young out of
the nest. It was a large grove of old pine trees, almost shut in with
a thick growth of thorn and holly, mixed with bramble and masses
of wild clematis. It was full of the crooning sound of turtle-doves,
and in the high firs several wood-pigeons had their nests. There
were several magpies and invariably on my coming to the spot they
would put in an appearance – quaint black-and-white birds, sitting
on the top boughs of the thorns, always with their decorative tails
behind them. A pair of carrion crows were there too, but appeared
to have no nest or young. Better still it was to find a family of long-
eared owls – two adults and three young, beginning to fend for

themselves. Best of all was a pair of sparrow-hawks with young in their nest; for the sparrow-hawk is one of my prime favourites, and the presence of these birds delighted me even more than that of the owls.

It was evident that these hawks did not associate my appearance with the quick sharp report of a gun and the rattle of shot about them, with perhaps the fiery sting of a pellet of lead in their flesh, for they were exceedingly bold and vociferous whenever I approached the nesting-tree. I visited them on several days for the pleasure of seeing and hearing them. The female was very bold and handsome to look at. Sometimes she would perch above me in such a position as to appear silhouetted against the blue, intensely bright sky, looking inky-black on her black branch. Then, flying to another branch where the light would be on her and a mass of dark pine-needles for a background, one could see the colouring of her plumage. Seen through a powerful binocular, she would appear as big as a goshawk, and as beautiful as that noblest of our lost hawks in her pigeon-blue wings and upper plumage, the white breast barred with brown, thin yellow shanks and long black claws, and the shining yellow eyes, exceedingly wild and fierce. Presently her little mate would appear, carrying a small bird in his claws, and begin darting wildly about among the trees, screaming his loudest, but would refuse to visit the nest. In the end my persistence would tire them out; gradually the piercing reiterated cries would grow less and less frequent, and finally cease altogether. The female would fly from tree to tree, coming nearer and still nearer to the nest, until at last she would perch directly over it and look down upon her young, and finally drop upon them and disappear from sight. And by-and-by the male, approaching in the same cautious way, would at length fly to the nest and, without alighting, just hovering a moment, drop his bird upon it, then dash away and quit the grove. She would then refuse to come off, even when I would strike loudly on the tree with

a stick; yet on my return on the following day the whole performance would be gone through again.

Watching these birds from day to day with an endless delight in
their beauty and vigour, their dashing flight, and shrill passionate
cries of anger and apprehension, I could not help thinking of all
the pleasure that hawks in general are to the lover of wild life in
countries where these birds are permitted to exist, and, in a minor
degree, even in this tame England – this land of glorified poultry-
farms. There is no more fascinating spectacle in wild life than the
chase of its quarry by a swift-winged hawk; and on this account I
should be inclined to put hawking above all other sports but for the
feeling which some of us can never wholly get away from, that it is
unworthy of us as rational and humane beings, possessing unlimited power over all other animals, to take and train any wild rapacious creature to hunt others to the death solely for the pleasure of
witnessing its prowess. No such disturbing feeling can affect us in
witnessing the contests of bird with bird in a state of nature. Here
pursuer and pursued are but following their instincts and fulfilling
their lives, and we as neutrals are but spectators of their magnificent
aerial displays. Such sights are now unhappily rare with us. At one
period of my life in a distant country they were common enough,
and sometimes witnessed every day for weeks at a stretch. Here
the noblest of our hawks are all but gone. The peregrine, the most
perfect of the falcons – perhaps, as some naturalists think, the most
perfect of the entire feathered race – maintains a precarious existence on the boldest sea-cliffs, and as to the hobby, it is now nearly
extinct. The courageous little merlin does not range in southern
England, and is very rare even in its northernmost counties. The
kestrel is with us still, and it is beautiful to see him suspended
motionless in mid-air with swiftly vibrating wings like a gigantic
hover-fly; but he is nothing more than a mouser and an insect-eater,
a falcon that has lost the noble courage of his tribe. The splendid

powerful goshawk, a veritable king among hawks, has long been
extinct; only his little cousin, the sparrow-hawk, lives on in ever-
diminishing numbers. But although small and, as his name implies,
a preyer chiefly on little birds, he has the qualities of his noble relation. In wooded places I am always on the lookout for him in hopes
of witnessing one of his dashing raids on the feathered population.
As a rule there is little to see, for the sparrow-hawk usually takes
his quarry by surprise, rushing along the hedgerow, or masked by
trees, then bounding like a small hunting leopard of the air on his
victim and, if the stroke has been missed, speeding on his way. Even
if I do not see this much – if I just catch a glimpse of the blue figure
speeding by, seen for a moment, then vanishing among the trees – it
is a pleasure to me, a satisfaction to know that he still exists, this
little living link with the better vanished past, and my day has not
been wasted.

Here, on the open downs where the small birds when feeding
have no close refuge into which they can quickly vanish at the sight
of danger, he may occasionally be watched chasing them as a dog
on the ground chases a rabbit; but the best display is when he goes
after a flock of starlings. At no other time does a company of these
birds appear so like a single organism composed of many separate
bodies governed by one will. Only when he is in the midst of the
crowd, if, in spite of their quick doublings, he succeeds in getting
there, do they instantly all fly apart and are like the flying fragments of a violently shattered mass; then, if he has not already made
his capture, he singles out one bird to pursue.

A still better spectacle is afforded by the fiery-hearted little bird-
hunter when, after the harvest, he ranges over the fields; when the
village sparrows, mixed with finches of several species, are out on
the stubble, often in immense congregations covering half a large
field from end to end. On such occasions they like to feed near a
hedge and are thickest on the ground at a distance of three or four

seconds' flight from the thorny shelter. Suddenly the dreaded enemy
appears, topping the hedges at its far end, and at the same instant
the whole vast gathering, extending the entire length of the field,
is up in the air, their innumerable, swiftly fluttering, translucent
wings, which produce a loud humming sound, giving them the
appearance of a dense silvery-brown mist springing up from the
earth. In another instant they are safe in the hedge and not a bird
is visible. In some instances the hawk is too intent on his prey to
hurry on to other fields hoping for better luck next time. No, there
are thousands here; he will drive them out and have one! Then,
heedless of your presence, he ranges up and down the hedge; rising
at intervals to a height of thirty or forty feet and, pausing to hover
a few moments like a kestrel, dashes down as if to descend into the
hedge to wrest a sparrow from its perch, and when just touching
the surface of the thorny tangle the flight is arrested and he skims
on a few yards, to mount again and repeat his feint. And at every
downward dash a simultaneous cry of terror is uttered by the small
birds – a strange sound, that cry of thousands extending the whole
length of the hedge, yet like one cry! If you then walk by the hedge-
side and peer into it, you will see the small birds crowded together
on branchlets and twigs as near the middle of the hedge as they can
get, each particular bird perched erect, stiff and motionless, like
a little wooden dummy bird, refusing to stir even when you stand
within arm's reach of him. For though they fear and fly from the
human form, the feeling is overmastered and almost vanishes in
their extreme terror of the sharp-winged figure of the little feathered tyrant hovering above them.

Undoubtedly it is a fine spectacle – one that lives in the memory
though less beautiful than that of the peregrine or other high-flying
hawk in its chase and conquest of its quarry at a great height in the
air; but in this matter of hawks and their fascinating exhibitions we
have long come to the day of small things.

Something remains to be said of the owls – or rather of the
long-eared owl, this being the only species I have met with in the
temples of the hills. Strange as it may seem to readers who are not
intimately acquainted with this bird, I was able to see it even more
clearly than the sparrow-hawk in the full blaze of noonday. The
binocular was not required. There were five of them – two old and
three young birds – and it was their habit to spend the daylight
hours sitting in a bush just outside the grove. After discovering
their haunt I was able to find them on most days, and one day had
a rare spectacle when I came upon the whole family, two in one
bush and three sitting close together in another. I stood for some
time, less than a dozen yards from these three, as they sat side
by side on a dead branch in the hollow of a furze-bush, its spiny
roof above them, but the cavity on my side. I gazed at them, three
feathered wild cats, very richly coloured with the sun shining full
on them, their long black narrow ears erect in astonishment, while
they stared back at me out of three pairs of round luminous orange-
yellow eyes. By-and-by, getting nervous at my presence, they flung
themselves out, and, flying to a distance of twenty or thirty yards,
settled down in another bush.

I had another delightful experience with long-eared owls at
another of the downland groves about fifteen miles distant from the
last. Here, too, it was a family – the parents and two young birds.
I could not find them in the day-time; but they were always out at
sunset, the young crying to be fed, the parents gliding to and fro,
but not yet leaving the shadow of the trees. I went at the same hour
on several evenings to watch them and experience pleasing little
thrills. I would station myself in the middle of the grove and stand
motionless against one of the tall pines, while the two young birds
would fly backwards and forwards from end to end of the grove,
perching at intervals to call in their catty voices, and then resume
their exercises. By-and-by a sudden puff of air would fan my cheek

or it would be slightly brushed with feather-ends, and an owl would
sweep by. This trick they would repeat again and again, always
flying at my head from behind; and so noiseless was the flight that
I could never tell that the bird was coming until it actually touched
or almost touched me in passing. These were indeed the most ghost-
like owls I had ever encountered; and they had no fear of the human
form, though it evidently excited their curiosity and suspicion, and no
knowledge of man's deadly power: for this grove, too, stood on land
owned by the person who farmed it, and he was his own gamekeeper.

Thinking on my experience with these owls in an unprotected
clump in Wiltshire, it occurred to me that owls of different species,
where these birds are not persecuted, are apt to indulge in this same
habit or trick, almost of the nature of a practical joke, of flying at
you from behind and dashing close to your face to startle you. I
remembered that in my early years, in a distant land where that
world-ranging species, the short-eared owl, was common, I had
often been made to jump by this bird.

It is sad to reflect that the few clumps which form bird refuges
such as the one described – small oases of wild life in the midst of a
district where all the most interesting species are ruthlessly extirpated – are never safe from the destroyer. A few years of indifference
or kindly toleration or love of birds on the owner's or tenant's part
may serve to people the grove, but the shooting may be let any day
to the landlord or shooting-tenant of the adjoining property, whereupon his gamekeeper will step in to make a clean sweep of what he
calls vermin.

Last summer I visited a hill-grove which was new to me, about
thirteen miles distant from the one where I met with owls and
sparrow-hawks and other persecuted species; and as it was an exceptionally large grove, surrounded by a growth of furze and black
and white thorn, and at a good distance from any house, I hoped to
find it a habitation of interesting bird life. But there was nothing to

see or hear excepting a pair of yellowhammers, a few greenfinches and tits, with two or three other feathered mites. It was a strictly protected grove, as I eventually discovered when I came on a keeper's gibbet where the pines were thickest. Here were many stoats, weasels, and moles suspended to a low branch: crows and rooks, a magpie, and two jays and eleven small hawks; three of these were sparrow-hawks – one in full, the others in immature, plumage – and eight kestrels.

This, judging from the condition, of the corpses – one or two newly killed, while the oldest were dried up to bones and feathers – was probably the harvest of a year or more. The zealous keeper had no doubt exhibited these trophies to the noble sportsman, his master, who probably rejoiced at the sight, though knowing that the kestrel is a protected species. This grove, its central tree decorated after the manner of a modern woman with wings and carcasses of birds and heads and tails of little beasts, was like a small transcript of any one of those vast woods and forests in which I had spent so many days in this same downland district. The curse and degradation were on it, and from that time the sight of it was unpleasant, even when so far removed as to appear nothing but a blue cloud-like mound, no bigger than a man's hand, on the horizon.

There is something wanting in all these same great woods I have spoken of which spoils them for me and in some measure, perhaps, for those who have any feeling for Nature's wildness in them. It has been to me like an oppression during my rambles, year after year, in such woods as Savernake, Collingbourne, Longleat, Cranborne Chase, Fonthill, Great Ridge Wood, Bentley and Groveley Woods – all within or on the borders of the Wiltshire down country. This feeling or sense of something wanting is stronger still in districts where there are higher and rougher hills, a larger landscape, and a wilder nature, as in the Quantocks – in the great wooded slopes and summits above Over Stowey, for example; the loss, in fact, is

everywhere in all woodland and incult places, but I need not go
away from these Wiltshire woods already named. They are great
enough, one would imagine, to satisfy any person's love of wildness
and solitude. Here you will find places in appearance like a primitive
forest, where the trees have grown as they would for generations
untouched by man's hand, and are interspersed with thorny thickets
and wide sunny spaces, stony and barren or bright with flowers.
Here, too, are groves of the most ancient oaks in the land, grey
giants that might have been growing in the time of the Conquest,
their immense horizontal branches rough with growth of fern and
lichen; in the religious twilight of their shade you might spend a
long summer day without meeting a human being or hearing any
faintest sound of human life. A boundless contiguity of shade such
as the sensitive poet desired, where he might spend his solitary life
and nevermore have his ears pained, his soul made sick, with daily
reports of oppression and deceit and wrong and outrage.

To the natural man they have another call. Like the ocean and
the desert they revive a sense and feeling of which we had been
unconscious, but which is always in us, in our very marrow; the
sense which, as Herbert Spencer has said, comes down to us from
our remote progenitors at a time when the principal activities of the
race were in woods and deserts. Given the right conditions and it
springs to renewed life; and we know it is this which gives to life its
best savour, and not the thousand pleasures or distractions which
civilised dwellers in towns have invented as substitutes. Here we are
away from them – out of doors, and able to shake the dust of such
artificialities from our souls. In such moods, in these green shades,
we are ready to echo every grateful word ever spoken of those who
for a thousand years in a populous and industrial country, the work-
shop of the world, have preserved for us so much of Nature's freshness. Doubtless they did it for their own advantage and pleasure, but
incidentally the good was for all.

A young American naturalist, writing to me some time ago, contrasted the state of things with regard to the preservation of wild life in his and this country. There, he said, the universal rage for destroying all the noblest and most interesting species, and the liberty possessed by every man and boy to go where he likes and do what he likes in utter disregard of penal laws, was everywhere producing a most deplorable effect. Whereas in this happier land, the great entailed estates of our old county families and aristocracy were like bulwarks to arrest the devastating and vulgarising forces, and had served to preserve our native fauna.

He spoke without sufficient knowledge, describing a condition of things which existed formerly, even down to about the thirties or forties of the nineteenth century. Then a change came over the spirit of the landowner's dreams; a new fashion in sport had arisen, and from that time onwards those who had been, indirectly, the preservers of our country's wild life became its systematic destroyers. For the sake of a big head of game, a big shoot in November, the birds being mainly hand-reared semi-domestic pheasants driven to the guns, they decreed the complete extirpation of our noblest native species:

> The birds, great Nature's happy commoners,
> That haunt in woods:

raven and buzzard, goshawk, kite, harrier-hawks, and peregrine. Besides these, a score of species of less size were also considered detrimental to the interests of the noble poultry-killer. Nor is this all. Incidentally the keepers, the men with guns in their hands who patrol the woods, have become the suppliers to the dealer and private collectors of every rare and beautiful bird they can find and kill.

But I wish now to write only of the large species named above. They are not very large – they might almost be described as small compared with many species in other lands – but they were the largest known throughout the greatest portion of England; they were birds that haunt in woods, and, above all, they were soaring birds. Seen on high in placid flight, circling and ascending, with the sunlight falling through the translucent feathers of their broad wings and tail, they looked large indeed – large as eagles and cranes. They were a feature in the landscape which made it seem vaster and the clouds higher and the sky immeasurably further away. They were something more: the sight of them and the sound of their shrill reiterated cries completed and intensified the effect of Nature's wildness and majesty.

It is the loss of these soaring species which spoils these great woods for me, for I am always sadly conscious of it: miles on miles of wood, millions of ancient noble trees, a haunt of little dicky-birds and tame pheasants bred and fed for the autumn shoot. Also the keeper laying his traps for little mousing weasels, or patiently waiting in hiding among the undergrowth to send a charge of shot through a rare kestrel's nest when the mother-bird comes back to feed and warm her young.

26 AUTUMN, 1912

Wells-next-the-Sea – A great man's reason for residing there –
The enviable chameleon – Black redstart – Antics of a squirrel –
The dreariness of desk-work – Observations on a pair of late-nesting
martins – Conflicting instincts – Swallows observed in mid-winter –
A curious story of nesting martins and sparrows

Wells-next-the-Sea, as I have already said in a chapter a long way back, in this volume, is one of the spots I love best to frequent in the autumn, chiefly to see and hear the wild geese that winter there in larger numbers than at any other point on the coast. This season of 1912 I had another object in going thither; there remained two or three weeks' work to be done in order to complete this book; and where, flying from London, could one find a place more admirably suited for such a purpose? A small, ancient, village-like town, set in a low flat land next the sea, or separated from the sea by a mile-wide marsh, grey in summer, but now rust-brown in its autumnal colour. The fisher-folk are poor, and their harvest consists mainly of shellfish, mussels, whelks, clams, and they also dig at low water for sand-worms to be sold for bait. They are, as I think I remarked before, like their feathered fellow-creatures, the hooded crows; and indeed they resemble crows when seen, small and black, scattered far out on the wide waste of sand. When the men are away at sea and those noisy little animals, the children, are shut up in school, you can imagine that there is no longer any life in Wells; you would not be in a quieter place on the wide brown marsh itself, nor on the low grassy sand-hills faintly seen in the distance, nor on the wide stretch of sand beyond, where the men, crow-like, are seeking their subsistence.

To Wells I accordingly went on October 17, yet was no sooner in this ideal spot than I began to think it was the last place where I could do any work, since even the noises and distractions of London would have a less disturbing effect than that low murmur, that familiar yet ever strange sound of the old old sea, that came to me by day and night, and the wild cries and calls of passing birds, especially the cries of the geese.

It is related of a man who has a great reputation in his day which is now ended, that he was once taken to task by a friend for having settled himself at Wells. You, his friend said, with your love of mankind, your noble ideals, your many talents, and especially your eloquence in addressing your fellowmen – how can you endure to waste your years in this dead-alive little town in a marsh?

The other answered that it was because Wells was the only town in England where, sitting at ease in his study, he could listen to the cries of wild geese.

To me, just a naturalist, these same cries were even more than to that famous man: to sit still and do any work where I heard them was the difficulty. Thus was I pulled two ways, and my state was that of being in, or between, 'two minds'. My wish was that these same two minds could have two bodies with sets of senses complete, so that each might be able to follow its own line. I envied the chameleon just then – a strange creature which is said to change its colour according to its surroundings. That, however, is merely a physical condition, one which it shares with certain other creatures without any mind at all, or in which the mind is dormant, as, for example, in some chrysalids. It is a minor mystery; the big mystery of the chameleon, the pretty problem for the students of animal psychology, is the divisibility of its mind, the faculty of being two persons in one body, each thinking and acting independently

of the other. Observe him in a domestic state, sitting on a branch
in a room, in appearance a deformed lizard, or the skeleton of one,
encased in a discoloured, granulated skin, long dried to a parch-
ment. The most remarkable feature is the head, which reminds one
of a grotesque mediaeval carving in or on some old church, of a
toad-like or fish-like human creature, with a countenance expressive
of some ancient, forgotten kind of wisdom. He is absolutely motionless, dead or asleep one might imagine; but on a closer scrutiny
you discover that he is not only awake and alive, but that he has
two lives in him – in other words, that the two hemispheres of his
brain are working separately, each occupied with its own problem. It
may be seen in his eyes – minute round lenses mounted on swivels,
or small fleshy or rubber processes, capable of being elevated or
depressed and pointed in this or that direction at will. They are
like the freely moving ears of a horse, but they do not point one
way, since each one, together with the half-brain which governs it,
is occupied with looking at a different thing. You see, for instance,
that one of the pair is now aimed like a spy-glass at some remote
object, also that it is continually moving, and you will presently
discover that it is following the erratic movements of a bluebottle
wandering about the room. This is not an idle amusement nor mere
mental curiosity on the chameleon's part; he knows that the fly is an
indefatigable traveller and investigator; that by-and-by, when he has
finished quartering the ceiling, running up and down the walls and
looking at the pictures, he will turn his attention to the furniture,
piece by piece, and eventually arrive at that very spot, that stand
or table with its counterfeit presentment of a branch, and upon the
branch the strange image of a monster, perhaps a god, of stone or
metal, dug up by some Flinders Petrie in some desert city, where it
has been lying buried in sand these several thousand years. Truly a
curious and interesting object for an inquisitive fly to look at! And
just as a little tourist will place himself in front of the Sphinx to

survey its countenance at a proper distance of forty or fifty yards, so does the fly settle himself before the face of the chameleon, at a distance of six or eight or ten inches. That is not too far for the tongue, which is as long as the body: the eye on a swivel has never lost sight of the blue wanderer; it is fixed on him even now; the tongue follows like lightning, and lo, the fly has vanished, and will buzz and look blue no more!

Meanwhile, the same chameleon, on the other side of him, has fallen into a doze, or reverie, or is perchance philosophising, the eye on that side being sunk into the skull. One could say that he is lying comfortably muffled up at home, lapped in rosy dreams, while his fellow-chameleon, the other half of him, is abroad hunting, practising all his subtle strategy to capture a shy volatile quarry. Yet at any moment these two, so divided in mind and indifferent to each other's doings and thinkings, can merge into one: they literally pull themselves together, and a single will takes command of the entire body, from the gargoyle head to the prehensile tail.

I can laugh now at the plight I was in just through not being made like a chameleon; but it wasn't a laughing matter when Conscience pointed sternly to the writing-table and at the same time a persuasive voice called to me from the door to come out, otherwise I should miss something never again to be seen. No hint as to what the wonderful thing was to be, nor when nor where it was to be seen: all I had to do was to be out all day, patiently waiting and watching!

The wonder is that when, in spite of conscience, I got away, I did witness some things which were actually worth recording. Thus, one day while sitting by the old sea-ruined coastguard station on the dunes, between the sea and the marsh, I noticed a small, unfamiliar bird, robin-like in appearance, but darker and without the red waistcoat, flitting in a sprightly manner about the old crumbling walls. By-and-by his flittings and little dashes after passing flies brought

him to a perch within five yards of me; and sitting there, curiously
eyeing me, drooping his wings and flirting a broad tail, he stood
revealed – a black redstart! A happy experience: in all that empty
desolate place I could not have met with a more engaging stranger,
nor one more friendly. For he is first cousin to our pretty firetail
with a sweet little summer song, only our redstart is a shy bird,
whereas this black redstart was tamer than any robin. I took it that
he was resting a day on the dunes after his perilous flight over the
North Sea, and that he came from Holland, where he is common and
breeds fearlessly in and on the houses. That is why he was so confi-
dent, also why he eyed me so curiously, for he knew by the look of
me that I was not a Dutchman. More than that he did not know, and
he had no letter tied to his wing; nevertheless, he had a greeting and
a message for me from that country and that people, who, among
the nations of the Continent, are most like the English in kindness
to animals as well as in some other things, but are better than we
are in their treatment of birds.

On another day I stole into the pine wood growing on the
sand-hills by the sea, and in the heart of the wood came to a deep
basin-like depression in the sand, and there I seated myself on the
rim or margin among the long grey marram grass, with the dark
red pillars of the pines standing all about me. It was marvellously
still in that hidden place in the wood; after sitting there for half an
hour, listening and watching, the thought came to me that I might
stay there half a day without seeing any living creature or hearing
any faintest sound of life. Yet before another minute had passed
something living flashed into sight, the woodland creature that is
most alive – a beautiful red squirrel with an exceptionally big bushy
tail. He slid swiftly down a bole, and straightway began leaping,
pirouetting, and dashing hither and thither about the floor of the
basin, not twenty yards from my feet. As I sat motionless he did not
see or did not heed me: he was alone in the wood, and was like the

solitary nightingale that asks for no witness to his song, and played his glad, mad game with his whole soul. Now with feet together he arched his body like a stoat, then flung himself out full length and dashed round in a circle, and as he moved there was an undulating motion, as of wave following wave along his back and tail, which gave him a serpentine appearance. On coming to a thick bed of pine needles, he all at once became motionless and spread himself out on the ground and looked like the flattened skin of a squirrel, with the four paws visible at the corners. When he had sufficiently enjoyed the sensation of pressing on the pine needles with the under surface of his body, he started up to continue his game, until he suddenly caught sight of a large, yellowish-white agaric growing some yards away, and, dashing at it, he tore it violently from the stalk with his two paws and began devouring it as if mad with hunger, taking huge bites and working his jaws like a chaff-cutter.

Sitting upright devouring his mushroom, he looked like a quaint little red man eating a round piece of bread-and-butter twice as broad as himself. Then suddenly, after a few more bites, he dashed the mushroom to the ground as if he hated the taste of it, and scampering off out of the hollow, vanished from sight among the trees.

With such things as these to be seen, the very thought of work gave me a sensation of weariness and disgust: to sit down to a pile of old note-books, some of them more than a year old, patiently and laboriously to sift out two or three observations worth recording out of every hundred, seemed an intolerable burden, and not worth the candle. Even the sight of a black redstart (with greetings from Holland) and the romps of a fantastic squirrel seemed more to me a hundred times than the sights of a year ago. To go back to such stuff was to leave living, breathing, palpitating nature to finger bundles of old faded photographs and muse on dusty memories. Why then go back? Why indeed! Ah! how easy to ask that question; how often we ask it and there is no answer but the old one; because of the eternal desire in us, which must have fretted even the hearts of the men who dwelt in caves; to reveal, to testify, to point out the path to a new enchanted realm which we have discovered; to endeavour to convey to others some faint sense or suggestion of the wonder and delight which may be found in nature.

We say – and I am here speaking of my own peculiar people, the naturalists – that birds too, like ourselves, may be pulled two ways, and that two conflicting impulses may be the cause of one of the most pathetic of Nature's innumerable little annual tragedies. This is when a pair of swallows are rearing a late brood, and before the time comes for the young to fly are themselves overtaken and borne away to the south by the irresistible migratory instinct.

It happened that on the very day of my arrival at Wells, October 17, I noticed a pair of martins still feeding their young in a nest under the eaves above a sweetstuff shop, within two or three doors of the Wells post-office. Now I shall see for myself, I said, resolving to keep an eye on them. There were no other martins or swallows of any kind in Wells at that date: a fortnight earlier I had witnessed the end of the swallow migration, as I thought, on the South Devon sea-coast. I saw them morning after morning in numbers, travel-ling along the coast towards the Isle of Wight, which is one of their great crossing-places, until they had all gone.

I kept an eye on the martins, visiting them very early every morning and two or three times later during each day. The young, it could be seen when they thrust their heads and almost half their bodies out to receive the food their parents brought, were fully grown and very clamorous.

'They will be out in a day or two,' I said confidently. The people of the house informed me that this same nest had been occupied, off and on, throughout the summer; and if we take it that eggs were laid at the beginning of May, it must be assumed that this pair of martins had been occupied almost continuously with the breeding business for six months, and were now rearing their third, or possibly their fourth, brood. A long period when we consider that they could not have had a worse season: bad everywhere in England, it was exceptionally so on the Norfolk coast, where the winds and cold were most felt and the flooding rains in August were greatest.

As the young birds did not come out during the two following days, I began to look for their abandonment, whereupon the women of the house compassionately offered to take them in and feed them, in the hope of keeping them alive until the return of warm weather, when they would be liberated. From that time onwards they and others in the town who had begun to take an interest in the birds helped me to keep a watch on the nest. Assuredly the young would be abandoned and that very shortly; the weather was rough and cold, food becoming scarcer each day; and for a month or six weeks the impulse to fly south, the 'mighty breath, which in a powerful language, felt not heard, instructs the fowls of heaven', must have been worrying the brains of those two overworked little martins.

But again the expected did not happen; the parents did not forsake their young, and on two occasions, one on October 25, the other five days later, they tried their best to get the young out. They came to the nest with flies a dozen times a minute, and instead of delivering the food into the open mouths, they would flutter a moment with beaks just out of reach, then drop off to circle round and repeat the action. All these enticing arts were of no avail; the young had not the strength or spirit to launch themselves on the air, otherwise they would have been saved.

On the following day, October 31, the weather was exceptionally bad; it was cold, with a strong wind, and rained heavily all day: the call of the young now sounded feebler from the nest, and the eager little black, flat heads and white throats were no longer thrust out. Yet the old birds still laboured faithfully to find them food, only on

this last day they did not go far in search of provender. They were
too anxious, or in some way conscious of the failing strength of the
young; they hawked after scarce flies up and down the street, always
near the nest, constantly giving themselves that quick little shake
by means of which the swallow throws the rain off his feathers.
There was another noticeable change in them: at intervals of about
a quarter of an hour one or both of the birds would fly into the nest
and remain there for a space of three or four minutes, doubtless to
warm the young. At all events, I don't think it was merely to rest
themselves, as on previous days I noticed that when they wanted
to rest they would fly into one of the empty martins' nests close to
their own.

That last day came to an early end, as it began to get dark at four
o'clock, and the old birds settled down with their young for the night.

The following morning, although somewhat chilly, was more like
April than November, with a light wind, a crystal clear sky, and a
sunshine with a magic in it to enliven the world and give renewed
life even to the perishing. The old birds had vanished and no faintest
sound came from the nest. I waited some hours, then procured a
ladder and took the nest down, and found two full-grown dead
young martins in it. One had died that morning, probably at two or
three o'clock, before the turning of the tide of life; the other looked
as if it had died about two days before.

This is but one case and it happens to be the only one of an
exceptionally late brood which I have had an opportunity of
observing closely, yet to me it does suggest the idea that we may
be mistaken after all in our belief that the migratory impulse or
passion will cause the swallow to forsake its late-hatched offspring,
leaving them to perish of starvation in the nest. More observation is wanted, but the case described inclines me to think that so
long as the young continue alive and able to emit their hunger cry,
the parental instinct in the old birds remains dominant and holds

the migratory impulse in check or in abeyance; that only when the
insistent cry ceases and the young birds grow cold the release comes
and the 'mighty breath' blows upon and bears them away southward
irresisting as a ball of thistledown carried by the air.

I see that Dixon, in his *Migration of Birds* (1897), page 112, says
that he knew of a case in which a pair of barn swallows abandoned
their young in the early days of November when they were almost
able to take care of themselves, whether in or out of the nest he
does not say. Nor does he state that the case came directly under his
own observation; if the young were in the nest it may be they were
dead before the parent birds set out on their journey. It is possible
that such cases do occur from time to time and have been observed,
yet they may be exceptional cases. We know that a few swallows
do linger on with us into the depth of winter each year; that they
become torpid with cold, and that occasionally one does survive
until the following spring. These rare instances gave rise to the
belief that swallows hibernate regularly, which was held by serious
naturalists down to the early nineteenth century: but we now know
that these cases of torpid birds are rare exceptions to the rule that
the swallow migrates each autumn to Africa.

While I was keeping watch on the martins when the fate of the
young was still hanging in the balance, there was a good deal of
talk on the case among my old fishermen and wild-fowling friends,
and about swallows generally. One man told me that last winter
(1911) he was at the neighbouring village of Warham, one bright
sunny day about the middle of December, and saw five or six swallows at a pond there flying about in a slow feeble manner over the
water. They perched frequently on a small bramble bush growing by
the pond and were so tame or stupefied by the cold that he actually
attempted to take one in his hand. He thought it was an extraordinary thing, but there is no doubt that a few swallows are seen
every year up to mid-winter somewhere in England although their

appearance is not recorded; also that these birds have been lying up in
a torpid condition until a bright warm day revived and brought them
out. Few of these stay-at-home swallows can survive to the spring.

Another curious incident was related by another man, a very
old wild-fowler of the place. He said that when he was a young
man living in his home, a small hamlet near Wroxham Broad, a
number of martins bred every year on his cottage. They thought
a great deal of their martins and were proud to have them there,
and every spring he used to put up a board over the door to prevent
the entrance from being messed by the birds. One spring a pair
of martins made their nest just above the door and had no sooner
completed it than a pair of sparrows stepped in and took possession and at once began to lay eggs. The martins made no fight at
all, but did not go away; they started making a fresh nest as close
up as they could against the old one. The entrance to the new nest
was made to look the same way as in the first, so that the back part
was built up against the front of the other. It was quickly made and
when completed quite blocked up the entrance of the old nest. The
sparrows had disappeared; he wondered why after taking a nest that
didn't belong to them they had allowed themselves to be pushed
out in this way. At the end of the season, after the departure of the
martins, he got up to remove the board, and the double nest looked
so curious he thought he would take this down too and examine it.
On breaking the closed nest open he was astonished to find the hen
sparrow in it, a feathered skeleton still sitting on four eggs!

27 WILD WINGS: A FAREWELL

An abundance of wild geese – Hooded crows – Their evening
amusements – A sociable mixed gathering – Herons at play – A ringed
dotterel's fun – Gull and pewit – Kestrel harried by starlings – Starlings
flying in company with wild geese – Behaviour of starling flocks –
Wounded goose and redshanks – An inquisitive crow – Evening return
of the geese – Migrant crows and fieldfares – Last sight of the wild geese

My anxious interest in the swallows did not keep me
from seeing and hearing the geese. They had arrived
as usual 'in their thousands'; the wild-fowlers said they
had never seen them in greater numbers than this autumn. One
reason for this was supposed to be the unusual abundance of food
on the farm-lands, where a great deal of the corn had remained on
the ground on account of the floods in August and September. The
farmer's loss was pure gain to the wild geese. The birds shot during
my stay were fat and their crops full of corn; certainly they appeared
happy; and when they passed over the town with resounding cackle
and scream one could imagine they were laughing in the sky: Ha!
ha! ha! it is a jolly life in spite of you wingless, wicked wild-fowlers,
so long as we remember when flying to and from the sea to keep
out of range of your hateful old guns! They didn't always remember,
and a goose was a great prize when one fell to the gun of one of
these very poor men; but when they sent me round a bird just to see
what a fine bird old So-and-so had got, and 'would I give him half a
crown for it?' I could only reply that it was indeed a fine bird, and I
congratulated my old friend on his luck, but I wasn't buying a goose.

I can eat sheep and pig and some other beasts, always excepting cow; also fowl, pheasant, and various other birds, wild and tame; but I draw the line at wild geese. I would as soon eat a lark, or a quail, or a nice plump young individual of my own species as this wise and noble bird.

The cries of the geese going inland to their happy feeding-grounds would come to me in my room before I was up in the morning, and again the same exhilarating sound was heard in the evening just after sunset, causing the women and children to run out of their cottages to see and listen to the passing birds. At that hour I was usually a mile or so out on the marsh or by the sea to have a good view of the geese as they came over. On some evenings they disappointed me, but there were always other birds to look at and enjoy, the chief among these being the hooded crow. He was a few days later than usual this year, but during the last ten or twelve days of October came in steadily, arriving, as a rule, in the morning, until he was as numerous as ever all along the coast. The best time to see these birds is in the evening, when they have been feeding all day on the marshes, and are as full of small crabs and carrion cast up by the sea as the geese are of corn, and when they have an hour before going to roost to spend in play.

One evening I was greatly entertained by their performance, when the tide was out, leaving a wide stretch of mud at the mouth of the river or small estuary which serves Wells as harbour; and here some sixty or seventy birds had gathered to amuse themselves before going to roost. Here would be a bird looking for something to eat, and when he found a small crab or other morsel he would make a great to-do about it, and hold it up as a challenge to others; then his next neighbour would set upon him and there would be a sham fight, and the crab would be captured and carried trium-phantly away, only to be used as a challenge to others. This was but one of a dozen different forms of play they were indulging in, and

while this play on the ground went on, at intervals of a few seconds
a bird would shoot straight up into the air to a height of eighteen or
twenty feet, then, turning over, tumble straight down to the ground
again. To drop vertically down seemed to be the aim of every bird,
but with a wind blowing they found it a somewhat difficult feat, and
would wriggle and flutter and twist their wings about in various
ways to save themselves from being blown to one side. At longer
intervals a bird would shoot up to a height of forty to sixty feet,
going up in a much easier way than the others, with a stronger
flight and falling more skilfully, almost like a stone. So great was
the difference between this display and that of the generality that
these birds were like old practised hands or professionals at the
game, and the others mere amateurs or beginners.

On describing what I had witnessed to an old fisherman and
fowler, he said, 'I've watched them playing like that many and many
a time, and have thought to myself, they're just like a lot o' children.'

I doubt if anyone who has observed birds in company closely,
especially when they have come together, as in the case of the
hooded crows, just for recreation, has not occasionally had this same
thought – just like a lot of little children!

It is, as I remarked in the chapter on the marsh warbler, a
delightful experience to a field naturalist to sit at ease, binocular
in hand, at a proper distance from a company of birds and watch
them at their little games. The right distance varies according to
the species and the nature of the ground; it should always be outside
the danger limit, so that if they see the spectator they do not heed
him and are practically unconscious of his presence. Whatever that
distance may be, a nine to twelve prismatic glass will bring them
within a dozen yards of his vision.

This delight was mine almost every day at the spots where the
birds were accustomed to congregate on the meadows and by the
sea. I could watch them by the hour and was never disappointed,

even when there was nothing particular to see, or at all events
nothing worth noting down. The more the species in a gathering
the greater the interest one takes in watching them, on account of
the marked difference in disposition they exhibit; but, speaking of
the birdlife of the meadows and shore, they have this in common,
that they all appear to take a certain pleasure in each other's
company. I notice, for instance, that if a pair of pewits are in a
meadow and a flock of starlings appear, after wheeling about as if
undecided for a few moments, they almost invariably drop down
where the pewits are and feed in their company. If rooks or fieldfares
come they too join the others. Even where there are only large birds
on the spot, geese or sheldrakes, for example, any small birds that
come to the place – starlings, thrushes, larks – will alight among or
alongside of them. They will appear to know each other, and if no
relations they are friends and intimates – geese, ducks, rooks, daws,
crows, pewits, thrushes of all kinds, larks, pipits, and wagtails; also
curlews, redshanks and other small shore birds during the intervals
when they leave the sea. On these meadows herons and gulls are
also included in the company. You cannot watch one of these gatherings for long without witnessing many little incidents that have
nothing to do with the business in hand – the search for small seeds
hidden on the surface and for grubs beneath it lying among the
fibrous roots of grass. It is an important matter, and it takes a long
time to get a satisfactory meal when each morsel or half-mouthful
has to be searched for in a separate place; but it does not take up
their whole attention; there is always some sort of byplay going
on, encounters friendly or hostile between two birds, mischievous
pranks and ebullitions of fun. The playful spirit is universal among
them; even the solemn gaunt heron, that stick of a bird, is capable
of it; I was delighted one day to, witness three of these birds that
formed part of a big promiscuous gathering all at once break out in
a wild game of romps. A heron at play differs from all other birds in

its awkward ungraceful motions, and when running about appears hardly able to keep its balance.

The heron's moments of abandonment are rare and he is rusty in consequence: the small shore birds on the contrary relax often and are as easy and graceful at play as any bird. One day when sitting on Wells bank I had only two birds in sight, two ringed dotterels, one quietly feeding on the mud-flat directly beneath me, the second bird running along the margin of the water forty or fifty yards away. By-and-by this one rose and came flying to his companion, but instead of alighting near him as I expected him to do, he paused in the air and hovered for three or four seconds directly over him, at a height of a couple of feet, then dropped plump down upon his back, almost throwing him to the ground with the impact, after which he folded his wings and stood quietly as if nothing had happened. The other bird, recovering from the sudden shock, threw himself into a belligerent attitude, lowering his beak and aiming it like a fighting ruff at his comrade, his whole plumage raised and his wings and tail feathers open; but he did not attempt to inflict any punishment; after all that show of resentment at the insult he contented himself by pouring out a series of prolonged sharp scolding notes. These ended, the two birds started quietly feeding together.

In the promiscuous gatherings one cannot but observe that although they all meet and mix in an easy friendly manner there is yet a great difference in their dispositions and in their ideas about fun, if it be permissible to put it in that way. In some of the most social species, small shore birds, starlings and rooks, for instance, their games are mostly among themselves and are quite harmless although there is often a pretence of anger. That is part of the game, just as it is with kittens and with children. The gulls mix but do not affiliate with the others and play no tricks on their neighbours, like the crow, just for mischief's sake. They want something more substantial. They must have it out of someone, and it is usually the pewit. He, the gull, flies about in a somewhat aimless way, then drops down among them to rest on the turf or walks about curiously inspecting the grass, perhaps wondering what the mysterious sense or faculty of the rook and starling is by means of which they know just which individual grass among a hundred grasses contains a grub in it roots – a fat morsel which may be unearthed by a thrust of the beak. The grass tells him nothing and in the end he finds it more profitable to watch the other probers at work. He sidles up in a casual manner to the pewit, pretending all the time to be honestly seeking for something himself, but watching the other's motions very keenly, to be ready at the prime moment when a grub is being pulled out to make a dash for it.

There was another bird who took no part at all in the work and play of the others – a kestrel who made the meadows his daily hunting-ground. What he was finding I could not discover as I never saw him lift a vole and it was too late for insects. Anyhow, he was often there and the other birds took not the slightest notice of him; even the smallest in the company, the larks, pipits, and wagtails, knew him for a harmless person. But one day while he was flying about, hovering at intervals and dropping to the earth, a flock of about fifty starlings came flying to the meadow and after circling round as if just going to alight they all at once appeared to change their minds – or mind – and mounting up again until they were about twenty yards above the kestrel, began following his movements, and when he hovered six or seven birds detached themselves from the flock and dropped like stones upon his back. He struck them angrily off and flying a little distance away began searching again; but they followed and no sooner did he hover than down again came half a dozen starlings on to his back.

After this annoyance had been repeated five or six times he flew away to another part of the meadow and resumed his hunting there. Again the starlings followed and repeated the former action

each time he hovered, until in anger and disgust he flew away out
of sight, while the starlings, their object gained, dropped down to
the meadow and started feeding. The action may have been inspired
by a love of fun or a spirit of mischief complicated with a sense of
irritation at the sight of a bird who was not of their society, whose
ways were not their ways – a feeling akin to that which occasionally
prompts a person of a primitive order of mind to heave half a brick
at a stranger. The feeling is quite common among birds, only the
heaving process is performed with such a precision and so gracefully
that it is a pleasure to witness it.

In marked contrast with this spiteful behaviour was another act
of a flock of starlings I witnessed at the same spot, showing the
different feelings entertained towards a stranger like the kestrel and
a comrade of the feeding-ground – a wild goose. A small gaggle
or company of a dozen or fourteen geese came flying from the sea
across the meadows on their way inland to the feeding-ground,
and at the same time a flock of about a hundred starlings, travelling at a much greater height than the geese, came flying by, their
course crossing that of the geese at right angles. Just as the flocks
crossed about thirty starlings detached themselves from the flock
and dropping straight down joined the geese. They did not merely
place themselves alongside of the big birds; they mixed and went
away among them, accommodating their flight to that of the geese.
Yet they must have been uncomfortably placed among such big and
powerful birds, fanned by their wings and in some peril of being
struck with the long hard flight feathers. With my binocular on the
flock I watched them until they gradually faded from sight in the
sky, the starlings still keeping with them.

What could have moved these thirty birds out of a flock of a
hundred to act in this way? Perhaps they were 'just like little children' and had said to each other, 'Come, let's play at being geese
and march solemnly to the sound of screaming and cackling to the

distant farm-lands, where we'll stuff our crops with clover and spilt wheat; and while some of us are feeding others will keep watch, so that no crafty gunner, hiding his approach behind an old grazing plough-horse, shall get within shot of us.'

One becomes so imbued with the notion of unity of mind in a flock of starlings – the idea that the whole crowd must act with and follow the leader, if leader there be – that one always wants to know why there is any divergence at all, as when a flock divides and goes off in different directions. Thus, from a flock proceeding steadily in a certain direction some of the birds, half the flock it may be, will suddenly drop down to settle on a tree-top, leaving the others to go on; or in passing over a field where sheep are grazing a certain number of the birds will come down to feed among them. In the first case, the sight of the tree-top below has probably suggested the need for rest to a single bird; the impulse is instantly acted on and a certain number of the birds are carried away by the example and follow, while in the others the original motive or impulse which sent them off to travel to some more distant place remains unaffected and they keep steadily on their way. In like manner, in the other case, the scene below tells sharply on some one bird in the flock; hunger is created by suggestion; the sight of feeding sheep scattered about in the moist green earth is associated in his starling mind with the act of satisfying his want, and down to the sheep he accord-ingly goes and carries some of the others with him.

The action of the starlings going off with the geese may perhaps be accounted for in the same way. An impulse due to an associate feeling caused those thirty birds to break away from the flock. These starlings were probably migrants from the north of Europe and were intimate with geese: they had perhaps even travelled with the geese over lands already whitened with snow and over the sea; they had also probably fed with the geese in green meadows and fields where both birds find their food in abundance. The sight of the flying geese became associated in their minds with some such past experience and they were instantly carried away by an impulse to join and fly with them, but only some thirty of the flock, the other seventy remaining unaffected or uninfected by the example.

My best evening was on October 29, for at the close of that day the sky cleared and the geese returned, not in detachments, but all together a little earlier than usual. I was out on the marsh towards Blakeney, a mile and a half or so from Wells, when, about half an hour before sunset, a solitary goose came flying by me towards the sea, keeping only foot or two above the ground. It was a wounded bird, shot somewhere on its feeding-ground, and, being unable to keep with the flock, was travelling slowly and painfully to the roosting-place on the sands. When it had got about a couple of hundred yards past me a few redshanks rose from the edge of the creek and, after wheeling round once or twice, dropped down again in the same place, and no sooner had they alighted than the goose turned aside from his course and, flying straight to them, pitched on the ground at their side. That is just how a bird of social disposition will always act when forsaken by his fellows and in distress: it will try to get with others, however unlike its own species they may be – even a goose with redshanks; and this, too, in a most dangerous place for a goose to delay in, where gunners are accustomed to hide in the creeks. It was evident that he was ill at ease and troubled at my presence, as after alighting he continued standing erect, with head towards me. There he remained with the redshanks for full fifteen minutes, but he had not been more than two minutes on the spot before a passing hooded crow dropped down close to and began walking round him. The crow will not attack a wounded goose, even when badly wounded, but he knows when a bird is in trouble and he must satisfy his inquisitive nature by looking closely at him to find out how bad he really is. The goose, too, knows exactly what the crow's life and mind is, and no doubt despises him. I watched them intently, and every time the crow came within a couple of feet of him the goose bent down and shot out his snake-like head and neck at him. If my binocular had been able to catch the sound as well as the sight, it would have conveyed to me, too, the angry snake-like hiss which accompanied the threatening gesture. And each time this gesture was made the crow hopped away a little space, only to begin walking and hopping round the goose again until he had satisfied his impudent curiosity, whereupon he flew off towards his roosting-place.

Then, after a few minutes, from a great way off in the sky came the sounds of approaching geese, and the wounded bird turned his breast towards the land and stood with head held high to listen to and see his fellows returning uninjured with crops full of corn, boisterous in their happiness, to the roosting-place. The sound grew louder, and presently the birds appeared, not in a compact body, but in three single lines or skeins of immense length, while between these widely separated lines were many groups or gaggles of a dozen to forty or fifty birds arranged in phalanx form.

I had been witnessing this evening return of the geese for a fortnight, but never, as now, united in one vast flock, numbering at the least four thousand birds, the skeins extending over the sky for a length of about a third of a mile. Nor had the conditions ever been so favourable; the evenings had been clouded and it was often growing dark when they appeared. On this occasion the heavens were without a cloud or stain and the sun still above the horizon. I could see it from the flat marsh like a great crimson globe hanging just above the low, black roofs of Wells, with the square church tower in the middle. The whole vast aerial army streamed by directly over me and over their wounded fellow below, still standing statuesque and conspicuous on the brown, level marsh. In two or three minutes more the leading birds were directly above the roosting-place on the flat sands, and at this point they paused and remained stationary in mid-air, or slowly circled round, still keeping at the same height; and as others and still others joined them, the whole formation was gradually broken up, skeins and phalanxes becoming merged in one vast cloud of geese, circling round like a cloud of gulls. Then the descent began, a few at a time detaching themselves from the throng and sweeping obliquely downwards, while others, singly or in small parties, with half-closed wings appeared to hurl themselves towards earth with extraordinary violence. This marvellous wild-wing display continued for four or five minutes before the entire multitude had come to the ground. Altogether it had been the most magnificent spectacle in wild-bird life I had ever witnessed in England.

It was not until all were down and invisible, and the tumult of the multitudinous cries had sunk to silence, that the wounded bird, after some moments of indecision, first taking a few steps onwards, then returning to the side of the redshanks, as if reluctant to part from those little unhelpful friends lest he should find no others, finally set off walking towards the sea.

There were no gunners out on the shore at this point just then and he would be able to reach the flock in a little while, although he would not perhaps be able to follow them to the farm-lands on the morrow or ever again.

Rough and rainy days succeeded that rare evening of a wild-wing display on a magnificent scale; then followed yet another perfect November morning like that on which the martins had abandoned their stricken nest. A clear sky, a light that glorified that brown marshy world, and a clear sharp air which almost made one think that 'miracles are not ceased,' since in breathing it in the shackles that hold and weigh us down appear to drop off. On such a morning it is only necessary for a man to mimic the actions of a crane or stork by lifting his arms and taking a couple of strides and a hop forward, to find himself launched in space, rising to a vast height, on a voyage of exploration to 'heavens not his own and

worlds unknown before'. It is the nearest we can get to the state of
being a bird.

On that side where the large sun was corning up the sky was
all a pale amber-coloured flame, and on it, seemingly at a great
distance, appeared minute black floating spots, which rapidly
increased in size and presently resolved themselves into a company
of hooded crows just arrived from their journey over the North Sea.
And no sooner were they gone journeying inland in their slow-
flapping laborious manner, than other crows and yet more crows
succeeded, in twos and threes and half-dozens, and in scores and
more, an endless straggling procession of hoary Scandinavian or
'Danish' crows coming to winter in England. And from time to time
fieldfares, too, appeared, travelling a little faster with an undulatory
flight, but keeping strictly to the crow-line; and these too appeared
to be fatigued and journeyed silently, and there was no sound but
the low swish of their wings.

A morning and a bird life to rejoice the heart of a field naturalist; yet this happiness was scarcely mine before a contrary feeling
supervened – the same old ineffable sadness experienced on former
occasions on quitting some spot which had all unknown been
growing too dear to me. For no sooner am I conscious of such an
attachment – of this queer trick of the vegetative nerves in throwing
out countless invisible filaments to fasten themselves like tendrils to
every object and 'every grass', or to root themselves in the soil, than
I am alarmed and make haste to sever these inconvenient threads
before they get too strong for me, and take my final departure from
that place. For why should these fields, these houses and trees, these
cattle and sheep and birds, these men and women and children, be
more to me than others anywhere in the land?

However, I made no desperate vow on this occasion: the recollection of the wild geese prevented me from saying a word which
could never be unsaid. I had planned to go that morning and bade a

simple good-bye: nevertheless my heart was heavy in me, and it was perhaps a prophetic heart.

The black straggling procession of crows, with occasional flocks of fieldfares, had not finished passing when the train carried me away towards Lynn, skirting the green marshes or meadows sacred to the wild geese. And here, before we came to the little Holkham station, I had my last sight of them. Looking out I spied a party of about a dozen Egyptian geese, on a visit to their wild relations, from Holkham Park close by, and as the train approached they became alarmed and finally rose up with much screaming and cackling and flew from us, showing their strongly contrasted colours, black and red and glistening white, to the best advantage. Now a very little further on a flock of about eight hundred wild geese were stationed. They were all standing with heads raised to see the train pass within easy pistol shot; yet in spite of all the noise and steam and rushing motion, and of the outcry the semi-domestic Egyptians had raised, and their flight, these wild geese, the most persecuted and wariest birds in the world, uttered no sound of alarm and made no movement!

A better example of this bird's intelligence could not have been witnessed; nor – from the point of view of those who dream of a more varied and nobler wild-bird life than we have now been reduced to in England – could there have been a more perfect object lesson.

INDEX

COLLINS NATURE LIBRARY

The Collins Nature Library is a series of classic British nature writing – reissues of long-lost seminal works. The titles have been chosen by one of Britain's best-known and most highly acclaimed nature writers, Robert Macfarlane, who has also written new introductions that put these classics into a modern context.

CURRENT TITLES IN THE SERIES

A Land
by Jacquetta Hawkes

Nature Near London
by Richard Jefferies